D0405531

Copyright © 2014 CelebrityPress® LLC

All rights reserved. No part of this book may be used or reproduced in any manner whatsoever without prior written consent of the authors, except as provided by the United States of America copyright law.

Published by CelebrityPress®, Orlando, FL

CelebrityPress® is a registered trademark

Printed in the United States of America.

ISBN: 978-0-9912143-4-1
LCCN: 2014933601

This publication is designed to provide accurate and authoritative information with regard to the subject matter covered. It is sold with the understanding that the publisher is not engaged in rendering legal, accounting, or other professional advice. If legal advice or other expert assistance is required, the services of a competent professional should be sought. The opinions expressed by the authors in this book are not endorsed by Celebrity Press® and are the sole responsibility of the author rendering the opinion.

Most CelebrityPress® titles are available at special quantity discounts for bulk purchases for sales promotions, premiums, fundraising, and educational use. Special versions or book excerpts can also be created to fit specific needs.

For more information, please write:
CelebrityPress®
520 N. Orlando Ave, #2
Winter Park, FL 32789
or call 1.877.261.4930

Visit us online at: www.CelebrityPressPublishing.com

CELEBRITY PRESS®
Winter Park, Florida

CONTENTS

CHAPTER 1

MAXIMIZE YOUR INCOME

BY BRIAN TRACY

You have the ability, right now, to earn vastly more than you are earning today, probably two or three times as much, just to start off. How do we know this? Simple. You are surrounded by people who are not as smart, ambitious or as determined as you are, but who are already earning more than you. In addition, all of these people started off earning less than you are earning today. In this chapter I will show you how to move to the front of the income line of life, faster than you ever thought possible.

One of the qualities of superior men and women is that they are extremely self-reliant. They accept complete responsibility for themselves and everything that happens to them. They look to themselves as the source of their successes as well as the main cause of their problems and difficulties. High achievers say, "If it's to be, it's up to me."

When things aren't moving along as fast as they want, they ask themselves, "What is it in me that is causing this problem?" They refuse to make excuses or to blame other people. Instead, they look into themselves, and seek ways to overcome obstacles and to make progress.

SEE YOURSELF AS SELF-EMPLOYED

Totally self-responsible people look upon themselves as self-employed. They see themselves as the presidents of their own personal service corporations. They realize that no matter who signs their paycheck, in the final analysis they work for themselves. Because they have this attitude of self-employment, they take a strategic approach to their work.

The essential element in strategic planning for a corporation or a business entity is the concept of "return on equity (ROE)." All business planning is aimed at organizing and reorganizing the resources of the business in such a way to increase the financial returns to the business owners. It is to increase the quantity of output relative to the quantity of input. It is to focus on areas of high profitability and return. Simultaneously, it is to withdraw resources from areas of lower profitability and return. Companies that do this effectively in a rapidly changing environment are the ones that survive and prosper. Companies that fail to do this form of strategic analysis are those that fall behind and often disappear.

To achieve everything you are capable of achieving as a person, you also must become a skilled strategic planner with regard to your life and work. But instead of aiming to increase your return on equity, your goal is to increase your return on *energy.*

Most people in America, and worldwide, start off with little more than their ability to work. More than 80 percent of the millionaires in America started with nothing. Most successful people have been broke or nearly broke several times during their younger years. But the ones who eventually get to the top are those who do certain things in certain ways. Those actions set them apart from the masses.

Perhaps the most important thing they do, consciously or unconsciously, is to look at themselves strategically and think about how they can better use themselves in the marketplace; how they can best capitalize on their strengths and abilities to increase their financial returns to themselves and their families.

YOUR MOST VALUABLE ASSET

Your most valuable financial asset is your earning ability, your ability to earn money. When properly applied to the marketplace, it acts like a pump. By exploiting your earning ability, you can pump tens of thousands of dollars a year into your pocket. All your knowledge, education, skills and experience contribute toward your earning ability, your ability to get results for which someone will pay good money.

Your earning ability is like farmland. If you don't take excellent care of it, fertilize it, cultivate it and water it on a regular basis, it soon loses its ability to produce the kind of harvest that you desire. Highly paid men and women are those who are extremely aware of the importance and value of their earning ability. They work every day to keep it growing and current with the demands of the marketplace.

One of your greatest responsibilities in life is to identify, develop and maintain an important marketable skill. It is to become very good at doing something for which there is a strong market demand.

WHAT ARE YOU GOOD AT?

In corporate strategy, we call this the development of a "competitive advantage." For a company, a competitive advantage is defined as an area of excellence in producing a product or service that gives the company a distinct edge over its competition. This "unique added value" enables the company to charge premium prices for its products and services.

To earn what you are truly worth, as the president of your own personal services corporation, you must also have a clear competitive advantage and area of excellence. You must do something, or several things, that makes you different from, and better than, your competitors. Your ability to identify and develop this competitive advantage is the most important thing you do in the world of work. It is the key to maintaining your earning ability as well as the foundation of your financial success. Without it, you are simply a pawn in a rapidly changing environment. But with a distinct competitive advantage, based on your strengths and abilities, you can write your own ticket. You can take charge of your own life. You can always get a job. The more distinct your competitive advantage is, the more money you can earn and the more places in which you can earn it.

THINK STRATEGICALLY ABOUT YOURSELF

There are four keys to the strategic marketing of yourself and your services. These are applicable to huge companies such as General Motors, to candidates running for election, and to individuals who want to accomplish the maximum amount possible in the least amount of time.

The first of these four keys is *specialization*. No one can be all things to all people. A "jack-of-all-trades" is also a "master of none." That career path usually leads to a dead end. Specialization is the key. Men and women who are successful have a series of general skills, but they also have one or two areas where they have developed the ability to perform in an outstanding manner.

THINK ABOUT THE FUTURE

Your decision about how, where, when and why you are going to specialize in a particular area of endeavor is perhaps the most important decision you will ever make in your career. The strategic planner, Michael Kami, once said that, "Those who do not think about the future cannot have one."

The major reason why so many people are seeing their jobs eliminated and finding themselves unemployed for long periods of time is because they didn't look down the road of life far enough and prepare themselves well enough for the time when their current jobs would expire. They suddenly found themselves out of gas on a lonely road, facing a long walk back to regular and well-paying employment. Do not let this happen to you.

In determining your area of specialization, put your current job aside for the moment, and take the time to look deeply into yourself. Analyze yourself from every point of view. Rise above yourself, and look at your lifetime of activities and accomplishments to determine what your area of specialization could be or should be.

KEEP YOUR MIND OPEN

You might be doing exactly the right job for you at this moment. You might already be specializing in an important area where people are eager to pay you a lot of money for what you do. Your current work might be ideally suited to your likes and dislikes, to your temperament and your personality. Nevertheless, you owe it to yourself to be continually expanding the scope of your vision and looking toward the future to see where you might want to be in the months and years ahead. Remember, the best way to predict the future is to create it.

You possess special talents and abilities that make you unique and different from anyone else who has ever lived. The odds of there being another person just like you—are more than 50 billion to one. Your remarkable combination of education, experience, knowledge, problems, successes, difficulties, challenges, and your way of looking at and reacting to life, make you extraordinary.

YOU HAVE UNLIMITED POTENTIAL

You have within you potential competencies and attributes that can enable you to accomplish virtually anything you want in life. Even if you lived for another 100 years, it would not be enough time for you to plumb the depths of your potential. You will never be able to use more than a small part of your inborn abilities. Your main job is to decide which of your talents you will exploit and develop to their highest and best possible use right now.

So, what is your area of excellence? What are you especially good at right now? If things continue as they are, what are you likely to be good at in the future—say one or two or even five years from now? Is this a marketable skill with a growing demand. Is your field changing in such a way that you are going to have to change as well if you want to keep up with it? Looking into the future, what could your area of excellence be if you were to go to work on yourself and your abilities? What should be your area of excellence if you want to rise to the top of your field, make an excellent living and take complete control of your financial future?

KEEP YOUR EYES OPEN

When 1 was 22, selling office supplies from business to business, I answered an advertisement for a copywriter for an advertising agency. As it happened, I had failed high-school English and I really had no idea what a copywriter did. I remember the executive who interviewed me and how nice he was at pointing out that I was not at all qualified for the job.

But something happened to me in the course of the interview process. The more I thought about it, the more I thought of how much I would like to write advertising. Having been turned down flat during my first interview, I decided to learn more about the field.

BACK TO SCHOOL

I went to the city library and began to check out and read books on advertising and copywriting. Over the next six months while I worked at my regular job, I spent many hours devouring them. At the same time, I applied for copywriting jobs to advertising agencies in the city. I started with the small agencies first. When they turned me down, I asked them why. What was wrong with my application? What did I need to learn more about? What books would they recommend? To this day, I remember that virtually everyone I spoke with was helpful to me.

By the end of six months, I had read every book on advertising and copywriting in the library. I applied to every agency in the city, working up from the smallest agency to the very largest in the country. By the time I had reached that level, I was ready. I was offered jobs as a junior copywriter by both the number-one and number-two agencies in the country. I took the job with the number-one agency and was very successful in a short period of time.

THERE ARE NO LIMITS

The point of this story is what I learned. I learned that you can become almost anything you need to become, in order to accomplish almost anything you want to accomplish, if you simply decide what it is and then learn what you need to learn. This is such an obvious fact that most people miss it completely.

Some years later, I heard about a lot of people who had gotten into real estate development and made a lot of money. I decided that I wanted to get into real-estate development as well. I used my same strategy. I went to the library and began checking out and reading all the books on real-estate development. At the time, I had no money, no contacts and no knowledge of the industry. But I knew the great secret: I could learn what I needed to learn so I could do what I wanted to do.

THE POSSIBILITIES ARE ENDLESS

Within 12 months, I had tied up a piece of property with a $100 deposit and a 30-day option. I put together a proposal for a shopping center, as explained in the books. I tentatively approached several major potential anchor tenants and several minor tenants that together took up 85 percent of the square footage I had proposed. Then I sold 75 percent of the entire package to a major development company in exchange for the company's putting up all the cash and providing me with the resources and people I needed to manage the construction of the shopping center and the completion of the leasing. Virtually everything that I did I had learned from books written by real-estate experts—books on the shelves of the local library.

THE SAME PRINCIPLES WORK

As you might have noticed, the fields of advertising, copywriting and real estate development are very different. But these industries, and every business venture I have explored over the years, had one element in common. Success in each area was based on the decision, first, to specialize in that area and, second, to become extremely knowledgeable in that area so that I could do the work well if I got a chance.

In looking at your current and past experiences for an area of specialization, one of the most important questions to ask yourself is, "What activities have been most responsible for my success in life to date?"

How did you get from where you were to where you are today? What talents and abilities seemed to come easily to you? What things do you do well that seem to be difficult for most other people? What things do you most enjoy doing? What things do you find most intrinsically motivating? What things make you happy when you are doing them?

INCREASE YOUR EARNING ABILITY

Your level of interest, excitement and enthusiasm about your particular job or activity is a key factor as you become more valuable, and increase your ability to get results that people will pay you for. You will always do best and make the most money in a field that you really enjoy. It will be an area that you like to think about, talk about, read about and learn about. Successful people love what they do, and they can hardly wait to get to it each day. Doing their work makes them happy. The happier they are, the more enthusiastically they work, and the better their work will be.

BECOME DIFFERENT AND BETTER

The second key to becoming valuable is *differentiation.* You must decide what you are going to do to not only be different but also better than your competitors in the field. Remember, you have to be good in only one specific area to move ahead of the pack. And you must decide what that area should be. What do you currently do, or what could you do, better than almost anyone else?

SEGMENT YOUR MARKET

The third strategic principle in capitalizing on your strengths is *segmentation.* You have to look at the marketplace and determine where you can best apply yourself with your unique talents and abilities, to give yourself the highest possible return on energy expended. Which customers, companies, products, services or markets, could best utilize your special talents and offer you the most in terms of financial rewards and future opportunities?

FOCUS AND CONCENTRATE

The final key to personal strategic planning is *concentration.* Once you have decided the area in which you are going to specialize, how you are going to differentiate yourself, and where in the marketplace you can best apply your strengths, your final job is to concentrate all of your energy on becoming excellent in that one area. The marketplace only pays extraordinary rewards for extraordinary performance.

In the final analysis, everything that you have accomplished up to now is a part of the preparation for becoming outstanding in your chosen field. When you become very good at doing something that people want, need and are willing to pay for, you will soon begin moving rapidly into the top ranks of the highest-paid people everywhere.

About Brian

Brian Tracy is Chairman and CEO of Brian Tracy International, a company specializing in the training and development of individuals and organizations. Brian's goal is to help people achieve their personal and business goals faster and easier than they ever imagined.

Brian Tracy has consulted for more than 1,000 companies and addressed more than 5,000,000 people in 5,000 talks and seminars throughout the US, Canada and 55 other countries worldwide. As a Keynote speaker and seminar leader, he addresses more than 250,000 people each year.

For more information on Brian Tracy programs, go to: www.briantracy.com

CHAPTER 2

YOUR GOLD MEDAL MOMENT AWAITS

BY APRIL HOLMES

For seventeen minutes, I laid facedown on the snowy railroad tracks at the train station in center city Philadelphia. While I was free to rummage through my mind's museum, I was trapped under the weight of a train. The pain of my leg being crushed by the train was unbearable, yet I remained confident that this was not the end. I had so many questions for myself and for God. I wondered if I would make it out alive? I questioned how I got there in the first place? I believed I would be given another chance to be great and do amazing things if I just held on and had faith. However, this time was different because I physically couldn't move.

My legs failed me. I could no longer depend on them solely to lead me to my destiny. I was lost. I was wondering, but traveling nowhere; I was still but my mind was racing around the world. While I had been unsure of my life's path before, this was different. I have no idea where the feelings of uncertainty, self-doubt, and insecurity come into our minds, but I was lying facedown in it.

I dozed off thinking this was a horrible nightmare, only to wake up in the hospital and learn the truth. I was now an amputee, whose leg was severed by the weight of a train. I was incomplete. I was inadequate. I was unable to be…me!

Time was racing as I was spiraling into depression. I had fallen, and unable to get up. On the outside, I was missing a leg but plastered on my face was a smile to hide the pain. My internal mirror was shattered. I needed help getting up, but around me were the mental bodies of people who were displaced from my fall.

There are times when we fall, times that we are covered with disappointment. Our actions have led to disgrace, anger, and confusion to those around us. We all have fallen. We all have feelings of self-doubt. We all have inadequacies. However, in our darkest moments, we feel like we are the only ones in the world going through this issue. Where do these feelings of isolation come from?

As I lay in the hospital bed, I needed a light to my path so I could continue to search for the new me; I was presented with several magazines about disabled athletes. As I turned the pages, I saw photos and read stories of athletes from the United States that had participated in the 2000 Sydney Paralympic Games. Eventually I stumbled upon the female amputee that had won the GOLD medal in the 100 and 200 meters.

My feelings of despair were quickly replaced with courage as I formulated three dreams in my mind:

1. I wanted to wear the USA uniform at the next Paralympic Games.

2. I wanted to be the fastest female amputee in the world.

3. I wanted to win GOLD medals.

Acceptance was now firmly in my heart, wisdom was in my mind and doubt was behind me. I just needed a leg to help me reach my destiny. Those magazines represented hope and hope is what I needed desperately.

Everything I did became about my dreams and my "gold medal moments." Despite my fall, my mishap, my perceived shortcomings, I now had to dig deep into my serenity chest and embrace my physical differences, and broken commonalities.

Was I really that different? The world is inundated with divorcees, dropouts, addicts, parents who have failed, individuals who have been fired, and adulterers – just to name a few. In fact, there is not one individual who can say that they had not fallen or failed at something. So, what ignites the intestinal fortitude in some to brush them off and reach the championship podium in life, while others are struggling to even appreciate the stitching on the uniform?

I learned the essence of being a champion while watching Dr. J as a child, Michael Jordan as a teen, and my mother as a woman. While they may have gotten knocked down, their spirit and goals remained at skyscraper status. They dusted themselves off many times in the eyesight of others and probably even more times in the closet of their inner being. However, they continually made changes to be better daily.

When I ventured along my journey to my "Gold Medal Moment," I learned that my dreams required a game plan. Imagine yourself in the fight for your life after you have just fallen to an unthinkable low. Dreams will get your mind going, but actions will help you change direction. You can't afford not to chase greatness. Think of something you want, think of something you need, consider yourself achieving something that will define this moment in your life. Think of something that will personify your existence.

Ready, Set, D.R.E.A.M.

D= Digest your possibilities. Always assess where you are and what you currently have in your arsenal. Preparation gives you the time, space, and opportunity to marvel at the effect you have on people's life. When I was lying on the train tracks and in that hospital bed, I knew I didn't have a leg. Instead of continually focusing on something I didn't have, I instead began to rely on things I did. For instance, I believe I had an internship in Championship 101 from watching my favorite teams and players all my life. They had a walk; I had a limp. However, I believed that practice would allow my limp to become a walk. In other words, I believed I could fake it until I made it. What do you have the chance to do right now that would be the defining first step in your dream?

R= Reinvent Yourself. Strive to be a better you than you were yesterday. With this simple goal, your "Gold Medal Moment" is no longer a distant future, but well within your grasp. While I had been running track all my life, I had never reached the pinnacle of greatness to declare I was the greatest in the world. Now, here I was missing my left foot, but declaring to the world and myself that I had the courage to embark and declare my mission to begin my "Gold Medal Moment." Who cares if you failed before! Who cares if you fail again! Get out there and exercise your right to be the winner of your dreams.

E= Evolve Ahead of Time. Great people find a way to bring their future success closer to the present. If your goals and dreams mirror that of your friend or foe, respect will be difficult to score. Champions define their goals; they don't allow their goals to define them. During rehab, I continued to think about accomplishing a goal instead of defeating a person. Imagine if my focus was the person and they ended up not being the best at the next competition? If all you desire is to be better than your co-worker, then you are competing against jealousy and envy, a race you will never win. Instead, if you consider the goal, that will remain constant and require greater focus for an ultimate reward.

A= Assemble a great talent pool. Surround yourself with innovative people so you remain relevant long after you/your product is gone. When you are in the midst of a storm, oftentimes you are unable to see very far in front of you because you are focusing on now. That is when a great coach becomes valuable. Imagine being able to trust someone that challenges, cheers and cherishes your journey. There will be days you don't love your journey coaches, but you will always respect their opinion and their commitment to your dreams. Give your permission to trust your coach and understand that no man climbs a mountain alone; we always need people to be stakes in our ground.

M= Market yourself/product. The best tool, product, or poster child to represent your brand or your image is you. Live who you are out loud, tell people about your dream as if it were your child. Dreams have an amazing way of manifesting themselves in conversation amongst friends and foes. Accountability produces champions, because we will be reminded of our actions. Think about your successes and failures and how often someone reminded you of them. I dare you to share them like we do our newborn baby pictures, then when you stand on the podium of success, you will appreciate the community support from your telling others about your dreams.

We all live dangerously close to both failure and success. Our actions define who we are and what we will eventually become. Who are you not to take a chance on a dream? Who are you not to take the walk of your life? Who said that you were not allowed to partake in the dream of your life?

Athletes find themselves training 7 days a week, 8 hours a day; even resting is considered training. When they are not training they are preparing their bodies and their minds to excel in their respective sport. Excellence would not prevail without 24/7/365 determination and a championship mindset. Like symbolizing excellence in athletics, greatness is a habit that requires exercise and constant positive reinforcement.

Athletes are very fortunate to have championships defined, without searching for that moment. We know what the ultimate medal, trophy, reward, prize, and celebration will look like. Others are not so lucky in that they have to define their "Gold Medal Moments" for themselves.

The Training. The Race. The Execution. The Finish – Repeat???

As an athlete stands atop the podium, with their right hand over their heart, reciting their national anthem as their own personal song as a single tear runs down their cheek, it represents so much more than winning a race. It is the sweat, the fight, the perseverance, the resilience and the tenacity they had to will themselves to that moment.

Sometimes we are unaware that our "Gold Medal Moment" is right around the corner for us. Will you fight for that moment or will you lie awake at night waiting to hit the dream lottery?

Ask yourself, what will you let define you? What will you push yourself to achieve when your energy and self-esteem are on empty? Do you have the passion, instinct, desire, and courage to dive into your life and produce something great? What are your chances of becoming champion?

While people may express the desire to be a champion, many lack the discipline to excel at winning. We can no longer afford to participate in the parades of our favorite teams while we sit on the sidelines in our own dreams. Buy your own jersey, build your own team and define your own championship, because you are one dream, one goal and one ounce of confidence away from your Gold Medal moment in life.

Ready! Set! Win!

About April

Raised with a hard work ethic, which she has honed with a will of steel, April Holmes has redefined what it means to be disabled. April was involved in a train accident in 2001 that resulted in the loss of her left leg below the knee. While she lay in her hospital bed, a doctor told her about the Paralympic Games and three goals were firmly implanted in her mind. She desired to wear the USA uniform. She wanted to break world records. She was determined to win gold medals.

Since her career in Paralympic track and field began in 2002, Holmes has continued to succeed, improving each and every step of the way. She has broken IPC World Records fourteen times and American Records eighteen times in the 100, 200, 400 meters and the long jump. Over her astonishing career, April has put together several undefeated seasons, and her first Paralympic gold medal in the 100 meters at the 2008 Beijing Games. Speed and quickness are her best friends as she continues to break her own world records every season. With a commanding lead over the growing field of competitors, Holmes continues to captivate track enthusiast with her grace and style. April put on the USA uniform again at the 2012 Paralympics in London and after a photo finish was awarded bronze in the 100 meters in front of a sold-out arena. April spends the majority of her time training in Orlando at Disney Wide World of Sports with her eyes firmly set on winning more gold medals at the 2016 Paralympic Games in Rio.

When she is not competing, April Holmes runs the April Holmes Foundation, Inc. a non-profit organization assisting people with physical and learning disabilities with scholarships and medical equipment. Having completed her MBA in Marketing, Holmes uses her education to improve the awareness of people with disabilities. April was recently named by the International Paralympic Committee as one of the "Top 10 Women in Paralympic Sport," a US Paralympic and US Anti-Doping Ambassador, and has assisted First Lady Michelle Obama on the "Let's Move" Campaign.

April is a well sought-after speaker and enjoys opportunities to share her life and GOLD medal with others. She has electrified audiences with messages of motivation, diversity, leadership, and marketing. Some of her clients include Deloitte, Disney, The Jordan Brand, The Hartford Insurance Company, Aflac, and BMW. April also assists companies in Olympic-themed sporting days to enhance the core values of teamwork, determination, discipline, and goal setting.

Given her expertise, education, and athletic achievements, Holmes has been featured on multiple media outlets including NBC Today Show, CBS Early Morning, Fox, ESPN,

BBC, Forbes, and Oprah's *O Magazine*. "Communicating Your Greatness" remains a staple in her life, both on the track and in the corporate workspace.

You can connect with April Holmes at:
Aprilholmes.com
Facebook.com/FanofApril
Twitter.com/aprilholmes
Linkedin.com/in/aprilholmes

CHAPTER 3

THOUGHTS ARE THINGS

BY JANIS BUTLER

One day when John was twelve, his dad overheard him complaining with disgust, "Well, what do you expect? My parents are divorced."

His dad took a red-faced John aside. "Don't ever again use your parents' divorce as an excuse." John had volunteered to lie down, angry, dejected, a candidate for failure. He was polishing his "ain't it awful." That dad cut John's "poor me" off, knocking guts and courage back into his boy. That dad was my father.

Now, what do I have to do with Mariah Carey, Barack Obama, Daniel a young poet, and—perhaps, you, or someone you know? All are dealing with lost or phantom parents, some successfully, others not so much.

- Mariah's parents divorced when she was three. Ugly fights ensued. Police were called. She said she grew up with nothing, with no sense of security.

- After Barack was born, his dad went back to Africa, leaving the boy to be raised mainly by his mother's parents.

- An outgoing, soft-spoken man, with the tall lean looks of a model, Daniel told me his brother died from cancer when Daniel was nine. Not knowing how to cope with grief, his parents skirted life for years, drowning in substance abuse, eventually divorcing. They left Daniel shuffling homes – on his own.

- My parents went missing early on. Daddy was gone to war during my preschool years. When Mother divorced him, he didn't know how to be a non-custodial dad. Because he lived nearer his office down the coast from Santa Monica, I seldom saw him. When I did, his discomfort was palpable. Gone was the Boy Scout Den Master easiness. Mother wasn't available much even when she was there. Mostly, she was off trailblazing, never having worked before the divorce.

You know kids who only appeared to have parents. Maybe you're one. Maybe a parent died, or skipped away completely, derelict in their duty. Or, maybe your parents were home but were overwhelmed, unapproachable, or worse, abusive.

ACCEPT WHAT IS

Put simply, it hurts. It is the kind of wistful, empty ache in the throat and chest that only complicated, painful feelings bring. We want to burst, like the skin of a ripe tomato, to relieve the pressure. We *must* mourn our loss, or even the parenting we never had. Finally, we are free to move beyond the unfillable void. Grieving, if allowed fully, has an end. Sir Winston Churchill said, "If you are going through hell, keep going." Because, surprise – hell is of our own making. Any horrible circumstance is compounded or relieved by what we think about it. No one escapes childhood unscathed. Even if you were well supported growing up, the money's on your having lived through some unhappiness. The key is to quit battling what *is*. Don't try to create a better past. My favorite Spanish professor would say, "You can't eat last Tuesday's lunch." Accepting what is, in this very moment, frees us to do something about it.

- That's what Mariah did. Rather than succumb to turmoil and insecurity, she threw herself into music.

- That's what Barack did. All the while searching for a sense of identity, he set high expectations for himself, sought mentors to advise him with his goals, and excelled in his studies.

- That's what Daniel did. Rather than sticking in hatred and depression, he aligned himself with his spirit, releasing through poetry. I asked Daniel what pulled him out of the chaos and despair. "Attitude. Attitude is 90%." It's as though Daniel read a quote by Charles Swindoll I had posted prominently in my Spanish classroom:

ATTITUDE

> Attitude…is more important…than education, money, circumstances, failures, successes, what others think, say or do…we have a choice regarding the attitude we embrace… We cannot change our past…life is 10% what happens to me and 90% how I react to it…we are in charge of our Attitudes.

No wonder I connected with Daniel. "And choice," he said. "I consciously chose not to be like my parents." And so did I. The sense of being controlled falls away when we realize choices. We can't always choose how we feel. We *can* choose what we do about it.

QUANTUM PHYSICS, HOLOGRAMS, AND—THOUGHTS?

It all begins with our thoughts. What we think about expands. The Law of Attraction states that we attract to ourselves the subject of our focus. The author of the best seller *Don't Sweat the Small Stuff*, Richard Carlson, says our moods are the source of our experience. Moment by moment, the way you feel is the result of your thoughts. I'll go further. You become what you think about all day. This isn't just self-help hooey. Science—specifically quantum physics—is confirming the power of thought to create our own realities.

What is quantum physics? Quantum refers to a very small, discrete packet of any physical property, such as energy or matter. Quantum physics says that everything is energy at its most basic level—or rather space filled with energy. Many scientists support the idea of the universe and humans as holograms of vibratory light and sound…energy. A hologram is a pattern of energy. Anywhere in that pattern, all the information exists to recreate that hologram. No matter the size, each part has everything it needs to reproduce its pattern. Each piece is a reflection of the whole.

If then our thoughts are a form of energy, they are reflected in the hologram (universe). Some scientists say the universal hologram is responsive to and receptive to our thoughts. Some theorize that this pattern of energy is Consciousness, or conceivably, the mind of God. At the quantum level, there is no separation between things, between *us* for instance. Energy here affects energy there and vice versa.

THE BUTTERFLY EFFECT

My son-in-law Greg is one of the most cheery people I have met. My daughter Emily said, "He wakes up every morning happy, whistling, a living steam kettle eager to pour into his day. He loves his work, whatever he's doing; even chores are OK. He may get frustrated, but it doesn't last. It's hard to be in a bad mood around him." Remember each piece reflecting the whole in the universal hologram? Emily might be grumpy, but because of interacting with up-beat Greg, she gets out of her funk. This creates a change not only in their corner of the world, but also in the whole of, say, Phoenix and even Arizona. This phenomenon is known as the Butterfly Effect. If a butterfly flaps its wings in Tokyo, a week later it may cause a hurricane in Florida. Our thoughts, feelings, and actions compound in ways we can't imagine—because of the hologram. This puts a big exclamation on the importance of our consciously creating what we want to experience, the kind of life we want to have. It's about more than me or you. Thank goodness.

The 2006 film *Babel* is an example of the Butterfly Effect. Drawn into a situation, shared because of a tragedy, are four groups of people from around the globe. In Morocco, Brad Pitt and Cate Blanchett are caught in an accident and the resulting turmoil. Linked are poor shepherds, two children and their caretaker, the caretaker's family in Mexico, as well as a father and his daughter in Japan. Babel's theme is barriers that separate humankind: barriers that stem from lack of communication and cultural misunderstandings—not sharing feelings, speaking different languages, not giving people a chance to explain, holding resentments, making assumptions, interrupting. One of the most heartbreaking segments is about the teenage Japanese girl who desperately wants to connect with someone. It's all emotionally frustrating until the end. It is the Tower of Babel played out. The Bible's Book of Genesis talks of such a tower in Babylon where because of a confusion of languages, no one could communicate.

Somewhere, maybe in the film's trailer, I heard this: "If you want to be understood, listen." *Oh my.* One of my posted notes reads: "Listening is a habit." I need to add "Listen to be understood."

We are learning how really connected we are, and science is offering how our consciousness might affect our experience of our world. Change our thoughts, and we change our world.

WHAT THE BLEEP?!

Do yourself a favor. Rent the DVD *What the #*!@*! Do We Know?!*, affectionately known as *What the Bleep?!* Follow Amanda down the rabbit hole into the quantum-field world of infinite possibilities. Upon learning how quantum physics affects our biology, Amanda moves out of depression and self-loathing into appreciating and loving herself. Interspersed, fourteen scientists and mystics discuss the Great Questions. We now know that our brains can't tell the difference between what we imagine and what occurs in our environment. Bleep shows us that what's happening on the inside creates our response to and experience of our outer world. The easy-to-grasp explanations are visual and funny, accomplished with animation.

At one point, Amanda is in the subway. A hysterical-looking woman with too much red lipstick is discussing large photographs of frozen water crystals. Japanese scientist, Dr. Masaru Emoto discovered that crystals change when specific thoughts and musical vibrations are directed toward them. Crystals exposed to words like "I hate you," "You fool," or heavy metal music, for example, look like deformed amorphous blobs. However, exposed to "You're cute," "I'm sorry," classical music, or The Beatles' song "Yesterday," the crystals are lovely. "Love and gratitude" produce the most exquisite and perfect ones.

A stranger approaches Amanda, saying, *"If thoughts can do that to water, what can thoughts do to us?"* Wow!

After all, our bodies are at least 70% water. Dr. Emoto's *The Hidden Messages in Water* is a small paperback, a third of which is photos. See for yourself how water records and distributes information, thoughts, and feelings.

SO WHAT?

What does all this mean to you? One of the physicists in *What the Bleep?!*, Dr. Fred Alan Wolf says, "We can indeed turn matter into feeling, feeling into matter…you can harness the power of quantum physics to transform any situation you find yourself in."

"Feeling into matter" has been documented only at the tiny subatomic level under controlled circumstances. However for twenty-five years,

Princeton engineering professor Robert G. Jahn has successfully tested volunteers' ability to influence physical objects by thought, albeit by only tiny amounts. His experiments are mainly notable because of the large number of trials and because they worked whether the person was close by or in Australia. Further, scientists have proven that the very act of observing events in one's life can change their outcome—The Observer Effect. We *can* create and alter our experience with what we choose to see or not see, with our thoughts and intentions.

CHOOSE IT!

So, thoughts and feelings are things, taking up space in our minds. Periodically, it's good to clean house. Reliving old thoughts prevents pathways to new ones. Science tells us Nature abhors a vacuum. If negative thought or emotion is not replaced by positive, the negative will return. We don't know why, it just does.

Sometimes, you have to consciously choose the positive. I know. For years, I posted a sticky note: "Choose It!" If you make it *your* choice, whatever is happening right now with you, your resistance fades away. Life becomes easier.

"I do what I love, and I love what I do," is another saying I use. Change it or choose it. One of my friends is perennially sunny. During a bleak time in my life, I asked Cody how she did it. "I work at it," was her succinct reply. Still, some days, "Choose It!" gets posted again. Accept and release.

YOU SHAPE YOUR STORY

Whatever has happened to you matters. Good or bad, though, it's not the end of your story. That was then. Our senior U.S. Senator from Arizona, John McCain, flew light attack aircraft in Vietnam. His A-4 Skyhawk was shot down. He was thrown in the prison known as Hanoi Hilton, infamous for its brutality. Upon hearing that his father was commander of U.S. forces in Vietnam, his captors offered McCain freedom. He refused. Honor was more important. He held to the code "First In, First Out." There were prisoners captured before him.

Interrogation, torture, and solitary confinement continued five more years. Today, Senator McCain is still incapable of lifting his arms above his head. Yet he claims that Vietnam was not the defining experience in his life. He has said, "I learned the futility of looking back in anger."

Nelson Mandela spent twenty-seven years in jail in South Africa for his people, for a concept, for a cause. He was educated as a lawyer and became a leading civil rights activist against apartheid. Meaning separateness, apartheid is the official policy of racial segregation formerly practiced by the government of South Africa (1948-94). Mandela emerged from prison without bitterness. Called the father of his country, he became the first democratically elected State President of South Africa. Mandela was awarded the Nobel Peace Prize for his stand against racism. Unwilling to let events dominate him, Nelson Mandela used more of who he was to conduct his life.

No victims here. It's not where you start, it's where you finish. Struggles and unhappiness can become a source of perspective and strength. They complete our identity. They can open us to compassion towards others. Looking past our own navel to someone else's need and extending ourselves not only is cathartic, but also adds a dimension of meaning to our own lives.

EXCUSES ROB YOU OF YOUR POWER

Think about this: if you argue for your limitations, you own them.

- Mariah persevered through major career problems, enjoying a successful comeback with "The Emancipation of Mimi" selling more than five million copies. She held the United States record for number-one singles of a solo artist and earned five Grammy Awards.

- Barack graduated from Harvard Law School, became an accomplished politician as well as the 44th United States President, recipient of the Nobel Prize, and is a responsible, loving father.

- My father didn't want John to define himself by a painful episode – his parents' divorce. I never heard John use excuses again, even when he lost his hearing at age fifty. He graduated from Stanford University, the University of Southern California Law School, and successfully practiced law in Sacramento.

- Today, Daniel is a man who's centered. He held several jobs while finishing a degree in Community Health; has a darling family; and has published his second volume of poems. He says, "I have accepted the hills and valleys for what they are—simply products of the experience of life."

Daniel's attitude shows. It is what draws people to him. I wish this for you.

If we believe things will work out, we'll see opportunities. If we don't, we'll see obstacles. Explore the Quantum Leap, which Dr. Wolf calls "the moment we transform possibility into reality." You are responsible for your own good day. Seize it.

About Janis

Janis Butler received a BA in history with a minor in French from Stanford University. Receiving a post bachelor's credential in elementary education, she taught language arts as well as substitute taught while she moved around the country. Once her youngest was in eighth grade, Janis received a BA in Spanish and taught Spanish for eight years at the high school and university levels. She is presently completing the second year of a master's degree program in spiritual psychology at the University of Santa Monica in California, for which she flies out monthly for classes. Janis contributed a chapter in the anthology *Pebbles in the Pond, Wave II – Transforming the World One Person at a Time,* complied by Christine Kloser. Currently she is writing *THE TWO YOUS: How to Awaken to Your Soul and Be Present to Yourself and to Life.* She lives in Scottsdale, Arizona.

You can connect with Janis at:
www.JanisFossetteButler.com
www.facebook.com/JanisWriting
www.twitter.com/JanisWriting

CHAPTER 4

IT'S A JUNGLE OUT THERE

BY JONATHON LEISE

During what has been referred to as the lost decade for investors, I have helped investors provide for their families, save for retirement, and generate income to pay their bills in their later years. This decade followed two decades of hard work to build my business, establish trust, and raise my own family. I grew up in a small town and went to the same high school as my parents - a baker and a housewife. Upon graduation, I went to college intent on becoming a lawyer. I worked several jobs to pay my way. Whenever I was home, I worked on the back of a trash truck. In the summers I also painted houses and cut lawns after the trash was picked up. At school, I gave campus tours and did odd jobs. I also sold my plasma at a local blood bank. I finished college with a degree in accounting.

When I graduated from college, I was too broke to pay for the application fees for law school. So I spent several days going into every office building in the area seeking a job. I then began working as a dishwasher at a local restaurant. After two weeks I received a job offer from one of the companies I had visited and accepted while standing in the kitchen of the restaurant. I became a financial analyst for a large company. While I was there I became involved in an investment club and began to develop an interest in stocks. I thought it might be a good business to get into. I also started going to night school for my MBA. One of the courses I took was Investments, taught by the director of research for a local brokerage firm. He was a great guy and we hit it off and I thought again I might want to get into the brokerage business.

I was introduced to my future wife, Debby, by a co-worker and soon fell in love. On our second date I informed her that she and I were going to get married and she might as well get used to the idea. We were married shortly thereafter and started a family right away. She left her job to raise the kids and we struggled financially. We then made two important decisions. First, we felt we should tithe 10% of my income to the local church. We believed that this act of obedience would invite financial blessing. I also decided to take the leap into the 100% commission world of stock brokerage. It was a chance to get into a field I was interested in and help people while I was at it. First, I had to make less money while I was building a clientele, but Debby supported me and I was not afraid to put in the work necessary to succeed. I borrowed some money to pay a consultant to teach me how to interview and landed a position with Dean Witter. It was harder than it looked - it still is - but slowly people began to give me a chance and a book of business began to evolve.

While I was building my business, we ate almost exclusively from our garden. Debby became a wizard at making zucchini, squash and tomatoes look and taste different every night. I drove our bright orange Vega wagon to appointments and parked around the corner so prospective clients would not see how poor I was. In reality, I was rich. I had a beautiful wife who believed in me and a growing family that we enjoyed, along with a God that was faithful.

After a few years of working 2 to 3 nights a week cold-calling, giving investment seminars, and begging for business, I felt I could spare one night a week to go back to school and finish my MBA, which I did in 1986. I also attained my Certified Financial Planner designation at the same time. Building any business is very hard work. Keeping it going and making it grow is even harder. I have worked very hard and also been very blessed to have met and been influenced by some truly wonderful people. The first and most influential was my father. He taught me many lessons growing up. Mostly, he taught by example, working long hours to build his business, provide for his family, send his kids to college, and to retire some day. Today in my practice, I apply some of his favorite phrases, which helps me to keep perspective and stay focused as we navigate uncertain economic times.

- *"It's a jungle out there."* To think that life and more specifically investing will be easy is naive at best. Accumulating, preserving, distributing and transferring wealth is not easy and should be entered into with the expectation that there will be many obstacles along the way. A well thought-out plan is a must to overcome those obstacles. That is why I believe the advice and counsel of a qualified and dedicated financial professional is essential.

I enjoyed watching my sons play baseball from Little League all the way to the College World Series. They were not big and strong, but they were real good hitters. The pitchers they faced threw hard, and also threw curves and sliders. They had about one second to decide whether or not to swing. So, how did they do so well? The answer is a disciplined approach, or process, to swinging the bat. There are several keys to hitting that also apply to the investment process. First, you need a plan. A hitter needs to know what he is looking to accomplish, before stepping up to the plate. Depending on the pitcher he is facing, how many outs, how many runners are on base, and even the score, the hitter's objective may differ. Does he want to be aggressive or "work the count?" Does he need to hit the ball deep or simply make contact?

An investor also needs to have a plan based upon their life circumstances. Does he need to be aggressive or simply preserve capital? Is he looking for growth or current income? The plan should take into consideration all possible scenarios: inflation and rising interest rates; bull or bear markets; deflation and falling interest rates; "Black Swan" events.

- *"More horse power, less horse sense."* My dad used this one to let me know that driving too fast was not smart or "slow and steady wins the race." In the investing world, it is more prudent and the odds of success are much higher if we try to accumulate wealth slowly, rather than try to beat the market with hot stock picks. You need to have a process that is scalable, repeatable, and flexible. While the plan is very important, it is the execution that is critical. In order to hit a baseball you have to see it, recognize the pitch, and decide whether you can accomplish your goal by swinging at that pitch. An investor also needs to "see the ball," by knowing what he owns, and how those things fit into his plan. Rather than accumulating a series of "hot tips," or wild swings, the portfolio should be designed to fit the investor's plan.

Disciplined hitting requires that you keep your hands back as long as possible so you can recognize the pitch and avoid "chasing" a pitch that looks "fat" only to curve or tail away. A disciplined investor stays with investments that fit his plan and avoids "chasing" deals or the latest hot fad. Chasing performance is like swinging at a bad pitch.

Most of the time, you will strike out. A good hitter should be prepared to hit all types of pitches and adjust accordingly. The good investor should be prepared to include all types of sectors and asset classes in his portfolio and adjust accordingly. A well-balanced portfolio, re-balanced and adjusted periodically, will increase an investor's odds for success.

• *"It's nice to be important, but more important to be nice."* My job is to help people meet their goals and objectives and I could not do that effectively if I did not truly care. Personal, caring, loving service will help more than a long list of credentials. If I am successful in helping people, then my income will take care of itself. A few years ago I came across an open letter in the local paper from a father thanking everyone for their prayers and support for his son who had just returned from Iraq. The last time I had been with them was five years prior. I was coaching a baseball team that was hosting a tournament with teams from all over the country. The coaches wanted the experience to be special, so we took the team out for meals and acted like we were on the road. The son was on the team and the father joined us at all of the meals. When the subject of work came up this father told us his employer would not let him miss work so he quit! He said we would never get to experience something like this again with our sons. Knowing that his son went on to risk his life to protect me and my family, I realize how right he was. Some things are priceless and matter more than money.

A few years later, when my son was enjoying his last college baseball season, I traveled to watch him play in a weekend series. I was happy to be near my son sharing the afternoon on a beautiful day. In the last game he struck out. As was my habit, whenever he had a bad at-bat, I would change my seat. So I walked around the dugout where I came upon another father sharing the afternoon on a beautiful day with his son. However, this father was pushing his son in a wheelchair. After the game I hugged my son extra tight as he got on the team bus and traveled home knowing that while my expertise is certainly important to my job, "caring" is what truly matters.

• *"Be good to the people you meet on the way up, because you may meet the same people on the way down."* This was one of my favorites and was his way of telling me to never forget where I came from. If we appreciate and remember the disciplines it took to attain everything worthwhile, we are more likely to keep growing professionally and personally. It is also important to remember all of the people who helped you along the way and thank them whenever you can. I incorporate this lesson by staying involved with local charities and organizations and through continuing to tithe to the local church. Among the many organizations I support is Coaches vs. Cancer, a program founded by the American Cancer Society and the National Association of Basketball Coaches that empowers coaches, their teams and communities to make a difference in the fight against cancer. Several years ago, I attended one of their events and met the local organizers and coaches. When I saw how much they cared it inspired me to get involved. I now sponsor and attend many of their events. If I can make a small difference in someone else's life or be a blessing to someone each day, then that day has been worthwhile.

I have had the pleasure of having friends as clients and clients become friends. What began in many cases as business became personal. I have been able to touch peoples' lives and have them touch mine in so many ways. I am grateful that so many have entrusted me with such an important part of their lives. I have shared in the joy of their children and grandchildren being born, and in the trials, tribulations, and triumphs of watching them grow up. I have suffered along with many through the extended illness or loss of a spouse and witnessed the anguish over long-term care decisions for loved ones. I have lost sleep worrying about their investments so they would not have to. I hope that I have made their lives better by taking some of the worry out of reaching their financial objectives. I resolve to stay armed with as much education, knowledge and technology as possible, stay excited about the business I am in and take advantage of every opportunity to improve. Finally, I will continue to give to causes that are important to my family, my friends and my clients.

About Jonathon

Jon Leise believes that the key to financial success lies in a holistic financial planning approach – which he implements by providing a variety of specialized products and services. He has developed a client service philosophy that focuses on highly personal and attentive relationships and customized, objective services. Jon joined Janney Montgomery Scott LLC in 1992 and serves as Executive Vice President/Wealth Management and Assistant Branch Manager of the Philadelphia office. He is a member of Janney's CEO Roundtable, former member of the Financial Advisory Council, a 2011 NABCAP Premier Advisor, and 2013 Five Star Professional Wealth Manager.

Jon is the founding member of the Leise Wealth Management Group of Janney Montgomery Scott. It is a family affair that includes his two sons and daughter as well as close friends. His daughter, Jenna, has worked with Janney since 1996 including seven years in the Retirement Plans Department where she received the Janney Meritorious Service Award. Jon Jr., does research and performance reporting and holds the Retirement Income Planning certificate from Wharton. His son Jake is focused on business development. Donna, Jon's registered assistant, has been with him for over twenty years. She is familiar with all aspects of the Wealth Management process. His friend Jim, who started with Jon in the business more than three decades ago, also is an integral member of the team.

Among its many tools, Janney offers a retirement income evaluator that allows investors to *"test drive your retirement."* This program enables people to sit in the driver's seat of their own retirement and personally test the feel and fit of their particular plan. With this tool, investors can better understand the effects of their decisions and determine the best course of action. Details can be found at: *LEISEWEALTHMANAGEMENT.COM.*

Before joining Janney, Jon worked as a financial analyst for the RCA Service Company and as a registered representative with Dean Witter Reynolds and Legg Mason Wood Walker. He received his Bachelor of Arts degree from Franklin & Marshall College and his Masters of Business Administration degree from Drexel University. Jon furthered his education by earning a CERTIFIED FINANCIAL PLANNER™ designation from the College for Financial Planning and the Accredited Wealth Management Advisor℠ certificate from The Wharton School of Business at the University of Pennsylvania. Jon is currently seeking his Master's degree in Gerontology from Saint Joseph's University.

Outside the office, Jon serves as an active member of his community. He is a former member of the Riverwinds Advisory Board, West Deptford Planning Board, the Woodbury Zoning Board, and the Collingswood Board of Education. Currently, Jon is very active in Coaches vs. Cancer, a program founded by the American Cancer Society and the National Association of Basketball Coaches (NABC) that empowers coaches, their teams and communities to make a difference in the fight against cancer. He also remains active in the West Deptford Little League baseball program.

Jon resides in West Deptford, NJ, with his wife Debby. They have three daughters, two sons, four grandsons and two granddaughters.

CHAPTER 5

UNDERSTANDING SUCCESS: AN INTRODUCTION TO THE REAL WEALTH EQUATION™

BY MALCOLM ROSS

Measure your wealth not by the things that you have but by the things that you have which money cannot buy.
~ Abraham Lincoln

I was born in Africa, the youngest of six children, into a family of privilege but not one of significant wealth. My father, a career civil servant, served much of his life in rural areas working with the African communities to build schools, clinics, and roads, specializing in community development. Later in his career he was a principal advisor to the government before the ravages of cancer steadily destroyed his health and claimed his life after a valiant four-year fight, the last part of which we nursed him as a family at home. Growing up, I was repeatedly reminded by him of the privilege and opportunity into which I had been born and I was acutely aware of the special family relationship that he developed with my mother, my siblings and me. While he was invested as Grand Officer of the Legion of Merit, the country's highest honour for his service to the nation, he was far more proud of the achievements and character of his children than of any award bestowed on him by the government. It gave him considerable joy to see his children fulfill their talents whether in being the youngest ever District Commissioner like my brother; artistic, ballet and academic success like my sisters, or representing province and country at sport as my sister and I did. When I was 17, a week before he died, he shared this with me: "Your mother and I can teach you a love of God, a love of family and we can give you a good education. After that it is up to you!" This was a true legacy, the value of which was only later fully evident to me.

Over the next few years, the civil war in Zimbabwe (then Rhodesia) claimed the lives of my older brother and of my brother-in-law, and I too saw combat action and narrowly escaped death from a land mine. I went to university in South Africa and was blessed with a good education. I trained as an accountant and by the age of 24 was made Financial Director and a minority shareholder for a group of engineering companies. I met and quickly married my wife Melanie (before she saw the real me!) who taught Agricultural Marketing at the University of Zimbabwe and together we built a wonderful life at our lovely 2.5-acre garden property with tennis court and pool, along with our share in a 440-acre mountain farm with 120 jersey cows and 40-acres of apple orchards. I remember on the day of my appointment as Financial Director, a close friend and mentor said, "Remember Malcolm, from those to whom much is given, much is expected!"

Later, when I had helped establish a Hewlett Packard Distributorship in Zimbabwe, the scourge of corruption steadily engulfed both government and business. As this became a daily reality and challenge, my wife and I determined that for the sake of our principles and for the future wellbeing of our children we would accept a two-year contract in South Africa and then move to Canada. This may sound a simple choice now, but it involved us leaving Zimbabwe with $300 and our furniture, making two international moves in twenty four months and leaving family and friends half-a-world away in Africa.

A year after arriving in Canada, the mining industry, in which I was involved in selling software, collapsed. Essentially broke, the other side of the world from family and with no real community, we were forced to rebuild our lives, relying heavily on the legacy our parents provided: *our faith, our family and our education*. It was a significant test when we lost my sister to cancer and my mother to a broken heart within our first two years in Canada.

To provide for my family, I joined the financial services industry and early in that career I was fortunate to hear two speakers who, at different moments, helped me shape my career. The first speaker was best-selling author Robert Kriegel of "If it ain't broke, break it!" fame. His inspirational story of Dick Fosberry "raising the bar above the competition and then flying over the bar" motivated me to raise the bar in my field. In the few minutes I spent with Robert Kriegel, he challenged me to be an educator and not a salesman, and to become the kind of professional that people would seek out when they wanted wise counsel. Although this was not easy as a "rookie" in Canada, many of the innovations I have helped develop in the planning field were sparked by challenging entrenched practices, something I learned from Kriegel's irreverent advice: "Sacred cows make the best burgers!"

An equally important influence for me was a co-author in this book, Brian Tracy, who retold the story of his journey as a young man by vehicle from Britain through Africa. Of particular significance was of crossing the sands of the Sahara beacon-to-beacon "one oil barrel at a time." For me this meant persistency, building my business deliberately and not expecting immediate success. Rather, his story helped me to understand that success could be a journey rather than just a destination.

My journey, through the loss of family, and my own encounter with mortality, made me want to believe that there was greater purpose in life than simply our transition through it. After having achieved our own relative financial success, only to then give that up for the future of my family helped me realise that finances were not the measure of real wealth. It was at this point that I started to develop the concept of Family Wealth Optimization™.

Upon arriving in Canada, I was quick to learn that taxation is often the largest ongoing expense and the most predictable investment risk for most affluent people. Any financial plan that does not fully factor in the impact of taxes is therefore almost certainly deficient. Generally, the people providing the tax advice rarely worked with financial products and the financial advisors rarely fully understood taxes. This is where I set about to differentiate my business. In 2002, I was recognized as the *Advisors Edge Magazine's* <u>Advisor of the Year</u> for British Columbia and the Territories.

Family Wealth Optimization ™ is the process by which client families actively set about to structure their personal and financial affairs to fulfill their values and purpose in the most tax effective manner. In order to achieve Wealth Optimization, meaningful discussions about the driving values must occur. To facilitate this discussion, I evolved a formula which I call *The Real Wealth Equation ™*.

Real Wealth (RW) is the **product** of Personal Fulfillment (PF) multiplied by Family Harmony (FH) multiplied by Financial Contentment (FC) multiplied by Social Contribution (SC). This can be depicted as follows:

RW = PF x FH x FC x SC

SOCIAL CONTRIBUTION

To get a better understanding of this equation, let's reverse engineer this formula and start by examining the last element – Social Contribution. We do not own the planet, its environment, its communities or its neighbourhoods, but if we don't look after them and leave them better off after our passing, then we leave it worse off for our kids and grandkids. Is that what we want? Almost universally the answer to this question is a resounding "NO!" This therefore introduces the concept of Stewardship. Making *stewardship* choices about how we manage and consume the earth's resources, caring for the disenfranchised in our streets and in slums, coaching a football team, all contribute to our *social contribution*.

FINANCIAL CONTENTMENT

The next element is Financial Contentment. John D. Rockefeller, when a reporter asked him, "How much money is enough?" responded, "Just a little bit more." If we try to put a number on a scoreboard of how much is enough, we will never be content and we will always be striving for more, especially as we live in an intensely competitive world. No matter how much we get on the scoreboard, we will always be looking to see how much others have. Comparing ourselves to those who have more, though, may actually reduce our level of contentment. The key, therefore, is to take a step back and ask, "What is Financial Contentment?"

Coming from Africa, I can attest to the fact that some of the most content people I have ever met were rural farmers, people who were not continually bombarded with advertisements for products that satisfied needs and wants they didn't even realize they had. They were fundamentally content with their lifestyle and with what they possessed. The secret to *Financial Contentment is not having what you want, but wanting what you have*!

Among these people, Financial Contentment is about understanding *sufficiency,* and this awareness manifests itself in the sense of hospitality those communities have, and their commitment to sharing resources to support community and family relationships.

FAMILY HARMONY

This brings me to the next element in our equation, namely Family Harmony. We all know that, "if mama ain't happy then no-one is happy." But then, "if papa ain't happy no-one is happy," and if the kids are being bullied at school then no-one is happy either. Because of these dynamics, investment in family *relationships* is essential, and this involves developing a real understanding and respect of the unique drives, passions and interests of each of the family members. Building communication and trust is often presumed in families, but regrettably, unless they are intentional, the distractions of work, social commitments, sport, peer pressure and addictions can fracture Family Harmony.

Many conflicts in spousal and family relationships relate to money. Many families reach the peak of this conflict when there is an estate settlement and perceptions of fairness and equity are examined when the will is read. How can this tension be avoided? Developing and establishing a common system of values is vital to building and sustaining family unity. There is no single right way to do this, but effective communication around money-related matters is essential.

PERSONAL FULFILLMENT

The first variable in the equation and the last we will examine is Personal Fulfillment. This naturally relates to the individual and to whatever the individual defines as Personal Fulfillment for themselves. Fulfillment implies a sense of purpose and so it is necessary to look at the individual's *sense of purpose*. For some people it is a spiritual question and relates to their faith and a sense of who they were created to be, whereas for others it is much more a unique/tangible definition of purpose aimed at particular goals. Either way, if people are subordinating their own purposes and always compromising their personal fulfillment for another person or system, there will ultimately be a lack of satisfaction. This, in turn, may well play out in seeking compensatory fulfillment in different ways. Yet personal fulfillment is something that we must empower in our children and families as well as in ourselves. *It is important we enable our children to seek their own purpose and to develop their passions and talents in the fulfilling of that purpose.*

LIFE IS NOT A ZERO SUM GAME

For much of our lives, we grow up believing that life is about give and take. We have an innate sense of equity and fairness. There comes a point, however, when we each come to understand that life is not fair, and the decisions we make may often have unintended consequences. I illustrate this in the Real Wealth Equation as follows:

Assume we have 40 units of energy to expend and that we assign 10 units of energy to each of the four components. Since the result of the equation is the product of the four components:

The result is 10,000 units of satisfaction = 10 x 10 x 10 x 10

However, if I have an imbalance in the way in which I apply my energy, for example if I take away from my Personal Fulfillment to pursue Financial Contentment, then look what happens to the equation:

The result declines to 7,500 units of satisfaction = 5 x 10 x 15 x 10

The more out of balance the resource allocation becomes, the lower the score. Moreover, mathematics teaches us that as soon as one component becomes zero the result of whole equation is zero.

0 units of satisfaction = 10 x 0 x 20 x 10

So, for example, I may achieve significant financial success, but if it is at the expense of compromised family relationships there may be little joy to be found.

WE ARE THE PRODUCT OF OUR DECISIONS

We are each unique with different talents and from different circumstances. I appreciated the Harvard Commencement address of J.K. Rowling where she said that if you are old enough to take control of the wheel, you become responsible for the decisions that follow. Often, we forget that by making the decision to do one thing, we are also choosing *not* to do something else, and the consequences of that exclusion may be very unexpected. For this reason I believe that the Real Wealth Equation has value in expressing the perspective that **our lives are not the sum of our choices but rather the product of our decisions!**

BALANCE – THE WINNING WAY

Understanding the Real Wealth Equation helps frame purpose, family relationships, financial sufficiency, and stewardship for ourselves, our children and our grandchildren. Communication about purpose, values, passions and dreams empowers families to grow into a better understanding and respect for each other, and develop lasting legacies built on common values. Our values are more enduring than the value of our assets - my parents' legacy is a simple example of that. In our materialistic, instant gratification, make-over driven society, taking stock of WHY we do things is essential. Through balance of purpose, relationships, sufficiency, and stewardship, we may optimize our family wealth and find a truly winning way!

About Malcolm

Malcolm Ross is a sought after Family Office Advisor to business owners and successful families. He helps navigate the difficulties of building successful businesses, preparing for business succession and the challenges of family wealth transfer. His belief is that Family Wealth Optimization™ is the process of aligning the client family value with that family's values.

Malcolm is a multiple-award winning Canadian Certified Financial Planner (*Advisors Edge Magazine* 2002 and 2013 Five Star Wealth Advisor™), a Chartered Life Underwriter, a Registered Trust and Estate Practitioner, a Certified Family Business Advisor, a CAFÉ trained Family Board and Council Facilitator and the Founder of Canada's first Virtual Family Office™. With over 35 years of international business experience Malcolm is unique in his ability to address family business and succession from farming, manufacturing, technology, hospitality, transport, retail sales, construction, industrial services, professional services and real estate. He has been selected as one of America's Premier Experts™ for his client-centred, process-driven, collaborative advisory approach for advising business families—which is at the core of the successful Virtual Family Office™ model which he pioneered in Canada.

He is an author and engaging international public speaker who has a spoken at conferences for Canadian National Christian Foundation and Advisors with Purpose, Canadian Association of Gift Planners, Society of Trust and Estate Planners, Canadian Association of Financial Planners, Vancouver Board of Trade, Opal Canadian Family Office Conferences and the First South African Family Business Conference. In addition he was the Founder of the Financial Advisor Network FAN Program which has provided professional development to over 750 professional accountants in British Columbia, Canada in the areas of tax and estate planning, family business succession and family wealth optimization. He speaks regularly on the subjects of Family Wealth Optimization™ and of structuring business for sale, succession and purchase.

Malcolm believes in involvement in local and global community service, having been a Past-President of Vancouver Arbutus Rotary Club, a former member of the Professional Advisory Committee to Sauder School of Business UBC Business Families Centre, lectured in Advanced Financial Planning at Trinity Western University, is a past Treasurer of St John's (Shaughnessy) Anglican Church, and Chairman of African Enterprise Canada. He is a proud husband of Melanie (who has suffered him for over 30 years), and father of Shaun (and Nicki) and Kathy, adult children who are a constant inspiration for faith, relationship and service.

You can connect with Malcolm at:
Malcolm@investaflex.com
www.twitter.com/TaxAlphaGuy
http://ca.linkedin.com/in/malcolmdross/
www.investaflex.com

CHAPTER 6

THE #1 RULE IN MARKETING...

BY MARK GAFFNEY

I am often asked at my training sessions and conferences, what are the most important strategies and concepts that we need to focus on in our marketing? My answer usually raises an eyebrow or two because the most fundamental premise of effective marketing is something that is unfortunately too rarely thought about. In fact, the majority of companies I consult for put this enormously important concept either low on the totem pole or it is completely non-existent in their planning.

To appropriately explain the *#1 Rule in Marketing*, I refer back to a conference I attended in 1992 during my early marketing days. At this time in my career, I was a musician trying to make it in the crazy world of the music industry. In addition to trying to make it myself, I was also assisting other groups with their music marketing. Who knew that the single most important premise of successful marketing was going to be picked up at a music industry conference?

The NYC hotel banquet room was filled with hundreds of musicians hungry for the essential industry information and advice to take their careers to the next level. The conference was conducted by a well-known music industry agent who handled the likes of Stevie Nicks and Don Henley to name a couple. Interestingly enough, the presenter opened up the seminar by saying, "Do yourself a favor and get out of this crazy business." He went on to say that your talent and song writing ability would only play a small role in your success. I thought success was all about talent and hard work, but to my dismay, I found out quickly that we weren't focused on the right dynamics of the industry to attain success.

Now it's time for a short marketing exercise. Please grab a pen and paper and participate in this with me. All you have to do is answer one question. I have asked this question to groups of three to three hundred in trainings all across the country just like it was asked to me back in 1992 at that NYC music industry conference.

Let's get started. Write the first ten things that come to mind (and don't censor yourself) when I say "Madonna". Please do not continue reading until you have written all ten of your answers. If you're like most of the groups I have worked with through the years (and I am willing to bet that you are) then your answers do not contain any of the following responses: great singer, wonderful song writer, great dancer or talented artist. Instead, your answers contain all of the memorable and sometimes controversial things that she's done throughout her career that are now burned into the American Psyche.

So how can it be that in a room of three hundred plus musicians, not a single person mentions her talent? She does have talent…right? Of course she does, but something has superseded her talent. So what is that and how does it pertain to us?

So there I was in my mid 20s attending a music conference only to find out that my talent, hard work and commitment were no longer the most important things in becoming successful. It was at that moment that I learned the #1 most important rule in marketing: *Image Is Everything!* Let me say it again while you twist in your chair like I did in 1992. *Image Is Everything!* So, let me explain this in a way that you can discuss this premise with your respective marketing teams. The headline should read like this: **In a marketing context, all things created equal, he or she with the best image wins.** So you are probably asking yourself right now, what does a pop diva and her image have to do with my business? The answer is: more than you may care to believe!

My consulting niche, since 2002, has been the financial services industry. This industry is filled with many talented, educated and multi-licensed advisors who have experienced very limited financial success on their own. Conversely, the vast majority of advisors who have excelled at the highest levels, have cultivated their image, brand and persona to a point where they are perceived as the most elite. It is this perception that has propelled them to Mt. Everest success levels.

So, would the "image" exercise we did earlier apply to the following financial celebrities: Dave Ramsey, Jim Cramer, Suze Orman and Clark Howard? You're darn right it would. That's because their celebrity image supersedes their talent. What can we learn from these seven-figure financial celebrities? Are they great advisors? Whether you believe that they are or aren't is totally irrelevant. That's because these individuals are perceived by millions and millions of Americans as the "go to" experts for financial advice. Do you think these financial icons and their respective marketing teams understand the importance of image, brand and persona? Not only are they thinking about it, but they are always trying to leverage it to achieve greater success.

So, in order to validate my point fully about image, let's take a moment to reflect on the 2012 Presidential Election between candidates Mitt Romney and Barack Obama. This was a referendum on image fought in the court of public opinion. In the modern era of 24-hour news cycles and the ever-present Internet, you had no choice but to be barraged by daily polls, soundbites and iconic images. Each candidate and their spin doctors worked tirelessly to win the hearts and minds of the American public hoping to influence the outcome at the polls. At the end of the day, the Presidential Election was about image and likability over substance, experience and talent. So remember… **the #1 Rule in Marketing is: Image is everything and all things created equal, he or she with the best image wins!**

So now let's take a look at four image tips that will help you go DEEP – (Develop, Elevate, Execute and Protect) – with your image, brand and persona.

IMAGE TIP #1: UTILIZE A GRAPHIC DESIGNER

Utilizing a graphic designer is the easiest way to jump start your image. Hopefully the days of having the office administrator paste Clip Art onto a Word document are over. For most of my clients, I recommend working with a graphic designer who can come to their office. This way, if the artist is good, they will become a true strategic partner in the business making real impactful changes on all marketing pieces both internally and externally. My secret for finding a really good artist is to contact a handful of local printers and ask them who they use on a regular basis. After you have the names, then check out their websites and have them bring in their portfolios examples. Graphic designers will typically cost between $60 and $150 per hour for their services. I assure you that once you find the right person or people, they will become worth their weight in gold. Also, a good graphic designer will help your business achieve an agency look without paying an agency price.

IMAGE TIP #2: CO-BRANDING

Associating your brand with other time-honored local and national brands will give you and your business instant credibility, trust and respect. All of your marketing materials should incorporate co-branding whenever possible. The reason is simple: you couldn't possibly invest the money and resources that these local and national brands have invested in developing and promoting themselves, so leverage your Image and Brand by riding the coattails of successful brands. The easiest and most cost effective way to establish a strong co-branding strategy is to secure the services of a good PR firm. One of the best PR firms in the country is Dicks and Nanton in Orlando, Florida. I have utilized their services on several occasions with excellent results.

IMAGE TIP #3: THE LITMUS TEST

Through the years I have developed a litmus test for all of the marketing materials that leave my office and my clients' offices. This litmus test is specifically designed for the financial services industry, but I have found that it works equally as well with other professional services companies.

The first thing I look for in our marketing is *elegance*. Few things are more attractive than elegance. The goal of being elegant is to outclass our competition. Let me tell you a quick story about a client I had recently who was wondering why his direct mail pieces weren't working. I had asked him if he kept a file of his competitions pieces so we could do a comparison. He broke out a full folder of multiple direct mail pieces; most of his competitors' marketing was designed to accomplish the same net result he was trying to accomplish. After the campaign was over, we put his marketing pieces out on the conference table with all of the others. It became crystal clear in seconds that his pieces were uniquely inferior to that of his competition. But the one thing that truly stuck out was that he was being outclassed by his competitors' *elegant* mail pieces. Since the "laws of attraction" dictate that we must become that which we wish to attract, you will need to market yourself and your business in an elegant manner.

The second thing I look for in our marketing is: does it radiate a *Rockstar* quality? Simply put, does our marketing exude a larger-than-life quality? That being said ... we do need to be careful. Today's regulatory agencies are red hot and the days of playing it fast and loose with compliance are over. So how do we construct a *Rockstar* marketing piece but stay within compliance? Easy. We simply turn up the volume on the truthful things that make us different and special. We do not lie and we do not embellish. With a little bit of initial discovery, I have always found the things about my clients that make them truly unique. Remember this: *Rockstars* attract other *Rockstars,* and *Rockstars* attract just about everybody.

Lastly, our marketing needs to be *messianic.* The pure definition of the word messianic means to be a deliverer or the one who will deliver. What does this mean in a marketing context? It means that it is simply not enough to tell your prospective new clients what you do. Instead, you need to inform them on how you are going to help them, educate them and assist them in achieving their goals and dreams. You need to compel them to the greater good and that greater good is you.

IMAGE TIP #4: REINVENT YOUR IMAGE

As you and your business gain more experience and become more successful, it is important to reevaluate and reinvent your current image, brand and persona. Remember earlier when I wrote about going DEEP (Develop, Elevate, Execute and Protect) with your image? The message you were conveying to the marketplace last year may not be relevant today. So don't be afraid to reinvent the image and the message. I have evaluated many companies where their image and message had gotten so lost over the years. In some cases, what they were putting into the marketplace had actually become harmful to current and future business. This is an area where obtaining the services of a good Ad Agency could have a significant impact on your business. Remember this: The starting place for all of your marketing campaigns is a well-developed brand and message.

For the last twenty plus years I have had the great fortune and opportunity to educate, coach and counsel wonderful companies, large and small, from coast to coast. Without fail, the first thing I look at, assess and discuss is **the #1 rule in marketing…**

IMAGE IS EVERYTHING, and all things created equal, he or she with the best image wins!

About Mark

Mark Gaffney is the co-founder of 20M Consulting LLC, a boutique consulting firm for the financial services industry. In his 20+ year marketing career, Mark Gaffney's list of credits include: Director of Marketing for one of the most successful independent financial firms in the country, Executive Producer of the syndicated television show *Strategic Wealth with Matt Dicken* (on ABC) and the syndicated financial radio shows *The Matt Dicken Show* and *The Road To Retirement*. He is also a sought-after marketing strategist, keynote speaker and author.

Mark's client list reads like a "Who's Who" of the financial services industry. Since 2002, he has coached, consulted and trained hundreds of financial professionals in over 30 states. Mark's "Image and Brand" advertising agency approach to financial marketing has made him a prominent authority throughout the national advisor community.

Mark has worked with multi-billion dollar corporations as well as start-ups and business entrepreneurs at all phases of development. His marketing strategies have returned hundreds of millions of converted assets for his financial clients. The top echelons of Mark's Private Client Group are proud members of his "$20 Million Dollar Club." Mark lives in Tampa, Florida with his wife Jennifer and, their three children Isabella, Alexandrea and Liam.

CHAPTER 7

DO SOMETHING SPECIAL TODAY

BY DARON DESTINY

"Do something special today," yelled Ms. Brown, the school bus driver, as she slammed on the brakes and pulled the black lever to open the door of the big yellow school bus. Almost everyday Ms. Brown would say kind words to motivate my classmates and I as we hopped off the bus and headed home after another long day of school. We were 6th graders growing up in a rough part of Fort Lauderdale, Florida, so Ms. Brown knew those kind words were needed because most of us as young black kids came from poverty-stricken single parent homes where the Mother worked two or three jobs just to make ends meet. Our sincere yet overworked mothers were so stressed trying to keep food on the table that such kind and motivating words often came few and far between, if at all. Fortunately, my mother was always very encouraging and supportive regardless of our situation. I was one of the lucky ones and I knew it.

As Ms. Brown drove away, the words 'Do Something Special Today' echoed over and over in my head. My friends and I and gave each other high-fives and parted ways, but then we heard a loud and blaring whistle. We looked over to the neighborhood park and saw Mr. Scott, the Park Recreations Director, waving for all of us to come to him.

We ran over because whenever Mr. Scott blew that whistle it meant he was organizing some type of event for us. Sometimes it was a basketball game for us to play against another park or he had free tickets to take us to a Miami Dolphins game or some other cool event to get us out of the ghetto for a few hours.

"Can you knuckleheads play soccer?" he asked. We all nodded that we could but the truth was that we only played it in P.E. class once every blue moon and none of us were very skilled at it. We only played basketball and football in our neighborhood. If you were caught dead with a soccer ball, then please be prepared to be the butt of all jokes for quite a while.

"Holiday Park has asked us to come play a soccer game today. You'll get your butts kicked, but it will be a learning experience for you and also I will take you to McDonald's after the game," proclaimed Mr. Scott. We were ecstatic. Butt-kicking or not, McDonald's was a rare treat in those days. I ran home, dropped off my books and left a note for Mom that I would be with Mr. Scott. I rushed back to the park and jumped in the van with my friends. As Mr. Scott weaved through traffic, my buddies debated on which sandwich was better: the Big Mac or Quarter Pounder with cheese. They all said which one they were going to get after the game. I stared out the window and ignored the arguing because I knew the Filet'O Fish sandwich was the one I was going to get with a large order of french fries. Heaven awaits.

Once we reached Holiday Park, Mr. Scott rushed all ten of us from the van to the field. As my teammates and I began to stretch and get loose, I noticed a small folding table packed with trophies that read:

> ### Ft. Laud Rec. Dept. Jr. Champs 1981

The design of the trophies was a Professional soccer player kicking a ball. They glistened so brightly it seemed like each trophy had its own Sun beaming down on it. They were beautiful.

Our opponents were across the field sporting red jerseys, white shorts and long red socks with chin guards. They all wore black cleats with white laces and some had on red wristbands and headbands. They looked professional. They were organized. They were a real soccer team. On the other hand, we looked like a bunch of guys headed to the Arcade Game Room to play Pac-Man and Donkey Kong for the rest of the day. Some of my teammates had on long pants and a few even had on the same dress shoes they wore to school. None of us wore cleats but luckily most of us at least had on shorts and sneakers.

Two white men approached Mr. Scott. "Thank you for putting together a team on such short notice," said the older gentleman with a beard that would rival Santa Claus. "This is a Championship Game but the other team had to cancel. However, the By-Laws of this Park forces us to have an actual game before we can award any trophies. That's why you all are here today so we can have a game and give them their trophies." Mr. Scott nodded his head and the man continued talking. "This here is the Photographer and we would like to have the Red team take pictures with their parents and the trophies before the sun goes down. This will save us time when awarding them the Championship trophies after the game." Mr. Scott agreed.

The two men rushed back to the table and the Red Team began taking pictures with their parents while holding the Championship trophy in their hands. They took a combination of team photos and individual shots. They even had a group shot with the coaches, players and parents all holding up the fore finger as if to say We Are Number One!

Our jaws dropped to the ground as the photos were being taken. I looked at my teammates and saw McDonald's had clearly left their mind. We felt disrespected. We felt violated. Obviously, the Red Team feels we had no chance of beating them. At that point, our focus changed. The leader in me began to strategize on how we might possibly win this game. As I huddled up everyone, all the greatest sports upsets I had ever read about or saw on television flashed before my eyes.

Suddenly, I could clearly see Muhammad Ali standing over Sonny Liston, as he won the heavyweight crown in 1965 when no one gave him a chance to last even one round. Images of legendary quarterback Joe Namath running off the field after his New York Jets beat the Baltimore Colts 16-7 in Super Bowl III also raced through my mind. Just one year earlier, I sat on my living room floor and watched the Men's USA Hockey Team win the gold medal in the 1980 Winter Olympics after upsetting Russia in the semi-final game. Now here I am with a chance to make my own sports history.

Finally, the Red Team stopped taking pictures and returned all the trophies to the table. As Mr. Scott stood to the side, I dropped down to one knee in the middle of the huddle like I was a quarterback. "Fat Mike, you'll play Goalie," I said. "Willie, Alvin, Richard and myself will play upfront and push the ball and try to score. The rest of you hang back on defense." We broke the huddle just as the referee signaled it was time to start the game. "Remember not to touch the ball with your hands," said Mr. Scott. Members of The Red Team laughed when they heard Mr. Scott yell those final instructions. Nonetheless, it was Showtime!

The Red Team kicked off and their second pass was intercepted by a streaking Richard Silvera who dribbled the ball through several defenders and shot the ball past the goalie with a thunderous kick. We scored! In less than a minute, we were up 1-0 and the Red Team knew they were in trouble. They looked dumbfounded and perplexed. The early smirks on their face had now turned to frowns.

The game was a battle. The fundamental soccer skill we lacked was made up for with our speed and aggressiveness. We complicated everything they tried to do. We never allowed them to run different plays or sets they were used to executing. We disrupted their system. They were overwhelmed by our quickness, tenacity and raw energy. Soon they began to argue among themselves and point blame at one another as we continued to score and play heart-pounding defense. I scored two goals. We won 7 to 5.

The parents of the Red Team were outraged. The Santa Claus guy had a meeting with the Red Team's coach and Mr. Scott. We couldn't hear what they were saying but I know the Red Team's coach was cussing like a sailor. Suddenly, Mr. Scott turned to us and said, "Come get your trophies boys." We each grabbed a trophy but the photographer would not take our picture. The parents were yelling and screaming as members of the Red Team were crying. It was total chaos. One parent even called us the "N" word. It was the first time ever I had been called that in my life. Mr. Scott rushed us to the van and we all piled in on top of each other. Some of the Red Team parents and players followed us to the van while calling us all sorts of names. They even threw stuff at the van as we drove off.

Honestly, I can't even remember us eating at McDonald's. I know we sat down and ate under those Golden Arches but it was all just a blur to me. I was so blown away by winning the trophy that everything was a daze until I actually got home and told my Mom the whole story.

I put the trophy next to my bed and stared at it for hours. As I finally dozed off to sleep, I could hear Ms. Brown's voice in my head saying "Do Something Special Today."

So based on what I learned, here are *5 Success Strategies* for today's entrepreneurs:

1. **Be Open To New Opportunities:** If my buddies and I were not open to trying new things then we would missed out on that amazing opportunity to play in the soccer game and win that trophy. Entrepreneurs need to constantly step outside their comfort zone to test new ideas because they may discover the next best thing – but first they have to get out of the box.

2. **Above Average Initiative beats Above Average Intelligence:** More often than not, Initiative trumps Intelligence. My team didn't possess the level of Soccer intelligence the Red Team had, but we had amazing initiative. In Business, many potential entrepreneurs never even start their new venture, because they are constantly compiling more information instead of getting just enough information and going for it. (aka: Analysis Paralysis.)

3. **Be Disruptive To The System To Be Successful:** We won that game because we were disruptive to the way a normal kids soccer game was played. We disrupted the system. Many great business empires are being dismantled by companies that disrupt the system. For example, Netflix's unlimited movies for one flat monthly rate deal destroyed Blockbuster's Video Rental business. Netflix was disruptive to the system. This is a great way to compete with the big companies. Be disruptive.

4. **Being Disrespected Can Be A Great Motivator:** My friends and I had no interest in winning that Soccer game until we felt disrespected by the Red Team taking pictures with the trophies before the game was even played. Football coaches love to get what is called "Billboard Material." It's usually a negative quote in a newspaper or online that an opposing player said prior to the game. The coach tapes the quote to the Billboard to get his team fired up to play the game. In business, entrepreneurs are motivated in various ways, but don't overlook the

power of being disrespected as a serious motivator to achieve great things.

5. **Be Able To Change Focus Instantly:** We immediately switched our focus from McDonald's to winning the soccer game. Based on varying circumstances, you must be able to change focus instantly and pivot your company, your idea or your venture to fulfill the needs that must be met at that time.

About Daron

Daron Destiny prides himself as the quintessential entrepreneur. After graduating from college, Daron embarked on an entrepreneurial journey that included successful concert promotions, record companies and independent film ventures. Currently he is CEO of Bedloo.com, the world's fastest growing social media voting platform. Daron is also the Publisher of the Moneymaking Opportunities Monthly Newsletter that was inspired by his friend and mentor, Don Perry, who published Moneymaking Opportunities Magazine for 50 years from 1962-2012.

Daron started his investing career financing small, urban, hip-hop, coming-of-age films and selling them at Blockbuster Video and Hollywood Video stores in the late '90's. He turned one $30,000 film into $10 Million in worldwide home video sales and also sold his record label BOOMIN' RECORDS to Scotti Bros./Freemantle Media who now owns the *American Idol TV Franchise.*

Daron's most recent film investment project *Confessions Of A Thug* was sold to Warner Bros. Films in 2007, and won Most Innovative Film and Best Director in prestigious film festivals, and was the only hip-hop musical ever to be featured on the cover of Billboard Magazine. Daron is also an award-winning author as a contributing writer in the book series *Wake Up: Live The Life You Love* with Dr. Wayne Dyer, Mark Victor Hansen and Deepak Chopra.

Daron is the author of Angel Investor Success Stories, a book that reveals how numerous Angel Investors got in early and made hundreds of millions of dollars in profits with Starbucks, Guitar Hero and more. He is fascinated with outside-the-box investing and people who invest early in successful companies, and the vision it takes to know if something is a Billion-Dollar idea.

Daron graduated with *Magna Cum Laude* honors from Bethune-Cookman University with a Bachelor of Arts Degree in Mass Communications. He is the youngest of three children and is an avid sports fan.

CHAPTER 8

NEW RETIREMENT REALITIES

BY DANIEL SHUB

The new reality in retirement planning is upon us. Gone are the days when a person worked at the same company for 35 years and retired with a gold watch and a pension. Today's retiree faces unpredictable markets, the erosion of defined benefits plans (pensions) and an uncertain future for Social Security benefits. Retirees also look forward to a longer life expectancy that is at once exciting at the prospect of living until 90, and threatening because their retirement plan may not last long enough. Indeed, after the 2008 market crash, many retirees are wondering if they will ever have financial security in retirement.

I understand retirees' fears; in fact, I watched my grandmother struggle in retirement. Her experience was the impetus that pushed me into financial planning. When the Soviet Union dissolved in 1991, the world cheered but on the inside, an economic downturn reared its ugly head. Changing currency in Ukraine devalued the savings people had acquired for their old age. My grandmother had amassed the equivalent of $40-50,000 U.S. dollars, enough to live off the rest of her life in Ukraine. She woke up one day to find that government shifts in currency had robbed her of her retirement savings. She had left only enough to buy a few loaves of bread.

As if my grandmother's story was not enough, in the last 16 years I have watched other couples lose their savings and live their retirement in fear.

Bill and Peggy Austin threw a big retirement party in December 1999. They had worked their whole lives, put in 90,000 hours, 65 years old, and in January 2000, they were to begin retirement. They planned to travel, help the grandkids, and take trips to Europe. Unfortunately, the market did not cooperate. The markets dropped. The Austins lost almost 50% of their retirement savings.

They shored up and decided not to take withdrawals from their retirement plans. They did not purchase the motorhome of which they dreamed, they did not take trips and they did not assist their grandchildren. They waited for the market to recover. Finally, by 2007, their investments had crept back up to slightly above where they had been in 2000. With a sigh of relief, the Austins decided to take an income from their retirement savings. The next thing you know, the market drops substantially and they lost it all again. Instead of the retirement of their dreams, Bill and Peggy have had the retirement of their nightmares for the first 10 years.

You will note that saving for retirement was not the issue for the Austins. They saved adequately. What they did not do was safeguard those savings by creating a distribution plan for retirement. Honestly, many people have difficulty making the psychological shift of saving for retirement to living in retirement. As a result, they use hope as their strategy; "I hope we will have enough money to last throughout our retirement." They have a "big pot of money" illusion that their $1 million in retirement investments will carry them through, having no real idea how to calculate how much they can spend each month in retirement, let alone being able to calculate how much they will actually need.

The financial services industry has done little to educate people that the oldies are not goodies when it comes to retirement strategies. Most retirees and many financial advisors are still operating under the assumption that if they can just manage to pick the winning stocks and mutual funds that they can withdraw 4% annually and not run out of money. Several new studies suggest, however, that a 4% withdrawal might be a little too aggressive and could result in only a 50% chance of not outliving your retirement benefits.

Imagine if you boarded an airplane for Detroit and the pilot got on the radio to announce, "The weather in Detroit is 72 degrees, we should arrive in two hours and we have a 50% chance of making it there." You would get off that plane as fast as you could, wouldn't you? A 50% chance of something does not sound very good anymore.

Some clients arrive at my office with brokerage accounts managed by someone else who pose the question to me, "How much should we take out of our retirement accounts each month?" because our broker told us, "You'll be fine."

"You'll be fine" is not a retirement plan. Many investment advisors do not take the time to advise their clients adequately. When you apply the "averages" of the market to your retirement years, you can run out of money very quickly. Retirees want guaranteed income for their basic living expenses in retirement. Retirement income includes social security benefits, pensions, and accounts to cover the gap that exists between those incomes and the expenses the retiree will have. When you are living in retirement, your retirement income should not depend upon market averages.

The most frequent problem I see when retirees come to my office is their reliance on "averages" in their accounts during the retirement phase. Averages no longer matter once you have entered the distribution phase. Sequence of investment returns is what matters. A client might have bad years in the beginning and good years later on, have an average of 7% return on their money and run out of money in retirement. If we take the same amount of money and the same average, but with the good years preceding the bad years, and the clients' money may last 30-40 years. What matters is the sequence of good and bad years in the beginning of your retirement.

Let's look at the example of some typical clients, represented in the chart below. Three people retired in 2000 with $1 million, each taking withdrawals to supplement income of $50,000 adjusted for inflation at 3%.

- First, we assume that they receive returns based on the performance of the SP500 Index. In 13 years, they have **only $17,435** left in their portfolio.

- Second, we reverse the sequence of returns (same numbers, just reversed) - they have **$499,793** in 13 years.

In both scenarios, the "average" is 2.53%! This is where most advisors and retirees make a substantial mistake, assuming the average and relying on it.

- The third example is based solely on the fixed 2.53% return-- assuming they have actually received that rate that they have assumed in their projections--the portfolio balance is **$459,159** after 13 years.

If the first 13 years of your retirement will be similar to what we have experienced from 2000 to 2013, you will have only $17,435 left in your portfolio. How are you going to live for the next 10 to 20 years?

Date	S&P 500 2000-2013 Historical Prices	Percent Change	Investment balance after withdrawal	Expenses Paid from Investments	Investment balance after withdrawal	Reversed sequence of returns	Investment balance after withdrawal at 2.53% fixed rate	Fixed 2.53%
7/17/2000	1510		$1,000,000		$1,000,000		$1,000,000	
7/17/2001	1214	-19.6%	$769,500	$50,000	$1,173,250	23.5%	$974,035	2.53%
7/17/2002	906	-25.4%	$538,500	$51,500	$1,153,159	2.8%	$945,875	2.53%
7/17/2003	981	8.3%	$524,291	$53,045	$1,361,941	23.8%	$915,419	2.53%
7/19/2004	1100	12.1%	$530,710	$54,636	$1,489,020	13.9%	$882,560	2.53%
7/18/2005	1221	11.0%	$526,623	$56,275	$1,068,828	-25.4%	$847,190	2.53%
7/17/2006	1234	1.1%	$473,345	$57,964	$831,941	-18.7%	$809,193	2.53%
7/17/2007	1549	25.5%	$521,190	$59,703	$969,159	25.5%	$768,453	2.53%
7/17/2008	1260	-18.7%	$372,354	$61,494	$916,742	1.1%	$724,845	2.53%
7/17/2009	940	-25.4%	$231,762	$63,339	$947,278	11.0%	$678,243	2.53%
7/19/2010	1071	13.9%	$189,836	$65,239	$988,766	12.1%	$628,513	2.53%
7/19/2011	1326	23.8%	$152,074	$67,196	$998,061	8.3%	$575,519	2.53%
7/17/2012	1363	2.8%	$85,348	$69,212	$692,921	-25.4%	$519,117	2.53%
7/15/2013	1683	23.5%	**$17,435**	$71,288	**$499,793**	-19.6%	**$459,159**	2.53%

| | | | | Average 2.53% | | | Average 2.53% | |

This is a hypothetical scenario for illustrative purposes only and does not represent a specific investment. You cannot invest directly in this index. SP500 is a registered trademark and service mark of the McGraw-Hill Companies.

The solution is guaranteed income streams. Our clients do not rely on the market or on "average" returns and hope for the best. They have reliable income streams guaranteed to be there for the duration of their golden years. We begin with their budget to determine the amount of money needed to cover basic living expenses. We select guaranteed income vehicles to cover those basic living requirements. We then take into account the inflation rate. Then we look at the ways to meet those expenses. First, we look at Social Security benefits and determine how to maximize those benefits. Next, we include their pension, if they have one. Finally, if there is a gap, we will look at guaranteed products to cover the gap between their avenues of retirement income and their necessary income. The rest of their money can be in the market, if the client choses.

Clients frequently ask, "What are the top 10 things we should know about planning for our retirement income?" The answers are as follows:

1. _Plan to Live a Long Life._ Life expectancies are increasing. A couple aged 65 today, has an 85% chance that one of them will live past age 85. The Social Security system wasn't built to sustain 76 million baby boomers for more than 20 years in retirement. Plan to provide yourself income for 20 years or more.

2. _Healthcare Costs will Increase._ We are not referring to overall costs of healthcare, but to a retiree's costs specifically. Seniors spend nearly as much on health care services and prescription drugs as they do on food. Build those increased expenses into your retirement budget.

3. _Create a Housing Plan._ Due to fluctuations in the housing market, your home may not provide the back-up plan for retirement income that you had hoped. In today's environment, the goal is taking a modest mortgage and paying it off before retirement. Secondarily, you should have a plan for housing away from home if you can no longer live independently.

4. _Plan for Long-term Care Assistance._ With longer lifespans come the increased need for assisted living and long-term care. Some annuity products will cover long-term care, only if you need it, by doubling your income when and if long-term care expenses become your reality.

5. _Inflation._ Many people do not realize that different expenses carry different rates of inflation. Healthcare, for example, has an inflation rate of about 8%, 2-3 times greater than the overall inflation rate. Many things will cost more than you had planned for in retirement. Planning for inflation now will give you peace of mind in retirement.

6. *Transition your Goals* from the accumulation phase to the distribution phase. Combine growth opportunities with guarantees to ensure your money lasts in retirement.

7. *Social Security Benefits.* When we host our seminars, we often ask attendees to raise their hands if they have a financial advisor. Generally, about 60% raise their hands. When asked if those same advisors have assisted them with their Social Security benefits, very few raise their hands. Social Security benefit planning is a very important part of the retirement planning process and should not be overlooked. There are 567 ways to claim Social Security benefits. If you do not know them all, find an advisor who does.

8. *Taxes in Retirement.* Tax rates may increase, but even if the rate does not increase, retirees must be aware of the taxes they will pay on their retirement benefits. Even social security benefits are taxed in certain circumstances.

9. *Distribution Strategies.* The first step is determining the sources of income you will have available to you to finance your retirement. Know that there is a difference between retirement planning and retirement income planning. The former specifically grows assets, while the latter incorporates a risk-management approach to distribute assets in an organized and disciplined manner.

10. *Paradigm Shift to Income Products and Strategies.* The way we design a retirement income portfolio has changed. The products that met your needs in the growth phase do not usually suit the goals of retirees. We look at all the available options for our clients and do not rule out anything viable. There are many new strategies available today to provide guaranteed income stream in retirement that allow you to stay in control of your principle.

How do we place your funds in a manner that will accomplish your goals? We have to position them so that they survive the next market crisis unscathed. We create strategies for our clients to make sure they are prepared for the worst. We make certain they keep what they have when the situation gets worse and take advantage of opportunity wherever possible.

The key words are safety and guarantees. Retirement success should never depend on the market; it should depend on mathematics. If you depend on a favorable market to provide income for your basic living expenses, consider your options if the market does not do well. Will you reduce your standard of living? Will you spend less, travel less or forgo helping your grandkids? Will you move in with relatives or return to work at age 70?

We rely on advancements on all areas of our lives. We shop and work from computers in our homes. We use cellphones where once we stopped at the nearest pay phone. We drive tiny cars that get phenomenal gas mileage, start with the push of a button and have navigation systems to direct us to the nearest steakhouse. We trust doctors who have cured everything from certain cancers to polio. Why then, would we apply antiquated financial strategies to our retirement investing?

Few of us would eagerly return to the days of pay phones, or worse, no telephones, as our grandparents had. Our grandparents' retirement strategies do not work anymore either. To have a successful and worry-free retirement, the first step is to create a written plan outlining your withdrawal and distribution strategy for bad times as well as good. If you do not have one yet, perhaps it is time to visit a specialist. You can, and should, live the retirement you dreamed and that you love.

Careful planning will take you anywhere your dreams do.

About Daniel

Daniel Shub is committed to helping better secure his clients' financial future in this challenging economy. His primary focus is to help retirees and aspiring retirees preserve wealth using innovative approaches, while designing retirement strategies that deliver predictable and consistent results.

Daniel B. Shub is the President at Shub & Company. Daniel is an independent financial professional and insurance agent who has helped hundreds of individuals and families to increase their confidence in their income strategies during their retirement years.

"When it comes to money, we believe that once you put a strategy in place, you should spend your future enjoying it — not second-guessing your choices. It all starts with a no-obligation assessment at our office." ~ Daniel Shub

Daniel has been actively involved in the Financial Services and insurance industry for more than sixteen years. He is a member of the National Ethics Association, the National Association for Fixed Annuities and qualifying member of the Million Dollar Round Table. MDRT is an international, independent association for leading life insurance and financial services professionals.

Daniel's approach for helping his clients achieve financial protection in retirements has found its way into countless newspaper articles, radio and TV programs, including *Bloomberg Businessweek,* CNBC, *Market Watch, Yahoo Finance* and many ABC, NBC and FOX affiliates across the country. His methods for designing a predictable, consistent and more secure retirement income have drawn significant attention and recognition throughout the local community and nationwide.

Daniel and his wife have one son and make their home in West Bloomfield, MI. As a father, a husband, a business owner and a financial professional, Daniel knows the value of trust, understanding and close relationships. He brings strong values to work every day in his family-centered Financial and Insurance practice.

Contact us at: dshub@shubandcompany.com or call us at 248-731-7729 today!

CHAPTER 9

NIDO'S LAWS FOR MAKING YOUR WAY THE WINNING WAY

BY NICK NANTON AND JW DICKS

Your present circumstances don't determine where you go; they
merely determine where you start.
~ Dr. Nido R. Qubein

Dr. Qubein's above quote is a winning way to approach your business. Qubein's philosophy has even more impact when you know his life story – he came to this country as a teenager with 50 dollars in his pocket and is now the president of High Point University, a board member for two Fortune 500 companies, a sought-after speaker, and a published author.

So where is the starting point for you to turn your present circumstances into the winning way that Qubein created for himself? We were fortunate enough to spend time with Dr. Qubein, visiting him at HPU (High Point University) while we shot a documentary about his life. From watching him in action we garnered what we like to call 'Nido's Laws' – Qubein's approach for winning in his business endeavors, at the university, and in his consulting with others to develop the success of their businesses. What follows are our interpretations of how he has done it and how you can create that winning way for yourself.

YOU BUSINESS WINS WHEN YOU CREATE VALUE

While he is an impressive guy in general, what blew us away was watching Dr. Qubein do a 90 minute presentation to potential freshman and their parents – consumers with hugely different needs and concerns. By the end of his speech the students were stoked about campus life, and the parents, who had come in getting ready to be bored to sleep (like they were at most university visits!) were hoping and praying that their child would have the privilege to attend the university and learn from such an inspiring leader.

How did he do it? Well, we've always said that *price is only an issue when value is a mystery*. If you don't create value, then you are just a commodity. High Point University stands out because Dr. Qubein shows his target market not just what HPU is, but what it can do for each of them. President Qubein has partnered with his faculty and staff to focus on offering experiential education and holistic, values-based learning. They want graduates prepared to live a life of both success and significance. Qubein even teaches a class to all freshmen titled, "The President's Seminar on Life Skills" where he shares the habits, skills, values, and practical intelligence that the students need to succeed in an ever-changing world.

Nido's first law is to create value. There are three ways we saw Qubein creating value in his businesses and at the school. The first is exactly what we experienced in the presentation for the potential students and their parents. By matching the vision and mission of the institution with the dynamic *persona* of the president, Qubein created a winning brand. Then he used that 90 minute speech to connect the parents and students to each other, to their goals, and to the vision of an HPU education. When you can create a brand that is identified with a 'celebrity' persona, you create value by connecting a person to the product.

The second way to create value is through creating a quality culture for your organization. Your company should make everyone from the CEO to the hourly worker responsible for putting value into the product. Motivate your employees to see their role as value adder rather than as the task-oriented machine operator or order processor.

Pride is a powerful motivator – everybody is proud of something! If you can find out what makes your people proud, you can use that insight to channel their motivation. As Robert W. Darvin, the founder of several winning companies, including Scandinavian Design, Inc. observes: "There's only one thing that counts in a business: building the self-esteem of your employees. Nothing else matters, because what they feel about themselves is what they give to your customers. If an employee comes to work not liking his job, not feeling good about himself, you can be sure that your customers will go away not liking or feeling good about your company."

When you have a culture of value adders, you empower everyone in your business to share the value of your product with your clients. Adding this kind of value makes your business more than a commodity – you will have a brand that clients feel connected to and trust.

YOUR CUSTOMER BASE GROWS WHEN
YOU INTERPRET THE VALUE

It doesn't do you any good to offer a service unless your clients are sure of how it benefits them. At HPU there is a Ruth's Chris-style steakhouse on campus that students can use on their dining plan to eat at once a week. The immediate reaction of each parent is, "What?! Is that how my money is going to be spent?" A totally reasonable response until you interpret the value – the steakhouse is a *learning lab* where students are allowed to come once a week. They must make a reservation, dress appropriately and be prepared to have an etiquette lesson. If they miss their reservation they are banned for a month! Students come away knowing how to host a client dinner or have a high level interview at a five star restaurant. Once the value is interpreted, the parents are not only onboard they are convinced this is vital to their child's success.

This is Nido's second law – interpret the value. Qubein says, "When we admit a student to HPU, we commit our full resources to ensure their success." That is echoed in the stories of the students, like Olivia French, a junior communication major. One of the first classes she took as a freshman was a first-year seminar called "The World is Flat: Globalization of Economics." HPU students get to know their professors in the classroom because the class sizes are so small (another win for the consumer). As a journalism major with an English writing minor, economics and any other science or math class was like a foreign language to Olivia. When she stepped into that classroom the first day and saw how small the class was, it did not seem like a win to her. In fact, panic set in. With a small, engaged classroom there was no place to hide and it would be easy for Olivia to be called on by the professor.

Dr. Suryadipta Roy not only managed to help Olivia understand globalization and economics (a feat in itself), he also managed to become one of her favorite professors during her time at HPU. Even in her junior year, she would see him on campus and he would ask how she was doing. She was amazed that he remembered not only her and her fears, but her name. To HPU's and Olivia's credit she was able to interpret the value of having a small class with an engaged professor who tailored his approach to motivate her to success. "He helped me to step outside of my comfort zone—a skill that is necessary for a journalist—and gave me the opportunity to understand concepts that I wouldn't have explored on my own."

Oprah would call Olivia's value interpretation an 'Aha Moment'. When your brand's values, and the people enacting those values align the value of your services, are interpreted for your clients—that is what enables those kinds of loyalty moments. So ask these questions – am I interpreting the value of my services from the POV of the buyer? Does our customer base understand how the value applies to them and their needs? Am I creating a win, a loyalty moment, for our clients when the value is interpreted for them?

YOUR BRAND WINS WHEN YOU CREATE A WINNING ENVIRONMENT

Michael Jordan, the great National Basketball Association superstar, showed his team spirit in the 1992 NBA playoffs when, after a stunning individual performance in which his team lost, he began feeding the ball to his teammates. Jordan's personal score fell considerably, but his team won.

Nido's third law is to create a winning environment for both your team and your clients. Qubein believes that the winning environment is created from within, by the staff first. When people in an organization compete with one another for glory, only the competition wins. When they cooperate internally, they become more competitive externally – and the entire organization wins. When you cooperate with your fellow workers, everyone is pulling for you to win. When you compete against them, they're all pulling for you to lose. In today's competitive world, nobody knows everything there is to know about the business. It's a win for your business to have a true team spirit and be able to tap into the expertise of everyone on the team.

Another way that Dr. Qubein creates a winning environment at HPU is by insisting that the campus and the staff get rid of all irritants. The price of tuition is all inclusive at HPU. On campus parking, housing, and tuition is all included in the price. They even have a concierge where students can go and get help on everything from how to load up their passport card (there's no cash on campus) to arranging a ride to the airport. The parents use the concierge as a way to get information to their student. No one has to fill out masses of paperwork on their own – they can call the concierge. By getting rid of all irritants, Dr. Qubein increases the value by making educating the student the main job of the student. Now that 40 grand starts to look like a bargain compared to the effort and extra costs of working with a state school.

A winning organization puts it all together for the customer, which makes the price make sense. As a consumer yourself, you know those irritants like extra fees and hidden costs. How many times does a customer have to click through a website to get to the Submit page? Any extra step that makes your prospect throw up their hands and say 'forget it' – those are the irritants that you have to not just reduce, but totally eliminate. Get rid of any irritants that decrease the value of your business. The ease that comes from doing business with you enhances your brand and is a product itself.

Finally, a winning environment adds 'Wow' to the experience.

When a potential student visits HPU for the first time they drive up to the college's sign and beneath it is a digital personalized welcome with the student's name and where they are from. Wow! After the presentation by Dr. Qubein every family leaves with a 'trail of tangibles' – HPU swag including a copy of Dr. Qubein's book. Wow! How many of those other 1800 colleges in HPU's market have that kind of take away? By the end of the first HPU visit there is literally no competition. Think back to Olivia's experience in economics – adding 'Wow' to your business can be done as simply as Dr. Roy did when he lived out the brand values of the organization. That behavior created a 'Wow' for the student.

The amazing thing about adding 'Wow' is that it makes people want to be a part of it. How many students do you think stop the car to take pictures under the personalized welcome sign? Right. Every one of them. Then they Instagram, Facebook and Tweet those photos, all with a hash tag that markets High Point University. Wow.

When you add 'Wow' it needs to have a purpose. Wow for Wow's sake doesn't work. Instead, differentiate with relevance. For instance HPU is building a Center for Student Success. They aren't building this innovative, modern facility just because it's cool. They're building it because internships and career connections are most relevant to their students. Yes, taking classes and working with career counselors in a building that Google employees would envy IS different. But the customer finds true value in the fact that the facility and its programs are instrumental in preparing them for success beyond graduation. You may offer something unique to your clients, but does it really benefit them?

It's up to you, not your circumstances, to determine which way your business goes. If you are looking for the way to win then use Nido's laws – create value, interpret that value, and establish an environment of value adders who eliminate irritants and add 'Wow'. By following these laws you can create the kind of winning culture that Qubein is famous for creating everywhere he goes.

About Nick

An Emmy Award-Winning Director and Producer, Nick Nanton, Esq., is known as the Top Agent to Celebrity Experts around the world for his role in developing and marketing business and professional experts, through personal branding, media, marketing and PR. Nick is recognized as the nation's leading expert on personal branding as Fast Company Magazine's Expert Blogger on the subject and lectures regularly on the topic at major universities around the world. His book *Celebrity Branding You®*, while an easy and informative read, has also been used as a text book at the University level.

The CEO and Chief StoryTeller at The Dicks + Nanton Celebrity Branding Agency, an international agency with more than 1800 clients in 33 countries, Nick is an award-winning director, producer and songwriter who has worked on everything from large scale events to television shows with the likes of Steve Forbes, Brian Tracy, Jack Canfield (*The Secret*, Creator of the *Chicken Soup for the Soul* Series), Michael E. Gerber, Tom Hopkins, Dan Kennedy and many more.

Nick is recognized as one of the top thought-leaders in the business world and has co-authored 30 best-selling books alongside Brian Tracy, Jack Canfield, Dan Kennedy, Dr. Ivan Misner (Founder of BNI), Jay Conrad Levinson (Author of the Guerilla Marketing Series), Super Agent Leigh Steinberg and many others, including the breakthrough hit *Celebrity Branding You!®*.

Nick has led the marketing and PR campaigns that have driven more than 1000 authors to Best-Seller status. Nick has been seen in *USA Today, The Wall Street Journal, Newsweek, BusinessWeek, Inc. Magazine, The New York Times, Entrepreneur® Magazine, Forbes,* FastCompany.com and has appeared on ABC, NBC, CBS, and FOX television affiliates around the country, as well as CNN, FOX News, CNBC, and MSNBC from coast to coast.

Nick is a member of the Florida Bar, holds a JD from the University Of Florida Levin College Of Law, as well as a BSBA in Finance from the University of Florida's Warrington College of Business. Nick is a voting member of The National Academy of Recording Arts & Sciences (NARAS, Home to The GRAMMYs), a member of The National Academy of Television Arts & Sciences (Home to the Emmy Awards), co-founder of the National Academy of Best-Selling Authors, a 16-time Telly Award winner, and spends his spare time working with Young Life, Downtown Credo Orlando, Entrepreneurs International and rooting for the Florida Gators with his wife Kristina and their three children, Brock, Bowen and Addison.

Learn more at www.NickNanton.com and:
www.CelebrityBrandingAgency.com

About JW

JW Dicks, Esq., is America's foremost authority on using personal branding for business development. He has created some of the most successful brand and marketing campaigns for business and professional clients to make them the credible celebrity experts in their field and build multi-million dollar businesses using their recognized status.

JW Dicks has started, bought, built, and sold a large number of businesses over his 39-year career and developed a loyal international following as a business attorney, author, speaker, consultant, and business experts' coach. He not only practices what he preaches by using his strategies to build his own businesses, he also applies those same concepts to help clients grow their business or professional practice the ways he does.

JW has been extensively quoted in such national media as *USA Today,* the *Wall Street Journal, Newsweek, Inc.*, Forbes.com, CNBC.com, and *Fortune Small Business*. His television appearances include ABC, NBC, CBS and FOX affiliate stations around the country. He is the resident branding expert for *Fast Company's* internationally syndicated blog and is the publisher of *Celebrity Expert Insider*, a monthly newsletter targeting business and brand building strategies.

JW has written over 22 books, including numerous best-sellers, and has been inducted into the National Academy of Best-Selling Authors. JW is married to Linda, his wife of 39 years, and they have two daughters, two granddaughters and two Yorkies. JW is a 6th generation Floridian and splits his time between his home in Orlando and beach house on the Florida west coast.

CHAPTER 10

THE WINNING WAY IN LOVE

BY JIMMY OCEAN

THE TOP TEN STRATEGIES FOR MAXIMIZING YOUR MOJO

To win in life you must win in love. I learned that the hard way. The good folks at Harvard took a different route.

A group of Harvard researchers conducted a seventy-five year study dedicated to unearthing the secrets of a happy and fulfilling life, following the lives of 268 men from childhood into old age. The study, known as the Harvard Grant study, is the longest and most in-depth of its kind and reveals a phenomenal conclusion.

It turns out, the Beatles were spot on when they sang: *All you need is love*. Dr. George E. Vaillant, the Harvard psychiatrist who directed the study from 1972 to 2004, puts it like this: "The only thing that really matters in life is your relationships to other people." He continues: "The conclusion of the study, not in a medical but in a psychological sense, is that connection is the whole shooting match."

I was always very much focussed on connecting. But I didn't learn the tools of connecting in a way that served me and others on a sustainable level until after what I refer to as, "My Big Fall."

My journey started about four years ago. It was the high point of my career as an internationally-touring recording artist. It was also the low point of my relationship. You could say that I was rich, famous, married and lonely. Quite literally, I was a suicidal millionaire.

I spent most of my childhood feeling "different". My parents divorced when I was five and I was raised by my mom. She did a great job of providing for me, but no matter how she tried, she could not replace my dad. I was bullied at school, taught that emotion is for girls, and I only had TV to teach me what being a man was all about. I felt disconnected as the out-of-town kid with divorced parents and an eclectic taste in music. I spent years trying to work out who I was, only to create a mask of what I thought people wanted me to be.

I learned to hide behind the mask I had created, but I always worried about being exposed as a fraud. By my teens, I was one of the most popular kids in high school. And later, even as I worked hard to develop a successful and award-winning music career, I still felt lost. I tried to fill the void in my life with sex, drugs, food, and my work. Having a deep desire to connect, I focused most of my free time on romancing women. I became an expert in seduction. After several years of following the rockstar lifestyle, I learned clearly that a thousand women and a million dollars could not bring me the happiness they seemed to promise.

My music career was like a dream come true for me. I was touring the globe, playing in front of thousands of people cheering me on. I reveled in the fame, travel and lifestyle. I was so grateful for the promoters who took such good care of us, the fans that were so lovely, the press who were very supportive, and the rest of the scene that I felt honored to be a part of. I felt proud to be winning awards, to be getting great press coverage, to hear my songs on the radio and in clubs, and most of all, to hear how fans had been touched, moved or inspired by my music. From the outside looking in, it seemed like I had it made. I was living my childhood dream as a globe-hopping recording artist. I lived in a paid-off city mansion in the center of London. My wife and I had enough money to never have to work again. On the surface, it looked like it just could not get better than that. The truth of the matter was that our marriage was in shambles, and I was miserable. I tried everything I could with the tools that I had at the time, but I just couldn't fix the situation. One day, I finally gave up.

I had just flown into New York City from an extensive tour of Australia and Southeast Asia. I was tired, lonely, and jetlagged. The city was so vibrant. So many people, so many lights and sounds passing me by. On the other hand, I felt like a ghost, completely disconnected from everyone and everything. I took the elevator to the rooftop of the high-rise, walked to the edge, and looked down. The car lights, street lights, and skyscrapers looked beautiful but unreal. My mind began to drift. I wondered what it would be like to jump off the building. I was surprised how little emotion was connected to such a thought. I asked myself, what it might feel like to soar through the sky, and if I would lose consciousness before hitting the ground. And then I had an experience that I could only describe as supernatural. I could suddenly see myself at the edge as if it were all part of a movie and the camera was zooming out. I could suddenly see how I was connected to everything that was going on in my life. I could see how I was not a victim of my circumstance, but at the cause of it. I realized that what I created, I could change. At that moment, I finally decided to take full responsibility for everything that was happening in my life. I committed myself to discover the key to sustainable success in love and life.

My wife and I parted, and I took a step back from the rockstar lifestyle. I decided to sell and donate most of my possessions and invest the rest into my personal research study as I embarked on a two-year sabbatical. I meditated in Japan, walked over burning coals, and studied with Tony Robbins in Fiji. I read a book a week in the areas of personal power, positive psychology, relational skills, communication, emotional intelligence, and masculine/feminine energy. I was blessed to be able to experience such powerful retreats as the Hoffman process, UPW, New Warrior Training and Solemate. I learned how to maximize my Mojo — the foundation to sustainable success in love.

Mojo is the core energy that moves through and out of us. It either attracts or repels people, partners and possibilities. Your Mojo affects how you feel and how others feel about you. Your Mojo determines your date-ability like nothing else. If you want to win in love, you absolutely must maximize your Mojo.

When I returned from my sabbatical, everyone marveled at how different I seemed. I marveled myself: how much easier it was for me to remain calm when girlfriends tested me; how less intimidated I felt by other men; how much richer my experiences were and how much deeper the connections. I noticed a fundamental difference in the quality of relationships I attracted. I also noticed how many people around me were struggling in their relationships. Some relationships were full of turmoil; others were lacking the warmth and intimacy that they deserved. Some men just weren't attracting any women at all. I also met a lot of women struggling to find the love they desire and deserve. These women were frustrated by the quality of man that they were attracting. To put it in the words of my coaching partner Marni Batista, they were "fed up dating the guys they got instead of the guys they wanted". I noticed a gigantic disconnect between the men and the women around me. And having realized that relationship is at the core of everything, I committed to my mission: empower men, liberate women, and build bridges between the two.

The success of your love life is not determined by clothing, pick-up-lines, or seduction tactics. Your date-ability is based mainly on your Mojo: How others experience you on an energetic level. Based on my personal experience and professional education, I offer the following advice on how to master your Mojo:

Set healthy boundaries
The ultimate core driver for the feminine is love. For the masculine, it is freedom. Many people misunderstand the concept of freedom. The highest stage of freedom is not being able to do whatever you want. This does not release you from the consequences of your actions. The highest stage is actually setting boundaries for yourself and deciding which things you will not allow yourself to do, in order to have the life you desire. Both men and women carry the masculine and feminine within them. I find it advisable to nurture and develop both aspects of one's core energies on the journey to wholeness.

Even outside of relationships, some of us tend to avoid conflict or put off decisions. This also drains our Mojo, as it strips us of our power and clarity. Good Mojo is centered, clear and confident.

Own your personal power

For a woman, this is often about self-worth: giving herself permission to recognize and cherish her true wonderfulness — a woman relaxes into her personal power with full acceptance, appreciation and acknowledgement of her innate worth. Radiating deeply from within, her beauty gives life and light to the world.

For a man, this is about becoming confident: having belief in himself, and trusting in his competence. A man steps into his personal power with clarity, confidence and charge. Deeply penetrating with powerful presence, this force of strength and skill opens the world up to new possibility and direction. He lays foundations, upholds values, contains, stabilizes and innovates.

Whether masculine or feminine, personal power feels fantastic. Personal power commands rooms and conquers hearts. And it demands results.

Conquer the LIEs

There are three ways in which your mind will play tricks on you and sabotage your Mojo: (1) **L**-Limiting beliefs, (2) **I**-Interpretations, and (3) **E**-Expectations ... **LIE**s.

A limiting belief is a perception about yourself or the world that restricts your thoughts or actions. With an abundant and empowering mindset you are able to open up to new experiences, attract a new quality of relationship, and exude more good Mojo.

Another important aspect is your tendency to interpret situations prematurely. If you get an email that just says, "We need to talk.", do you start worrying about what you may have done wrong? Do you start to worry about the other person? Or do you approach it with open curiosity? Free yourself from interpretations and judgements that are destructive, and your Mojo can flow more freely.

It has been said that "Expectations are disappointments waiting to happen." Your Mojo rises when you are able to enter situations with detached involvement: being fully involved in the process yet detached from the outcome.

Drop the boxing gloves

We have all experienced heartache and would like to avoid future pain. There are, however, no guarantees in life. Running through life with boxing gloves up, fighting for what you want, protecting you from all harm, is not only incredibly tiresome, it also repels others.

I coach a lot of men and women in the corporate world and the guarded, ambitious competitive edge serves them in the law firm or the finance world. In intimate relationships, not so much.

Women open up when they feel safe. When a man wants a mind-blowing connection with a woman, he needs to make sure that she feels safe and that he is coming to give, not to take. She needs to make sure that she is in a position to allow that to occur.

Dating is the dance of potential lovers. Relationship is the dance of intimate lovers. Would you rather dance with someone with wide open arms or in a fighting stance with gloves covering their face? Mojo flows through open arms. Step into the vulnerability, drop the gloves and open your arms.

Forgive

Were you raised to live with a lot of shame and guilt? Did you grow up with high expectations or even perfectionism? Learn to let go of that. We are all just perfectly perfect. Everybody is doing the best they can with what they've got at the time. And that goes for you, too. Be gentle with yourself.

Being able to forgive is crucial to having a healthy heart and a happy life. One thing I learned at the Hoffman Process is that "Resentment is like drinking poison, hoping your enemy will die." Resentment hardens the heart and sends an unconscious signal of bitterness and unavailability. Forgiveness and compassion are fundamental to experiencing love. Forgiveness is a gift to yourself and the forgiven.

Choose happy over right

The heart wants to be happy. The mind just wants to be right. Choosing happiness over being right can be difficult because we spend so much more time in our heads than in our hearts. The more you choose happiness over being right, the more happiness you experience — and the more pleasant you become as a current or future partner.

It is hard to let our Mojo flow when we are stuck in our minds. So breath. Deeply. Bring attention to your breath. And your core. Center yourself. Now you are in your body and in your heart. Now you can choose happiness. And love. Now you are powerful and centered and strong. That's hot.

Develop a wider perspective

As humans, we have this false perception we're at the centre of the universe and everything revolves around us. Don't take things personally. That funny look someone had was probably not about you. The more you cultivate the capacity to see the greater picture, the more you liberate yourself. And a liberated person is more successful in love.

Take full responsibility

You can either be a victim of your circumstances or at the cause of them. The choice is yours! Refusing to play the victim role and taking 100% responsibility gives you power and confidence. The truth is that you are in charge. It is your life and you are responsible for what goes on inside of it. Uncover your core values and align your choices with them. Dream big and live your dreams. Showing up in the world in an authentic and empowered way is the sexiest thing you can ever do.

Communicate Deeply

Learn how to become a masterful communicator. Communication is the foundation of relationship. A woman's deepest desire is to be seen and heard. When a man listens to a woman on a deep level, he gives her his greatest gift: his presence. As Stephen Covey put it: "Seek first to understand, then to be understood."

A man's deepest desire is to be respected. When a woman is able to communicate with a man in a way that honors him, it really brings out the king in him.

Create Polarity

One of the most important elements of maximizing your Mojo is creating polarity. Polarity triggers (sexual) attraction. Polarity happens when you step fully into your natural masculine or feminine power.

I liken positive masculine energy to that of a lighthouse... Standing firm at the edge of the ocean... Bearing witness to the sway of the water. Whether gentle tide or fierce storm, the lighthouse stands firm, bears witness, and guides by shining light on that which never changes. When a man manages to be with a woman the way a lighthouse is with the ocean, he will win in love.

Positive feminine energy is radiant and nurturing. It flows freely, replenishes, and inspires. Like the ocean. It is mesmerizing just by being.

There is no control, no direction, no effort. When a woman manages to let go of her anxiousness, of her desire to control and manage, and just relaxes into her radiance, she becomes irresistible. When a woman is able to rest into her radiant beauty and freely shine as the amazing woman that she is, she will win in love.

MOVING FORWARD

I will end with a quote by my mentor, Tony Robbins: "I challenge you to make your life a masterpiece. I challenge you to join the ranks of those people who live what they teach, who walk their talk." The love of your life craves the best version of you. Let it shine.

It's my fervent wish that you achieve the fullest success in life and in love.

About Jimmy

Jimmy Ocean is known as the most sought after personal power expert in the dating and relationship arena. He is famous for helping men and women attract and sustain fulfilling relationships. His personal mission is to empower men, liberate women and build bridges between the two.

As an international award-winning recording artist, Jimmy Ocean seemingly had it all, but like so many talented artists, he struggled with a feeling of disconnectedness and isolation. Rather than allow himself to spiral downward, Jimmy went on a personal quest to master love and life.

Having undergone extensive training by IPEC, Tony Robbins, Lauren Mackler, David Deida and participated in the Hoffman Process and the Mankind Project, Jimmy is now a certified professional dating and relationship coach and creator of "The Polarity Method."

Jimmy's dating and relationship coaching career is focused on his philosophy that: "To win in life, you must win in love." His goal is to help his clients to step fully into their own power and maximize their Mojo. This way they can naturally and sustainably attract new qualities of relationship and connection.

Jimmy is the founder of NewMacho, a podcast dedicated to redefining masculinity for the 21st century. Jimmy also functions as the Male Expert Coach at DatingWithDignity, a site dedicated to helping women find the love of their lives. Jimmy has also won numerous awards in the music and new media world and has been quoted in *Headliner, Knowledge* and *DJ Magazine*.

You can connect with Jimmy at:
www.JimmyOcean.com
www.PolarityMethod.com

CHAPTER 11

WORDS CAN CHANGE THE WORLD: ARCHETYPES OF INFLUENTIAL SPEAKING

BY NINA IRANI

Watch your thoughts, for they become words. Choose your words, for they become actions. Understand your actions...for they become your destiny.

~ Ralph Waldo Emerson

Change is something we all want every day of our lives. We want to feel better, look better, live longer, lose weight. We want more time with family and friends. We want to make more money, change our relationship with our boss, (or we might want to change bosses altogether).

Human beings are driven by the need to change. We hate stagnation. Our brains our wired to want more, and we yearn to evolve into ever-greater versions of ourselves.[1] Consequently, we seek to change things about ourselves and the world around us, minute by minute. If we're not actually trying to create change, we are wishing for it. Think about everything in your life you've wished was different, in the past few

---

1 *Words Can Change Your Brain*. M. Waldman and A. Newbert, M.D. Penguin Group, 2012

minutes. The length of your list may surprise you.

I began my career as an executive coach in 1989, focusing on high stakes communication. This included public speaking, media interviews, grooming executives to advance to partner or C-level positions and crisis management. Soon I began working with politicians and public figures in the entertainment industry. (You'd be surprised at how many Academy Award nominees say they'd rather not win if it means making an acceptance speech in front of their peers!)

It didn't take long for me to realize that the need for change drives businesses as much as it drives individuals. Whether I was working with an executive at Microsoft, a gubernatorial candidate, a film director, or the sales team at a local startup – every mission was to create change in some form. We were either boosting sales, improving a reputation, strengthening relationships, or motivating people to action. What followed was always a change to better results and an improved situation.

There is an important distinction between the kind of change that *happens to us*, and the change *we choose to create*; such as change within ourselves, within a small group or change that affects the entire globe, like the quest to cure cancer. No matter how big or small, self-generated change is by far the most fulfilling. There is an alchemy that happens within the psyche when you begin a quest, travel on a journey, then finally reach your goal. I often hear stories from clients who started out with a grueling professional mandate, and at the end of our project, tell me how utterly fulfilled and joyous they feel on a personal level. I am always inspired by this, but never surprised.

No matter who you are, if you desire to affect any type of lasting change in yourself or your world, it always starts with the right steps in the proper order. Most people make the fatal mistake of going about change starting with...ACTION! This is like building a house with the roof first: the roof is crucial but there's nothing holding it in place. What is the foundation and overall structure of the house?

Self-generated change always starts with words. Every time, no exceptions. Whether it's a marriage proposal via flash mob, or words whispered softly minutes before your yearly review, "This time, I am going to speak up about..." The words may be carefully crafted for networking events or social media. They could be spoken freely in a circle of trust. Or, your words may be uttered in secret and in silence at the altar of your own imagination. In fact, Albert Einstein said, "The world as we have created it is a process of our thinking. It cannot be changed without changing our thinking and imagination."

THE STORIES WE TELL OURSELVES

If I may be so bold, I believe Einstein would agree that our thinking (the words we tell ourselves) affects our confidence, motivation, happiness, and strategic abilities. "Self-talk" within the mind is almost constant. Neuroscientists estimate that we think approximately 70,000 words per day.[2] That's a lot of silent words and most of them slip by, just below the radar of our awareness. They can be extremely subtle - as hard to notice as an ant on a black cat at midnight. Once we do become aware of them however, we gain entry to a new world of leverage and power.

Before every word spoken aloud, there is a series of thoughts within the mind. They may result in a resolution, concern, musing, strategy and attitude - together these form a mindset.[3] When we seek change, the comfort of the familiar no longer holds reign over our thinking. A new possibility beckons and allures, it calls us forth. With this comes a journey needed to make the new possibility manifest, and we begin a quest.

This could be the reflection leading up to your commitment to finally start that new business, or the inner landscape Dr. Martin Luther King traveled to recognize his life mission, fighting for racial equality. As our self-spoken words change, so do the neurochemicals in our brains, affecting us physically, mentally and emotionally. How we translate this shifting network of thoughts and biochemical reactions into spoken or written words will make or break our chances for success.[4]

INFLUENTIAL SPEAKING

Our Spoken words affect our level of influence and persuasion. They shape relationships, reputation, credibility, and earning potential. In short, they create the results and outcomes of our lives. Volumes can

---

2 A.W. Toga, M.D. http://www.loni.ucla.edu . Laboratory of Neuro Imaging, UCLA

3 *Processing Emotional Pictures and Words: Effects of Valence and Arousal*, E. A. Kensinger and D. I. Schacter. *Cognitive, Affective, & Behavioral Neuroscience*, 2006, 6 (2.)

4 *Positive Affect & the Complex Dynamics of Human Flourishing* B.L Fredrickson and M.F. Losada, *American Psychologist*, 2005 Oct. 60(7): 678-86

be written on exactly how this works. Here, we will touch on a few key principles.

In persuasive speaking, or the language of change, there is a three-pronged purpose which must be present in every presentation or interaction. The three aspects work symbiotically to create an alchemy in your listeners' hearts and minds, and move them towards greater possibility, new ideas and action. They exponentially increase your ability to close a deal, build relationships, motivate a group or alter marketplace perception. Without them however, your message never reaches its fullest potential.

Your communication needs to **Express**, which is a heartfelt declaration of anything meaningful to you, such as, "When I first saw the new operating system, I couldn't believe how different it looked!" This adds authenticity, emotion and conviction. It's especially important during technical topics, like big data, for example. Steve Jobs was a master at weaving Expressive Language into his presentations.

Your message also needs to **Inform** - update, add knowledge, interpret facts, increase awareness. This is the bulk of most business meetings, and it's where you get to demonstrate your clarity, knowledge and expertise.

Finally, communication needs to **Motivate** - spur action or new ways of thinking. This is what listeners find most memorable in an interaction. It makes them feel more alive and connected to you.

While many conversations contain more than one communication category at a given time, any communication meant to affect change must contain all three.

THE FIVE ARCHETYPES OF CHANGE™

How do you Express, Inform and Motivate without feeling like you're constantly juggling word balls in your head? Within each of us is a bevy of communicators waiting for release. There are five Archetypes of Change, and while we tend toward certain ones, we possess all of them within us. Each Archetype represents different aspects of your personality, affects different regions of your listeners' brains and has a unique and powerful effect. When used in combination within a single discussion, these Archetypes are powerful change tools and you can draw upon each one as needed at any given moment to achieve your desired effect.

I. Visionary (also Icon)

The Visionary Archetype within us is idea centered and loves to empower. It motivates and creates possibilities. This Archetype conveys ambitious goals, the bigger picture, grandeur, symbolism and speaks to peoples' potential. It embodies aspirational speaking. Consequently, the audience feels respected, inspired, stimulated, their imagination is spurred, and they feel a sense of belonging. The Visionary can be controversial, but never forgettable. This relates to the brain regions that process inspiration and connection to something larger than life (middle inferior orbito-frontal cortex and caudate nucleus).[5] Without the other Archetypes to add balance however, the Visionary may appear to be ungrounded, out of touch or stubborn.

President Kennedy, Abraham Lincoln, Dr. Martin Luther King and Steve Jobs were perfect examples of Visionaries. This aspect of thought and word suffused their speaking and approach to their message.

Almost every political candidate I've ever coached has been tempted by the same trap: underestimating their opponent. At some point in the campaign, these candidates get hit by the blinding reality that their opponents' strengths can no longer be denied. Many never recover. Part of my job is preventing this by tactfully pointing out the strengths of their opponents from the very beginning. (My self-talk at this point is usually a fervent prayer!) Generally the candidate first resists the information, then accepts it with dismay. What comes next, however, is golden. The candidates use this to make themselves smarter and stronger, by becoming more grounded in their vision and speaking with even greater aspiration. When this happens, their speech and demeanor take on a whole new level and they become more invigorated. I call this the 3-inch rule, because people often comment that the candidate looks a few inches taller!

II. Ruler (also Leader, King or Queen)

The Ruler deals with parameters, rules, systems, resources and consequences. It focuses on a specific group and conveys *gravitas* and confidence in times of crisis. People feel safer around someone demonstrating the Ruler Archetype. When in balance, the Ruler's speech calms the fear center of the brain, called the Amygdala, with

---

5 . *Buy-ology*. M. Lindstrom. Doubleday, 2008, p. 107 (Nurturer)

strength, poise and rational thinking. In excess, however, the Ruler is threatening or harsh, which can alienate and bring out the rebel nature in otherwise cooperative people. Former Secretary of State Donald Rumsfeld and Governor Chris Christie are good examples of the Ruler Archetype, both in speaking style and demeanor.

Years ago, I was called to coach a CEO of a F500 firm. He was a smart, strong leader behind the scenes but in public crisis he often lost his gravitas. When a situation arose that he needed to address in front of the media, he panicked. (Yes, this happens to CEO's too!) At our first practice session he tried to overcompensate by raising his volume and increasing his gesticulation, a common mistake. He looked more like an angry rioter than a poised and credible leader. That's The Ruler out of balance.

We worked on the qualities that comprise the true Ruler Archetype - the body language and breathing; clear, succinct and direct language; and calm certainty in his delivery. The more we rehearsed the more he said, "I feel like myself again." This is because the Archetypes, in their true form are nothing less than expressions of our core strengths and values. This rioter turned Ruler nailed his media appearance and all those that followed.

III. Teacher (also Sage)

The Teacher is the informational, analytical aspect of the language of change. When was the last time you learned something new and couldn't wait to share it with someone? That's your Teacher Archetype at work. This is the pre-frontal cortex (rational, discerning part of the brain) in action. Detail oriented, concerned with data and processes, the Teacher adds value by conveying information, forecasting trends, making sense of information and identifying relevancy. Listeners become informed and curious for more. The Teacher is impressive and commands credibility. Without the Visionary and the following two Archetypes however, the Teacher can sound dry, boring or condescending to the listener. Former Secretary of State Hilary Clinton and Secretary of State John Kerry are two examples of Teacher Archetypes.

I once received a phone call from a prominent financial expert who is highly sought after to speak in front of large audiences and the media. His opinions are well respected and he is widely regarded as a thought leader in his field. He was not, however, exactly known for his ability to thrill an audience or rock the house. This distinguished expert had just accepted an invitation to give the commencement address at an Ivy League University and wanted his speech to be relatable to a younger audience. He said, "Nina, I don't just want to give an informative talk. I want to inspire and motivate. Can you help me do that?"

In addition to the Informing Language he wielded so masterfully as a Teacher Archetype, we added Expressive Language. He let people see who he is. It was a foreign experience at first. However, as he became more comfortable with it, his words flowed more easily. This transformation gave him the freedom to speak from the heart about what motivated him to his meteoric rise to success and continues to motivate him to this day. His natural warmth came through. Lo and behold, he even discovered he had charisma! It was a milestone event for him and a moving experience for his audience. Soon after the address he received a letter from one of the graduating students saying, *"...Your speech was one of the most motivating and inspirational moments of my life...".*

IV. Nurturer (also Healer)
Generous and emotionally aware, the Nurturer seeks to connect, comfort and reassure. "You did a great job, I appreciate that." They welcome, encourage, relieve pressure, and empower. Have you recently told someone, "Just do your best, that's all you can do."? Did you notice the deep breath that followed? The Nurturer inspires a feeling of relief, safety, intimacy and loyalty. This is related to the soothing, bonding hormone oxytocin and the brain's limbic system, which processes a sense of well-being.[6] This speaking often focuses on smaller groups or individuals. Without the Teacher or Ruler, however, the Nurturer can appear to be lightweight, not taken seriously. Oprah Winfrey gracefully displays the Nurturer, as does Senator Elizabeth Warren. Regardless of political beliefs, many people agree that President George W. Bush and President Obama embodied the Nurturer to grieving families and people in need after the September 11th attacks and Hurricane Sandy, respectively.

---

6 *The Brain Changes Itself.* N. Doidge, M.D., Penguin Books, 2007

I once coached an executive listed as the third most powerful woman in Los Angeles. She confided in me that she was afraid of expressing the Nurturer for fear of not being taken seriously at work. By suppressing this natural and necessary part of her psyche, her personal brand was being distorted and she was alienating the people around her. When she began to gradually and appropriately express the qualities of the Nurturer that came naturally to her, not only did she feel more comfortable in her own skin, but she also gained more trust and respect - the very things she was afraid of losing. This is a common phenomena among professional women. Many men, on the other hand, are learning how important the emotionally intelligent Nurturer is, and incorporating it into their communication with great efficacy. Well done, gentlemen. Ladies, don't hold back. The Nurturer gives you balance when you need to show your strength or give constructive feedback.[7]

V. **Entertainer** (also Storyteller)

The Entertainer employs visual, emotional language and Expressive Communication. Using stories and humor, this Archetype relieves tension, engages the audience and make people think. The Entertainer also uses personal traits such as humor, charm and wit to be highly persuasive and turn an audience around. They can grab someone's attention quickly and sustain suspense. They activate Brodman Area 10, known as the brain's "cool spot", related to social belonging and high status. The Entertainer also interacts with the neurotransmitters acetylcholine and dopamine - which cause a feel-good, lasting impression. Without the Visionary, Ruler or Teacher however, this Archetype can seem empty, superficial or irrelevant. An overabundance of the Entertainer can have a clown-like effect. At times, Vice President Joe Biden has been known to display an excess of the Entertainer Archetype.

One of the most common questions I get from leaders of all shapes and forms is, "How do I attract talent and keep teams engaged during all the ups and downs?" While the answer is complex and must be addresses on several levels, some of the lowest hanging fruit is proffered by the Entertainer, who displays passion, takes an active interest in people, connects unlikely dots, and helps reframe events

7 *Neuronal Plasticity: Building a Bridge from the Laboratory to the Clinic.* J. Grafman and Y. Christen. Berlin: Springer-Verlag

to add new perspective and meaning. This contributes to a culture of engagement, and compels people to stick around because they simply want more.

In the final analysis, no matter what you are trying to change - gaining freedom for an oppressed people, damage control after a product recall, or increasing your social media presence, the power of words is the same. Words create an aperture into the unseen mysteries of humanity. I've had the privilege of working with clients in 23 countries, in numerous industries and I've witnessed in awe, how the Archetypes of Change transcend culture, age, gender, race and religion. They are simply human. They unite and uplift. And they remind us that at the core of every human being, is the same ability to change our own world and the world at large.

About Nina

Nina Irani is the Founder and CEO of UniqueSpeak, and the creator of the highly acclaimed "Ground of Being" Methodology™, an innovative presentation platform for Fortune 500 executives, politicians and public figures to communicate their messages effectively, with impact.

Her journey began as a Communications and Theatre Arts major at New York University.

Then a chance encounter changed everything. Nina was asked to help a struggling high-level executive with his speechwriting and onstage presentation. The results were remarkable and word spread quickly. Executives, spokespeople, and political candidates began knocking on Nina's door and within months, there was a waiting list.

With a holistic perspective and gold standard methodology in communication, Nina founded UniqueSpeak Consulting in Los Angeles, which specializes in integrating the forefront of neuroscience with time-proven communication techniques, to create a hybrid for high performance in all levels of communication and leadership.

Nina assembled a stellar team of talented specialists in leadership and executive coaching that provides clients with the winning foundation to reach their goals.

As creator of the internationally-lauded Ground of Being Methodology™, Nina has taught numerous coaches and consultants her innovative techniques. She has led programs in 23 countries on 5 continents and guest lectures internationally at institutions of higher learning and conferences on topics related to communication, influence, leadership, brand delivery and the hottest topic of all...the differences between the male and female brain.

CHAPTER 12

HUG IT, TO WIN IT!!!

BY SOUL ONGOIBA

As I was screaming and crying, in vivid pain from my broken nose being "fixed" with a teaspoon, I thought: who was to blame? The sports medicine doctor at this weekend tournament or the pain itself? Or my opponent who broke my nose "accidentally" on the mat while trying to escape my offensive move when I tried to throw him?

From what I remember, this was a pain and fear I had never experienced my whole life. Without anesthesia, the French doctor in the Parisian Judo suburb tournament said I had two options: Fix the broken nose right away while the wound was still "fresh" without anesthesia, or wait two to three days to explore the surgery option since the International tournament took place during a long holiday weekend, hence medical services were limited.

What to do? I had two more tournaments within the next four weeks before my final Olympic qualifier tournament. Fear, victimizing non-empowering questions, and pain ran through my brain, spine, and every cell of my body as the doctor tried, without success, to realign my nose. My world seemed upside-down. Maybe even unfair? Why me? Why now? With all the sacrifices I made to pursue my Olympic dreams, I was rewarded with an injury that would weaken me physically and psychologically. Was I being stupid almost a year ago to have voluntarily left a promising career I had as an analyst in the San Francisco Bay area?

As the excruciating pain rose, the FEAR got worse; one minute was like eternity.

Doubt, frustration, fear, sweat, blood, anxiety, anger coursed through my body and mind until I asked the doctor for a break. I needed to reevaluate my decision before his second attempt. While sitting on the hard brown bench, frightened, I had about 2 minutes to make up my mind as the "apathetic" doctor needed to go back to the mat area. I felt totally naked; naked from my perfectionism, my excuses, my illusions, but most importantly naked from my fear of being seen and exposed to the possibility of not qualifying for the Olympics!

I closed my eyes and took a "broken" deep breath; I remembered an enduring lesson from my father while growing up: "Whatever you do son, you need to know what you want." This grounded me! My intentions were to share my deep belief and message with the world; I believe that each of us deserves to live our best lives!!! I wanted to communicate to the world a simple message: Dare to dream and Live Your Power! Don't let mediocrity, anybody, any event or circumstance "bully" you into giving up. I truly believe that our human spirit and right to life is to manifest the glory within each of us!!!

As these organic intentions rose from my heart to my mind, I could start stirring my fear. Contrary to the mainstream belief of overcoming and crushing your fear, Judo teaches its practitioners to be "accepting and flowing with the forces coming at you." I needed to welcome the fear; I needed to utilize that "fear"; I needed not to fight it but hug it and redirect it.

As I **hugged my fear**, I found courage to let the doctor proceed with his second attempt, which was somewhat successful.

Over the next three weeks, I went on to compete in the two remaining tournaments. I was proud and humbled at the same time. I had both bad and great performance matches. In May, about 11 months after I quit my corporate job to start training full-time, I was reaching my peak performance, as I was able to defeat the world silver champion by Ippon (full point) within a few minutes. That victory match was a highlight for me, as it inspired the spectators and fellow judokas; especially since it wasn't by chance but done with class and style. I silently hoped this victory would give me enough points to qualify for the 2008 Beijing

Olympics, but I didn't accumulate enough points to be among the top three (in my weight category – 178 LBS) over the preceding four years (technically one year for me, as I had only started full-time in the competition circuit and training camps the year before).

It was a breakdown for me. I felt like a failure. What had been the focus of the previous year was gone. It was devastating; all those countless hours of sweat, tears, injuries, personal financial chaos, sacrifices and social isolation just vanished like a tornado with no source and no destination. Even worse, my hope – that winning the gold medal would have given me the opportunity to share my message of "Live Your Power" – seemed gone. No gold, no Beijing 2008. I really didn't know what to do for a few months. Was I supposed to shut down my life's message? Even though I started interviewing again, going back to corporate was the last thing in my heart; I felt I had found my life message through the process of living My Own Power. I was at a crossroads where I felt like hibernating in a den. The confidence from competing at world-class level was replaced by doubts, unsure about everything which led me to a 5-year stretch of being a student again. Not only was I soul searching, I was diving deep into motivations, peak performance, and business. While leveraging my engineering background and systematic approach, I immersed myself in materials, seminars of masters in human potential, human psyche, business, marketing, finance and entrepreneurship.

I couldn't see it five years ago, but not qualifying for the 2008 summer Olympics was one of the best things that happened to me, as it opened new soil for me to cultivate. I got married and built a wonderful family, and I am a privileged father of two. These five years provided me the necessary grounding for my life's message to flourish. During my journey, I never had time to stop, reflect, and connect with people. It would be arrogant for me to pretend I could help people with their fears, hopes and dreams if I couldn't understand them. Even worse, what were my chances of success in my life's message if I didn't explore helping and connecting with people?

In fact, during these five years, not a **single day** would pass that I wasn't conflicted with doubt and FEAR. On one side, I wanted to teach people to Live their Power; on the other who am I? (Since I didn't make the Olympics.)

Psychologists call this a "self-worth" problem—"I'm not good enough."

Despite this "freezing" FEAR I was living with, I still held strong to the belief that "each of us is endowed to live our best lives," and I yearned to convey this message "Live Your Power."

"Actually I felt so strongly about my life message that I even dared to tell my wife that Tony Robbins, who had been doing this for a living since I was 10 years old, had stolen my idea."

Understanding, accepting people, and "developing compassion" were what I needed in order to share my message.

The gift of self-awareness was revealed before my eyes so I could live my own message: transcending my own fears of self-worth, which in itself was a true test. Now I understand what being vulnerable means. I understand failure, compassion, business and entrepreneurship; I understand having a family, responsibility. I can systematize life complexities into something simple.

I now see the similarity between the FEAR I had when I broke my nose, and the current fear of not acting and living in my own power. I could see the gift being handed to me by the Universe. Many spiritual messages say: "You need the experience until you get the lesson." Most people are chained to their fear and their weaknesses; I was.

I needed to "help myself" before "pretending" to help others. I remembered: Hug your fear to WIN.

Looking back, I realize how my journey prepared me in being a catalyst for others to help them live their best lives. My experience equipped me to align myself with my two deepest inner values - compassion and excellence - which I inherited respectively from my mother and father. Let me share *three steps* about how winning your FEAR is the winning way in your life. They will help you live your life on your own terms. As you transform and hug your fear, everything around you will transform too, and you will live your power.

Used properly, these steps will help you have a sustainable transformation. The process is based on my five years of research, personal experiences, business, entrepreneurship, and over 25 years of martial arts practice and understanding peak performance.

Since fear is the number one reason people don't take action, let's revisit **FEAR.**

Fear is a function of the ego, a framework of our identity, and the foundation of survival. Basically fear begins where our ego ends. It's a reaction of our psyche protecting the survival of our identity, perceiving that the ego is at "risk" of being extinguished, an indication that "I" am in danger. That's why fear is a function of our mind, since our subconscious mind mainly regulates our survival.

The most powerful force in people is the need for humans to be consistent with their identity. Our identity is what is known by our subconscious mind, it is our comfort zone. Ultimately our fear defines what we do and who we are. **The bigger your identity the smaller your fear; the smaller your identity, the bigger your fear**. The more you associate with your ego, the stronger your fear. To disassociate yourself from your ego is art and science, in order to move beyond the fear.

Let's dive in! **Step1. Acknowledge and "give a name" to the FEAR. MIND LOOP**

Key questions here are based on our identity being defined in context of our world:

What is it about me that am I trying to protect? What am I trying to get the world to believe about me? What am I afraid of?

The answers will reveal the nature of your fear. Give that fear a name and start the process of disassociating yourself from it and deliver it from your subconscious. In my case, it was that I don't have a weakness and I'm not vulnerable (belief developed growing up in the street). This wasn't congruent. I called my fear, *Lucas.*

Step2. Love Intent. HEART LOOP

This step anchors your intent in a place of love, which reveals that our "excuses" for not acting are the "reasons" and the cure to our fears. Per Tony Robbins, there are **two basic fears in each of us: "I'm not enough, and so I won't be loved."** Essentially, the heart loop roots us in the present moment; there's no fear in the "now." Fear is that anticipation of a "negative probable future." The heart loop allows people to disassociate themselves from their ego (values +beliefs). In fact, that is where courage stems from ("coeur" in Latin means "heart").

We step towards that "intent." We act from the place *"I'm enough and I'm infinitely loved."* It's our heart ruling our psyche.

What do I want to help people with? What values can I add? What can I give and contribute to humanity with my pure intent?

In my case, being rooted meant connecting with my intent: to help and coach people to live their power. But I felt I wasn't enough to help people, since I didn't make the Olympics. The irony was that I was advocating that you don't need anyone's approval to live in your power as long as you are aligned with your true intent. I found the cure to my own fear.

Step 3. HUG IT!! QUANTUM LOOP

The QUANTUM LOOP invites us to act from a higher plane of being an observer (as Einstein puts it, a problem cannot be solved at the same level where it was created). In any stage of growth progress, one should expect fear, as it is how the universe expands our "limitation sphere." The secret is to act from a higher place of understanding fear from the viewpoint of being an experiencer/observer.

I told *Lucas*: "I know you are trying to protect me, but I have a bigger mission/intent to accomplish, and I need your help in guiding me."

Great questions I learned from Michael B. Beckwith:

- Where am I supposed to evolve?
- What qualities should I give birth to in order to move forward?

Even for an agnostic, it's clearly a quantum probability, not a mere wish. Quantum physics demonstrated that observers can alter the reality of observations – as the observer and observed are part of the same quantum energy field. These questions above trigger empowering beliefs and create strong meanings.

In my case, I realized that in order for me to reach and help a broader audience, I needed to learn how to be vulnerable and authentic. A person who can face his own imperfections can understand.

To live your power is to take the road from fear to freedom. Change is the only constant, but how can we command deliberate progress and promote guided change? Consider Coach Wooden's words about winning and success: *It's really about doing and being your best* (growing from your fears). Earl Nightingale sums it up well: *Success is the progressive realization of a worthy ideal.*

Don't forget, courage doesn't exist without fear. **Our real power resides in hugging our fears.** In fact, I'm willing to push it further:

The winning way is the progressive realization of a worthy ideal, in living life on your own terms, and setting your own standards.

As it is in Judo, in using proper leverage, the winning way is using fear itself to your advantage.

Simply – HUG IT TO WIN IT!

About Soul

Soul Ongoiba was raised in a family of educators where teaching, compassion, self-reliance and excellence were fostered by his parents.

Soul believes that each of us deserves to live our best life. Along with The Golden Rule and the motto of: 'Teach them how to fish so people can feed themselves for a lifetime' have been the guiding principles in his upbringing.

Engineer by trade in both Electrical and Industrial Engineering, Soul has been able to leverage his background to approach the human potential and human mind in a very systemic and optimal way.

Very familiar with peak performance as a former elite Judo athlete, and was on his Alma Mater university SJSU judo varsity team. Soul has been practicing Judo for over 25 years and was promoted to second degree black belt in 2001 by THE NYAC club.

As an entrepreneur, with his financial and coaching practice, Soul helps his clients change the quality of their lives significantly, and most importantly, helps them live their lives on their own terms. Soul encourages people to tap in into their own resources and strength to become entrepreneurs, as he believes it is the fastest way to "freedom." Completing his certificate with the Robbins-Madanes Center for Strategic Intervention, and NLP certified, Soul uses cutting-edge tools of human transformation to help his clients live their lives on their own terms.

As an entrepreneur, author, speaker, athlete, and martial artist, Soul is first a family man, married with two children, with a deep passion for humanity.

Soul's vision is to create a world of "aware" empowered individuals with tremendous compassion to help humanity move forward. To guide leaders that have a drive to live their lives on their own term and to pursue excellence in their own standards... Building, training and coaching people to that pursuit is his life passion, mission and purpose. Soul strives to be that catalyst in all his endeavors, particularly in his financial and coaching practice (www.ultimatepeaktransformation.com) and podcast *Transmute Your Destiny.*

With his eclectic background, Soul's approach to change and transformation is quite innovative, as it blends a scientific-based approach and at the same time, promotes self-expression and intuition, leading his clients to be raving fans.

You can connect with Soul at:
yourauthenticpower@gmail.com
Twitter.com/Soulsj
Linkedin/soulman ongoiba
www.facebook.com/Soulman Ongoiba or at: www.UltimatePeakTransformation.com

CHAPTER 13

RETIREMENT INVESTING FOR THE 21ST CENTURY: DIVIDE AND CONQUER

BY STEVE HANSEN

I have a confession to make – My name is Steve Hansen and I'm a financial planner! There, I've said it out loud and I'm proud of it. I love what I do and I'm good at it!

I was fortunate enough to attend college on a football scholarship. I wanted to become a Minister and my dad wanted me to become an engineer (he was a design engineer for the Turkey Point nuclear power plant). So when I attended college, I chose Theology as my major and to keep Dad happy, I chose engineering as my minor.

Forty some years later, and I find I'm working with retirees and pre-retirees helping them have everlasting income or income for life. (Funny, that sounds a lot like how an engineer helps solve complex mathematical problems and how a Minister helps people discover life everlasting...)

Like many advisors, I came to it later in life having previously worked in the corporate world in avocations that involved banking, coaching football, insurance, and the markets. Staying educated has always been important to me – although I didn't necessarily love school. Somewhere in the back of my mind, I knew in the future my background would serve me and others well. I haven't stopped studying, in one form or another, since graduating from high school.

I studied part-time while working and raising three sons as a single parent. I immersed myself into anything financial. I was determined to learn how to avoid being poor. Sometimes I think there will be no more study now that I've reached my 60s, but deep down, I know that I'm only kidding myself.

It was while I was working for Krogers Corp. and raising my three sons, that I had an epiphany. I had remarried and we had our first daughter (Haley) in 1983. At that time, my wife's grandfather had just lost his entire life savings (more than $1 million dollars) to an investment scam.

Shortly afterwards he passed away from lung disease. Not long after that, we had to put grandma in a nursing home. Grandma passed away a short time later. Her wishes were to leave a small inheritance to her four children, one of them being my wife's father. The only asset left after the investment scam and Medicaid taking the rest of her cash was her home.

The children put the home up for sale and it quickly sold for full asking price, but at the closing, even though the mortgage had long since been paid off, there were no proceeds for the children.

What had occurred was that once grandma spent all of her money for nursing home care, Medicaid started paying the bill. Medicaid then placed a lien on the home for the amount paid by Medicaid for her care. After closing costs and fees and paying the Medicaid Lien, there was nothing left for the heirs.

I was studying a Retirement Planning unit in preparation to take the test to become licensed in property and casualty insurance and I realized I'd discovered my calling – financial planning! I had no idea how the industry worked or how to start. Lucky for me, I met a great person, Dave Meckenstock, who was very successful financial advisor and he gave me my start. That was 22 years ago and I've loved it ever since.

Like many advisors, I get great satisfaction every day from working with people to make their lives easier. My motto is, "I'll sort it all out for you." There is no better feeling than meeting people and knowing that I can lift a weight off their shoulders and show them everything's going to be alright. Explaining issues and concepts that aren't always straightforward, in a way that people can understand, is gratifying. When I see people nodding along and relaxing in the office, I know that I'm making sense to them and they are starting to see the potential and possibilities.

Everyone's circumstances are different and you don't have to be a millionaire to see an advisor. One of my clients recently asked me how I would describe what I did. He knows that I make his life a lot less stressful which gives him time to do things he wants to do. I likened my role to that of a personal trainer. Most people know they need to exercise, they even know the right exercises to do, but life gets in the way and motivation is lost. If you have a personal trainer you're more likely to show up, do the exercises properly and with more effort. And you get the results you were looking for.

I truly love what I do which is a blessing. For this reason I am motivated every day to acquire the best information on retirement income planning and guiding my clients to the life they want. So here is a glimpse into one of the strategies I teach and employ for my clients I call *"Divide and Conquer."*

Young investors can be aggressive when investing in stocks and mutual funds. However, once you attain an older age and paychecks stop because you have retired – to pay your bills you will need reliable sources of income. The transition to conservative from aggressive investing should begin around age 50.

The million dollar question is: How do you make this transition? As we begin retirement it is a complicated question that needs to be answered correctly. To start, you will need to know how much annual income you will need to retire comfortably. That amount is what you will need to generate from a safe, dependable bucket. These funds will cover your essential expenses, such as housing, utilities, auto, food, clothing and taxes. Lifestyle expenses – travel, gifts, entertainment, and hobbies should come from your growth bucket.

The retirement investor has three main strategies to choose from when constructing their investment portfolio. Each of the strategies has advantages and disadvantages, and your goal should be for your money to last longer than you do.

STRATEGY ONE: TOTAL RETURN INVESTING

The first and more traditional approach — known as "total return investing" — uses the famous 4 percent rule. You own a portfolio of diversified stock and bond funds, with roughly 50% in each. At retirement, you withdraw 4 percent of your assets in the first year, and raise that amount each year by the inflation rate.

Due to our current volatile stock market and today's low bond yields, 4 percent is too high. According to William Bernstein's study, a 65-year-old should probably take just 2.5% to 3 percent, to protect his principal. (*The Ages of the Investor* ~ William Bernstein)

STRATEGY TWO: SAFETY FIRST

The second method of funding your retirement is to take a safety-first approach. (*Risk Less and Prosper*, economist Zvi Bodie) Mr. Bodie advises you to cover all your essential expenses with guaranteed sources of money, including Social Security, a pension, lifetime-payout annuities, I-bonds (inflation-adjusted U.S. savings bonds), short-term bond funds and certificates of deposit. If you're married, your safe investments should cover you and your spouse.

If your safe investments won't produce enough income to cover your "floor" expenses, the answer is to rethink and reduce your expenses, Bodie says. You can't afford to gamble on stocks for growth. You might lose capital or run out of money.

This strategy presents a problem for many retirees because they simply do not have enough assets to create the needed income with this strategy. Currently the best rate a 5-year CD is paying is around 2% and 10-year treasury rates are hovering around 3.0 %. A retiree with a $500,000 retirement portfolio could only draw around $15,000 per year or $1,250 per month.

The obvious problems are twofold: One, this strategy does not allow for portfolio growth, thus many would have to cut their spending down to a bare minimum. Cutting out things they planned on doing during their "Golden Years" such as vacations, gifts and entertainment. Secondly, if they draw more than 3.0% they will be eating into their principal and they now run the risk of running out of money .

OPTION 3: THE DIVIDE AND CONQUER STRATEGY

Our approach is simple yet sophisticated, and recent research by Wade Pfau of the American College of Financial Services is solid confirmation that the Divide and Conquer Strategy is superior to the *Total Return Strategy* and the *Safety Strategy*.

The *Divide and Conquer Strategy* is constructed from two simple accounts—first we use a low-cost fixed index annuity with a lifetime income rider (Hybrid Annuity) which grows at 5% - 8% while in deferral and once the income rider is turned on, pays <u>GUARANTEED INCOME FOR LIFE</u> to the owner and their spouse. The second part of the portfolio is allocated into a managed growth portfolio.

In the American College of Financial Services study, Mr. Pfau applied the 4% rule for a couple aged 65 with a $500,000 portfolio. The Hybrid Annuity will pay out more than 4% so the excess funds are placed into the managed growth portfolio. All of these portfolios – whatever the proportion of annuities to stocks—met the couple's retirement spending in almost every situation. The *Divide and Conquer Strategy* also left more money at death than both the *Total Return* and *Safe* portfolios. Your retirement target should not be a "Magic Number" like $500,000 or $1 Million. Rather, you should be targeting a specific and attainable annual income amount.

To pursue the *safety-first* solution, you have to be a black-belt budgeter and saver. Work as long as you can, including part-time work; put off taking Social Security (the delay increases your future monthly income); cut spending and pour savings into guaranteed investments. Consider TIPS (Treasury inflation-protected securities), but not now — wait until interest rates go up, both Bodie and Bernstein say.

A *total return* investor is taking a greater risk for a better lifestyle. You should limit your annual inflation adjusted withdrawals to 3% and you will have a better chance of not outliving your retirement savings. However, if you are unlucky enough to start retirement in a year like 2008 or if there are repeats of 2008 during your retirement, you will either run out of money or you will have to reduce your income dramatically.

In summary, according to Wade Pfau's study, the *Divide and Conquer Strategy* portfolio never ran out of money and always had more money left for your loved ones regardless of interest rate or market performance. Understanding these facts, why would anyone not adopt the *Divide and Conquer Strategy* **to create retirement income**?

About Steve

A financial professional since 1991, Steve Hansen founded Altitude Planning Group – intent upon providing the personalized financial services retirees and pre-retirees need to achieve the retirement they envision. He emphasizes personalized service, because all of his clients have different financial goals and are best served by strategies customized for each client's unique needs.

Steve's ability to help his clients derives from extensive education and the kind of in-depth knowledge that comes from over 20 years of financial services experience. His passion for assisting people stems from what happened to his wife's grandmother. Because of inadequate planning, she became destitute after losing her husband and died penniless after her assets were spent down due to Medicaid.

Steve's mission is to help others avoid that nightmare. "We strive to offer financial solutions that can help you manage risk while growing and protecting your retirement assets," he says. "Altitude Planning Group's philosophy is preservation of wealth, both in the accumulation and distribution stages of wealth planning. We provide our clients a clear road map as to how to achieve their individual financial goals."

Due to his advice and services, Steve has been named a Five Star: Best in Client Satisfaction Wealth Manager, as seen in 5280 and Denver Biz magazines. An even greater tribute to him is his loyal clientele, which continues to grow – thanks to his clients' referrals.

CHAPTER 14

MAKING MEANING AS YOUR WINNING WAY

BY WAYNE D. PERNELL, PhD

Your Winning Way fully depends on how you show up for other people. Since you're reading this chapter, you're a person of positive influence, not a brick in the wall or a wrench in the works. You're not the person who complains or tells others why a plan won't work. You know people who do, but you will never be the one to slow things down by pointing out all that is, or could go, wrong. You are also not likely to be the person who just shows up to punch a clock and do the job with the goal of simply getting through the day. Your personal style is more directed and dedicated. Even if you're someone without a corporate title, you are making a difference because you *choose* to make a difference. Do not underestimate that act. Choosing to make a difference becomes the basis of your power and your Winning Way.

Leaders inspire, not because they demand of others, but because of what their actions indicate they stand for. Their values are apparent in all they do. People with titles are not *de facto* leaders. Those who hold positional power do not necessarily inspire others to follow. People align themselves behind a person or a cause they can believe in and nurture. Your Winning Way shows through your *congruent,* visible actions and communications.

Can anyone inspire or lead? Consider an adult neighbor from your childhood. Reflect back on your second-grade teacher. Did they affect you in some way? If not the neighbor or teacher, think about someone who perhaps influenced you when you were eight, ten, or twelve years old. Perhaps it was a friend of your older sibling, an aunt or uncle. It's likely that what affected you was that they demonstrated their passion about something they felt strongly about. You connected with their enthusiasm. In an embrace of emotion, from a place of vulnerability and authenticity, you found something to care about. That person created a meaningful moment.

So who can be a Meaning Maker Leader?

You, dear reader, as you venture forth to make a difference in the world. Leadership is about influence. Anyone who influences another IS a leader. If you have children, coworkers, or community members who look to you for any sort of guidance or advice, you are a leader. Whether a thought leader or strategist, whether a soccer mom, CEO or unique combination, your presence and your demonstration of what matters to you, make a difference.

People follow you because of the contribution you make in the present moment. You engage in a way that says others matter, the journey matters, the individual and collective investment matters, and the Vision is worth holding on to and fighting for. True leadership stems from our ability to make a positive difference in someone else's life. This is the essence of Meaning Maker Leadership™.

Seven core concepts give insights on what it truly *means* to be a Meaning Maker Leader. Outlined here, one can explore these critical criteria.[1]

Concept #1: Definition of Self
Knowing who you are, having true clarity about yourself, your presence, and your level of influence – both personally and professionally – allows you to live authentically and congruently.

At the core of defining one's *self* is the need for authenticity and congruence. The notion of the Authentic Self has percolated through various writings over the past several centuries.

Our determination of who we are "supposed" to be is often based on the expectations of others.

The journey of the brave is one of self-reflection; an inner journey of acknowledgement of true passion, desire, and even calling. What are you drawn toward, and how can you more greatly serve others more consistently? These answers change over time, and so the journey to answer them takes a willingness to engage in growth.

Definition of self isn't static. In fact, our ability to adapt to who we are becoming is what makes us strong leaders. Consistently bringing forth our authentic self requires both strength and vulnerability.

These qualities pave the Winning Way for you to make meaning for and with others.

Concept #2: Direction
Do you know where you are headed? Do you know what you want? Most people have a somewhat general idea. They're clearer on what they don't want. Meaning Making magic happens when you become very clear about what you want and the trajectory you're taking to get there.

Getting clear allows you to set and hold an intention without fear of reprisal or judgment, providing a glimpse into your personal Vision, breaking it free of being a solitary hallucination. Letting others know where you're headed and what outcome you're after gives them the opportunity to support you, come with you, or merrily send you on your way. Yes, you WILL get opposition. When you overcome the first obstacles and show that you won't be stopped, that is when your Winning Way shines through and you have the opportunity to truly become a Meaning Maker Leader. You're essentially saying, "This is my path. Come with me or don't." Strong statements with clarity become compelling, and with your clarity, you cannot be stopped.

Concept #3: Daring
Daring to dive in means you're taking action, moving from discussion to doing. Having the courage to take on the "hard stuff" makes a world of difference to those whom you serve and ultimately lead, and they are watching you. Recognize also, that all you do may not be seen by those who need to know. Keep lines of communication open, and open lines of communication if they don't exist! Doing so entails a certain amount of daring or courage.

Almost 30 years ago, as a relatively new manager, I thought I was doing a great job. My days were full, my team seemed happy, and my customers – internal and external – were being served. I was working on projects and creating the next step for our division. I was so busy being busy, however, I forgot about the importance of communicating. Since no one knew what I was doing, I might as well have been doing nothing. A leader out of touch is not leading. What are you working on that you haven't let your family, friends, team, or tribe know about? Dare to have people judge your direction, your thinking, and your efforts. Dare. Then DO. Then Dare some more!

Concept #4: Duty

As a parent, you recognize your involvement and commitment to the project called "grow this young human into an adult." As a Meaning Maker Leader, you recognize how any project you start resembles your "baby." You have a duty to give this living thing every chance to succeed and thrive.

Whether you are a crossing guard, a cashier, or a neurosurgeon, duty is about involvement and commitment. More than that, it's about a calling.

Demonstrating your involvement and commitment in the name of "duty" to what you *must* do calls upon each of the previous steps: finding your authentic self, getting clear about where you need to head, and then mustering the courage to take action.

For some, duty is a job they are given and becomes a chore to check off of a list. For the Meaning Maker with a Winning Way, duty is a personal calling that must be fulfilled. It's time for an inventory of what you are doing and why. Check in with your authentic self and make the necessary personal adjustments.

Concept #5: Determination

There will always be competing and compelling reasons to sway from your path. Somebody needs your help. Something shiny and new comes along. People judge you. You may begin to question whether where you're heading is really "right."

At this point it is time to take inventory again. Since a true self grows and evolves over time, is it possible you're now on the "wrong" path? More likely you are doubting yourself based on what others cannot or would not do. Other people are often kept from moving forward because of their fears, and are usually more than willing to share their fears in an effort to keep you from your path .

Whatever reason they have to not do something has no bearing on why you need to! Remember your calling? Yeah, go DO that – involve others, and be a Meaning Maker Leader on your Winning Way!

Concept #6: Divination

When you are on a path and know deep down that you must follow it, you start to get clues about what is coming. Divination isn't something talked a lot about in leadership. It IS a part of your Winning Way, though. True leaders who follow their authentic selves and recognize their calling actually have an idea about what's coming. This ability only looks magical because most people are so focused on manipulating and manufacturing, that they forget about how to be in alignment with whom they are. Divining the future doesn't make you a witch; it makes you perceptive. Listen to yourself, and recognize patterns and possibilities based on experience and research.

Calm clarity turns to excitement when you have a "gut feeling" that something might turn out a certain way… and then it does. Validation of what we know truly *is* exciting. As Meaning Maker Leaders, people count on our ability to perceive things they can't. As we gain clarity, others appreciate our perspective more and more.

Take a moment at the beginning of every day to simply check in with yourself. For what are you grateful? About what do you have true clarity? Others may find it spooky. As you relax into it, you'll find alignment with external energies very reassuring. Seeing things that others cannot makes you a very potent Meaning Maker.

Concept #7: Denotation

There are so many demands on each of us, and our ability to stay connected via technology has separated us from our humanity. The Meaning Maker takes the time to pause in the moment simply to make that moment matter. To denote or demarcate a moment as special invites others to enjoy it with you. We are here to make a difference in other people's lives. Take a moment to do that!

"Look at where we are!" It doesn't matter if it's a grocery store, coffee shop, or mountain top. Pause with another and point out the value of the present moment. It's not the *doing* that counts; it's the *sharing* that counts. Being a Meaning Maker leader means paying special attention to what might otherwise be just another moment passing by.

Say a kind word. Make a kind gesture. Notice where you are and whom you're with. Taking a moment in time to make the moment matter makes you a Meaning Maker Leader and paves your Winning Way in business and in life.

CHAPTER SUMMARY

Recognizing that we each have unique strengths puts you, as an individual, in a very special place. Keeping in mind all that you are makes you a person of influence. You have responsibilities to yourself and others, as others watch what you do and how you are (serving to make up *who* you are).

Seven components of the Meaning Maker Leader intertwine and build upon each other. When one component is missing, the others weaken. Reflect on whether you have changed someone's life for the better today, by encouraging, guiding, or collaborating. Yes, you can shout your way to getting something done, but bullying isn't leadership. People have to know who you are and what you stand for, before you start some behavioral technique of softly selling or persistently pushing. Your Winning Way is founded on your ability to make each moment matter. In doing this for and with others, you have truly taken on Meaning Maker Leadership.

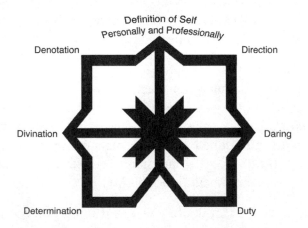

Core Concepts:

Definition of Self –requires an inward journey

Direction – means having clarity and choosing the steps to take

Daring – mustering up the courage to take on the hard stuff

Duty – recognizing a personal calling compels involvement and commitment

Determination – continuing on even though distractions abound

Divination – developing a sense about what may be coming

Denotation – the ability to pause and make the moment matter

References:

1. www.MeaningMakerLeadership.com

© 2014 by Wayne D Pernell, PhD

About Wayne

Insightful, witty, and playful, Dr. Wayne D. Pernell brings more than thirty years of experience helping leaders at all levels to draw on their emerging strengths, helping them to define and then set strategic pathways to attain clear success. Dr. Pernell knows the power of clarity and focus as foundational elements in relationships and leadership.

As an internationally acclaimed Author, Speaker, Certified High Performance Coach, and morning television guest, Dr. Wayne D. Pernell's work has helped thousands of people across the globe.

A native of California, Wayne grew up on the beautiful Palos Verdes Peninsula grateful and inspired each day by the magnificent sunsets over the water. Encouraged to explore topics about which he was curious, he began studying hypnosis and martial arts at the age of twelve. He knew he had found his calling as he understood deeply that *what the mind can conceive, a person can achieve.* Wayne's father, a dentist and entrepreneur, encouraged his academic pursuits. His mother balanced his humanistic interests, supporting his passion to enter the field of psychology to contribute to the arenas of human potential enhancement and transformational leadership.

After earning his doctorate in clinical psychology, Dr. Pernell began working with leaders across a broad array of organizations and, in building bridges between line staff and leadership, organizational efficiency ensued. Dr. Pernell's efforts have included relationship counseling, leadership coaching, and even holding senior management level positions, himself.

Throughout his journey, Dr. Wayne D. Pernell continues coaching individuals and consulting with organizations, always looking for ways to help people step into their greatness to share their unique gifts and talents.

As a fourth-degree black belt, coach, and author, his influence spread to the community. As Sensei Wayne, his students learn to continually assess available options in an effort to best minimize or eliminate conflict. Drawing on concepts from Bushido (the "Way of the Warrior"), Sensei Wayne helps his clients (and his readers) get through tough spots and reduce conflict in their lives by emphasizing the power of choice even during extremely high-pressure situations.

Also affectionately known by friends and family as "Dr. Wayne" or "Dr. P," this man of many talents is no stranger to the stage. In addition to his work in coaching individuals and organizations, speaking, and training groups of all sizes internationally, Dr. Pernell is an accomplished magician. These days he's likely to engage you in *Choosing Your Power* (the title of his first book) or pull out a "M.A.G.I.C." formula (as he explains in his morning TV segments) in the service of helping his clients.

When not on the road, Wayne is happily at home in Northern California just south of Napa Valley with his wife and his two sons, daughter, and two bonus daughters grow further into their independence in the world.

Dr Pernell invites you to keep moving forward, enjoying the challenge and rewards that come from Choosing Your Power as you create Your Winning Way!

To receive tips and updates from Dr Wayne D. Pernell, please find him online at:
www.Facebook.com/WaynePernell

and be sure to see what's new for you at:
www.WaynePernell.com.
contact info: DrP@WaynePernell.com and at: 415-336-1777

CHAPTER 15

USING EDUCATIONAL MARKETING TO BUILD RAPPORT, CREDIBILITY AND CRUSH OBJECTIONS

BY GREG ROLLETT

Everyone's favorite question to answer at cocktail parties, family reunions and networking gatherings is the infamous, "So, what do you do?"

Some people have it down pat. "I'm a personal injury lawyer," or "I'm a real estate agent."

Others, not so much. "I'm a writer…a blogger…and I help people manage the social web."

When we started the ProductPros, I found myself in the difficult position of trying to explain what it is that I do and how I help people in their business. Creating information products has a place at the forefront of the information marketing business, but not so much for nearly everyone else on the planet.

For prospects and potential clients, we had to take it a step further. While they understand what an information product may be, the concept of "We'll build your product for you" is lost on many people. In comes the power of using educational marketing to help paint a picture in our prospect's mind as to what we do, how it can help them, and why we are the expert, and the company they need to hire in order to get the results they desire.

Throughout our marketing campaign, we do this in a variety of ways – from live and recorded webinars, where we place an emphasis on education for 60-90 minutes, to free reports and manifestos. We also use the media to leverage their audience to share our story and our message, providing education through print, TV and online media outlets.

One such outlet that we recently used to our advantage was working with Andrew Warner and Mixergy.com. Mixergy is an online publishing company that interviews successful CEO's and entrepreneurs in an effort to help other CEO's and entrepreneurs build successful businesses. Mixergy has interviewed the likes of Tim Ferriss, Gary Vaynerchuk, the CEO's from Kiva, Groupon, Wikipedia and more. And now, it was my turn to help out.

Our interview was focused on creating and developing information products, even if you are not a guru. The interview was actually constructed as a step-by-step system for building, recording and releasing a first information product. The interview between Andrew and I lasted about 2 hours and was the definition of using education to gain interest, trust and rapport with a community.

After the interview was aired, numerous viewers contacted me inquiring about my work. They loved the interview and the information that I shared. The interview built a bond with the audience, as they saw my face (it was a video interview), my passion and my voice. I gave them everything that I knew about the subject.

When you are free to give value to an audience, and you over-deliver through education and information, you can quickly gain control of an audience. There is something about being vulnerable that opens you up to bonding and trust. This type of educational marketing will quickly allow you to do three powerful things in your business:

1. Build Rapport With Your Audience

2. Build Unmatched Credibility With Your Audience

3. Crush Objections That Your Market Might Have about You and What Your Business Does

In the Mixergy interview, I was able to do all of these three things through the education I provided in the content. The results from this interview alone have translated into $15,500 in new business, from clients that had never heard of me before the interview. That is very powerful indeed.

Let's explore how you can use education in your marketing in each of these three areas.

BUILDING RAPPORT WITH YOUR AUDIENCE

Today, more than ever, people are constantly being hit from every angle with advertising, information, ideas and brands. New companies, solutions, advertisers and experts are popping up literally every minute. How can you not only grab their attention, but also connect with them emotionally, making them remember you and take the next step or action?

This is done through rapport building. Wikipedia defines rapport as: "The relationship of two or more people who are *in sync* or *on the same wavelength* because they feel similar and/or relate well to each other."

In other words, in your marketing, you need to educate your marketplace that you know your market better than they do. You need to make them feel that you are just like them, that you understand them and that they can come to you when faced with a problem.

Education is the best way to do that. Think about your favorite teacher in grade school or high school the one that opened your eyes on a subject. This teacher found a way to connect with you, to get past the bad feelings about class work, and actually got inside your head, got you to pay attention and take action (in that case, passing your exams).

You need to now do this in your marketing. A great example is from Chris Guillebeau and how he builds rapport at The Art Of Nonconformity. Chris has been blogging about his life and his business since 2008. It started as a place to speak freely about his quest to travel to every country in the world before his 35th birthday. He is now only a handful of countries away from accomplishing this goal.

Along the way, Chris has built an online and offline publishing business that allows him to live his desired lifestyle of travel and creative production (books, blog posts, training programs and events). As he began to build his tribe, he needed to create a reason for people to follow him. He had an incredible story to tell and a movement that would resonate with a global audience that wanted more from their existing lives.

As the blog grew, Chris wrote his World Domination Manifesto, which explained his story, his travel ambitions and his new outlook on what work and life should be all about. The manifesto instantly connected with thousands of people from all over the world who were now hung up on every word Chris wrote. They were hungry for more.

Chris then developed a series of "Unconventional Guides," his first suite of products for this audience. Had Chris not educated his market about his mission, inspired them through his own journey and ambitions, and let them into his world essentially building rapport with a hungry audience, they would not be so eager to buy his "Unconventional Guides," to help elevate his books to *New York Times* Best-Sellers, to purchase tickets to his sold-out annual World Domination events and use his game changing products.

The rapport he built is so strong and focuses on a 90% educational and informational strategy, and only 10% sales. The trust with his tribe is immense and is difficult to match in his marketplace.

In your business, you may not have the luxury of delivering 90% free and useful educational content, and that's okay. What you do need to do and understand is that you cannot underestimate the power of connecting emotionally with your audience and how they are feeling.

This can be a manifesto, a book, vulnerable blog posts, videos and even webinars or events where you can connect on that emotional level. That connection can be unmatched and can help you to build a loyal tribe.

BUILDING UNMATCHED CREDIBILITY WITH YOUR AUDIENCE

The second piece to educational marketing is showing your audience that you, and you alone are the sole expert that can solve their problem. You do this by educating them about your credibility in your marketplace. People today do business with people that they know, like and trust.

They are buying you for *who* you are, *not what* you do.

Maybe businesses focus on the *what* part of their business the features and benefits that make their product great. While it is important to be great at what you do, you need to spend more time educating people on *who* you are. What is your core story? What are your values? What makes people connect to you on a human level?

In building unmatched credibility, you also need to educate people on what you have done and the results you have achieved for people just like them. Remember, in building rapport, we were able to connect with people on that emotional level. Now it's time to show them that you are the right solution for them.

People really do relate to things that they are familiar with. In knowing that, be sure to showcase your media mentions, major awards that resonate with your market, high profile people and businesses you have done business with, and other accolades that would draw the attention in the brain of your target client or customer. All of this plants the seed for credibility.

Now, we want to take it to that next level and blow them away with our ability to help them get results. People pay big money for results. How can you create educational pieces that drive results for your clients? When I talk about product creation I always tell my audience that you need to make the first step very easy and actionable and that will deliver near instant results for your audience. You don't want to do, what I call the "P90X Pass Out Plan." This is where after seeing your material, or going through your program they are so exhausted or overwhelmed that they cannot go on, take action or get any results because their mind or their body has been completely shut down.

One great example of using education to build credibility and ignite action is from Ramit Sethi's *I Will Teach You To Be Rich.* I love this example because Sethi has two major objections to overcome from the moment someone see his name or visits his website. First, is his ethnicity. American society is not accustomed to seeing or hearing from a guru with his cultural background. India is not seen as a country where you would want to learn about financial information. His second major roadblock is the name of his site and business. It sounds like a "get rich quick" program, which it is far, far away from being in reality.

In order to overcome these obstacles, Seithi created an amazing educational series that viewers can receive right from the homepage of his website. When you visit his homepage, you will see references to major media he has been featured within and also a note about his *New York Times* best-selling book. This is an instant credibility booster. Then, instead of a traditional free report, which many people relate to *give me your email address, and I will send you a bunch of promotional e-mails to buy my stuff,* Seithi is actually giving away the kitchen sink and then some. When you opt-in to his newsletter you instantly receive content that is better than many expert or guru's paid content. It includes:

- The 80/20 Guide to Finding a Job You Love
- The 30-day Hustling Course with interviews, worksheets and exercises
- The Idea Generator PDF and MP3
- Successful Client and Student Case Studies
- The first chapter of his NYT best-selling book and more

...all of this just to get an email address. That is very impressive and one look into the material and the credibility factor for what he does and teaches goes through the roof!

In your business, look for ways to over deliver and drive results for your clients before you ask them for money. Showcase your credibility in a way that helps them to accomplish their needs and desires in life and business. Once you do this, the selling becomes superfluous.

CRUSHING PROSPECT OBJECTIONS

You can use education to advance the conversation in the head of your prospect to move them one, or multiple steps closer to choosing you as the person to help them solve their problem. You have seen that with the first two steps, building rapport and building credibility. Even if you get through both of these detectors in the brains of your market, they will still have objections and red flags floating around in their minds. This is where the third and final piece of the puzzle comes together.

Everyday you hear objections as to why people are not yet ready to buy your products or services. Maybe it is price or that they don't fully understand your offer. Maybe something is conflicting in their mind, or they feel they don't have enough time to put it into play. No matter their objective, you have the ability to educate them on why their objective is not the answer and that your solution is.

Having an objection to a product or service that your market needs really means that they don't have the right education as to how it will impact their life. Your job is to educate them by teaching strategic points that paint a vivid picture in their minds that you are the right man (or woman) for the job.

If you have gotten this far, I want you to spend a few moments writing down every objection that you have heard as to why someone is not committing to your product or service. Talk to team members, write things down on a white board or just make a list on a sheet of notebook paper.

Now think about stories, case studies and information that will help to overcome each of these objections. What does your customer *not know* that is causing them to say "Not right now"?

A great example of overcoming objections in action is from Celebrity Press Publishing (CPP). Nick and his team put together a list of reasons people might not be using their publishing company. He turned those objections, or reasons, into a stellar report called "The New Rules of Becoming an Author: The 7 Myths Of Publishing Success." When someone wants to learn more or raising one of the key points mentioned in the report, the team at CPP can instantly send over the report as a PDF or mail a physical copy via FedEx that they can see, feel and read to overcome the objections that they might be having in their minds.

Nick is using educational marketing to showcase his expertise and build rapport with the audience. He showcases his credibility by telling stories of successful authors and then crushing objections. This becomes a powerful sales piece that is used as marketing. Again, it allows the prospect to come up with their own conclusion that Nick and Celebrity Press is the right solution to help their business.

THE POWER OF EDUCATIONAL MARKETING

I hope you can see how powerful using education can be in your business. It allows others to make up their minds about what you do and how you can help them. Even better is that you get to create the message and the materials. You control the output.

And if anyone ever asks you again at a party or event what you *do*, you will now be able to educate them and help them understand who you are and what you do.

About Greg

Greg Rollett, @gregrollett, is a Best-Selling Author and Marketing Expert who works with experts, authors and entrepreneurs all over the world. He utilizes the power of new media, direct response and personality-driven marketing to attract more clients and to create more freedom in the businesses and lives of his clients.

After creating a successful string of his own educational products and businesses, Greg began helping others in the production and marketing of their own products and services. He now helps his clients through two distinct companies, Celebrity Expert Marketing and the ProductPros.

Greg has written for *Mashable, Fast Company, Inc.com, the Huffington Post*, AOL, AMEX's Open Forum and others, and continues to share his message helping experts and entrepreneurs grow their business through marketing.

Greg's client list includes Michael Gerber, Brian Tracy, Tom Hopkins, Coca-Cola, Miller Lite and Warner Brothers, along with thousands of entrepreneurs and small-business owners across the world. Greg's work has been featured on FOX News, ABC, NBC, CBS, CNN, *USA Today, Inc Magazine, The Wall Street Journal*, the *Daily Buzz* and more.

Greg loves to challenge the current business environment that constrains people to working 12-hour days during the best portions of their lives. By teaching them to leverage marketing and the power of information, Greg loves to help others create freedom in their businesses that allow them to generate income, make the world a better place, and live a radically-ambitious lifestyle in the process.

A former touring musician, Greg is highly sought after as a speaker, who has spoken all over the world on the subjects of marketing and business building.

If you would like to learn more about Greg and how he can help your business, please contact him directly at: greg@dnagency.com or by calling his office at 877.897.4611.

CHAPTER 16

DESIRE BETTER HEALTH? EAT CHOCOLATE!

BY DR. BERNARD PRESS

If I told you that you could eat chocolate everyday to become healthier and lose weight, you would probably think I am crazy. Consider though, that growing up you might never have envisioned an iPhone or a tablet computer, or, if you are old enough, you might never have dreamed a computer would exist at all! Now, I am not advocating that you run down to the corner store to buy up all the chocolate bars. The secret is not chocolate itself, but the antioxidants in cocoa, the key ingredient in chocolate.

Naturally-occuring substances hold the key to better health for millions of us. Eating a healthy diet packed with nutrient rich food certainly is one right step toward optimal health, but the nutrient calorie ratio is important too. Spinach is loaded with antioxidants, however, most people would be hard-pressed to consume the pounds of spinach, broccoli or kale required to get the appropriate antioxidants to reverse damage in the body. How do we know how many antioxidants are contained in each food? We use the ORAC Test.

The ORAC (Oxygen Radical Absorbance Capacity) system measures the amount of antioxidants in foods. Tests are performed at independent laboratories and have been done on thousands of the foods we consume daily. Some foods such as tomatoes have a relatively low level of antioxidant with an ORAC value of 300 per 100 grams. At the top of the scale are unprocessed cocoa at 26,000/100 grams, drak chocolate at 13,000/100 grams, fresh Acai berry at 18,500/100 grams and freeze-dried powdered Acai berry at 44,000-61,000/100 grams. You would need to consume nearly 50 times the amount of tomatoes to get the same benefit as you would the dark chocolate!

You have probably heard or read a million stories about antioxidants. If you have been skeptical, I understand. Therefore, let me better explain what antioxidants do and why. It all begins with oxygen. We need oxygen to survive, but some of the oxygen we breathe has been damaged. The damage creates free radicals, damaged oxygen molecules that are missing electrons. These free radicals search for electrons to complete them and attack other, healthy cells to steal their electrons. The free radicals can attack any cells in our bodies from brain to skins to intestines. Antioxidants supply these rogue, free radicals with the electrons they need so that simple oxygen does not break down cells and cause damage.

What damages our much-needed oxygen to begin with? Free radicals are created when oxygen become damaged through two major sources, sunlight and pollution. Sunlight is, of course, naturally occuring and unavoidable. Consider, however, the fact that as we have damaged the ozone layer we have intensified the sun's dramatic affect on our oxygen supply. As to pollution, the more we pollute the environment, the greater the free radicals created to wreak havoc in our bodies. Free radical damage can be linked to conditions ranging from heart disease to dementia to diabetes or arthritis.

Antioxidants are available from a variety of sources. As mentioned before two of the top sources with the highest concentrations are cacao and acai. Let us look first at cacao. Cacao is the mother source of cocoa used in chocolates. Cocoa contains flavanoids, antioxidants that reverse free-radical damages. Studies show that flavanols, a variety of flavanoids, are particularly effective; but they are not absorbed well and thus require higher concentrations to achieve maximum effectiveness. The amount of flavanols in cocoa is dependent on the processing used. Fermentation, roasting and high temperatures—the processing used by most commericial chocolate manufacturers—decreases the amount of flavanoids in cocoa. Cold processes, on the other hand, such as blanching or cold pressing, can yield eight times the amount of flavanols.

Generally, the darker the chocolate, the more antioxidant properties it contains. Flavanoid-rich dark chocolates are purported to have many health benefits:

- Encourage healthier cardiovascular function
- Helps promote respiratory function
- Helps promote joint flexability and ease of motion
- Decreases LDL (bad) Cholesterol
- May act as histamine blocker
- Increases serotonin levels making you happier
- Encourages dental health
- Helps suppress cravings
- Encourages healthy elimination
- Natural sexual stimulant
- Skin benefits

Some of you might be laughing right now, because you have said for years that chocolate made you happier. Now there is scientific data to prove it! I want to focus here on the top seven benefits of dark chocolate consumption.

Aging
Chocolate contains double the antioxidants of red wine and up to three times more than that of green tea. Korean scientists demonstrated that free radicals contribute to the development and onset of dementia.

Cardiovascular health
Hundreds of studies have indicated that cocoa and chocolate aid the cardiovascular system. A Yale University study found that ingesting dark chocolate increased function of endothelial cells in the blood vessels and lowered blood pressure. Chocolate also stimulates production of nitric oxide to relax blood vessels and relieves inflammation while helping to control blood sugar and insulin levels.

Brain Health
Antioxidants minimize inflammation that contributes to strokes and dementia and protects brain cells, blood vessels and tissue. It improves mental cognition, enhances mood and decreases depression.

Diabetes

Antioxidants in chocolate will not eliminate or cure diabetes, but it can assist by protecting blood vessels from scarring of excess glucose. Findings in a 2008 double-blind trial, reported in Journal of American College of Cardiology, indicated that cocoa countered vascular damage common to diabetics. Moreover, cocoa can minimize symptoms of neuropathy.

Inflammation

Chronic inflammation is linked to many diseases including cardiovascular disease and gastrointestinal disorders. Cocoa, however, offers some strong anti-inflammatory agents. Flavanols in cocoa inhibit the very messengers that signal an inflammation response in the body. Italian scientists found that even small amounts of dark chocolate could result in lower levels of C-reactive protein that is a key marker of inflammation.

Weight Control

Turn on any news station and you are likely to hear about the obesity epidemic in the United States. In fact, one-third of all Americans are overweight. Free radicals have been labeled a culprit in weight gain. As the free radicals bounce around the body like the ball in a pinball machine, they leave a path of destruction in cells, tissues and organs. Ultimately, the free radicals damage so many body processes that the body no longer manages even simple functions like digestion or absorbtion of food properly. The good news is, you can consume some chocolate and have it benefit your weight and health. Some studies indicate that chocolate may regulate the genes that control weight gain. Chocolate appears to have appetite-suppressant qualities too.

In addition to the antioxidants, chocolate also contains other chemicals that just plain enhance your mood and make you feel better. These mood-altering ingredients include:

PEA can boost production of serotonin and endorphins. Both brain chemicals decrease depression and elevate mood. They can reduce sensitivity to pain and increase feelings of contentment.

Arginine is an amino acid and natural sexual stimulant, therefore, the arginine found in cocoa might improve libido.

Vitamin B6 is essential for production of hormones serotonin, melatonin and dopamine. It is helpful in reducing and reversing depressive symptoms and PMS related symptoms.

Magnesium found in cocoa in high levels, helps raise progesterone levels, which is one reason women tend to crave chocolate during their menstrual cycle.

Tryptophan the precursor to serotonin also helps increase serotonin production. It is no accident that some of the most prescribed pharmaceuticals in America increase available serotonin in the brain. Tryptophan also aids in production of neurotransmitters that help produce restful sleep.

Theobromine is a cousin to caffeine that provides a natural burst of energy, improves mood and improves blood flow.

MAO inhibitors are chemicals that fight depression. Their natural occurrence in cocoa suggests that cocoa consumption might be beneficial for those with depression, mood issues and attention deficit because they calm cravings, elevate mood and improve neurotransmitter activity.

I became interested in antioxidants and their affect on the body when my wife of 30 years was diagnosed with high blood pressure. I learned that inside our bodies, a battle is constantly raging. The healthy cells fight against the damaging effects of free radicals. When we are young, our bodies easily win the battles, but as we age, our cells lose the battle and some of them die. What some of us so readily accept as a natural progression in aging: arthritis, high blood pressure, muscular degeneration and dementia, are all losses on the battlefront. By shoring up our bodies' defenses, we prolong our bodies' natural ability to fight the enemy. I researched the products available on the market and found that most were lacking in efficacy and the science backing them. Xoçai was different.

As I previously mentioned, dark chocolate and acai berry both contain high concentrations of antioxidants and other chemicals that aid in achieving optimal physical and mental health. Can you imagine the effect of combining the two into one product? The effect would be similar to the mult-tasking power of the iPhone or Android. What if you could combine all the nutrients of an entire meal plus all the antioxidant power of cold-pressed cocoa into one product? You can. Xoçai provides it.

REAL HEALTH BENEFITS

Xoçai is a leader in the healthy chocolate market because their products deliver real health benefits. Regular commercially prepared chocolates use cocoa that has been heat processed which destroys the phytonutrients and antioxidants and, thus, the health benefits as well. Their chocolates use unhealthy oils, milk solids, waxes and fillers and remove the natural cocoa butter found in the cacao bean. Xoçai uses cold-pressed cocoa beans, retains the natural cocoa butters and incorporates low-glycemic index sweetners into their products for maximum health benefit. Xoçai is so confident in the benefits their product provides that they have enrolled in Brunswick Lab's certified program. Brunswick is an authoritative, third-party-assurance system that certified products for their ORAC values. What this means to consumers is consumers can better discern the claims of a company's antioxidant values.

Ideal for Busy People
What do all these benefits and certifications for Xoçai mean to you? Busy professionals, executives and entrepreneurs barely have time to eat a proper meal, let alone make sure that meal is packed with essential nutrients. And when you are barely squeezing in a quality meal, often those meals you do get are packed with empty calories and are not comprised of the nutrients your body needs. Xoçai to the rescue.

Ideal for Athletes
Xoçai is perfect for athletes. Xoçai products boost energy, accelerate recover and enhance mental performance. The appetite suppressant properties are ideal for athletes to stay in shape, and Xoçai is natural and does not contain any of the ingredients banned by anti-doping agencies and major athletic associations.

Ideal for Weight Loss
Xoçai's weight loss products satisfy your body while they boost how you feel. The cacao-based products are not "chocolate flavored" like many other weight loss shakes and products. They contain actual cocoa fiber as the primary fiber source to promote satisfaction and suppress appetite. Other ingredients like blueberries deliver antioxidant protection, whey protein isolates promotes healthy blood sugar, and chia seed oil delivers omega-3 fatty acids. Machiel N. Kennedy, MD and Steven E. Warren, MD, DPA, CIME, FABFP, FABHPM, FAPWCA

studied Xoçai X-ProteinMeal Shakes for their effectiveness. The study's findings were revealed in the American Journal of Bariatric Medicine.

The Xoçai products include meal replacement shakes, chocolate X Power squares, XoBiotic (probiotic) squares, Omega squares for omega-3 delivery, peanut butter snack cups and energy drinks. Unlike high-calorie, fat-laden fast food meals and vending machine snacks, Xoçai products cost less per serving and provide optimal nutrition. Three X Power Squares, for example, provide the same amount of antioxidants as 6.5 lbs of tomatoes or 1.6 lbs of spinach. I don't know about you, but I find it difficult to load 6.5 lbs of tomatoes into my office fridge!

My wife's death taught me never put off until tomorrow what I can do today. Today is your day too. Start replacing the bad with the good in your life. Start with your health. If you are an athlete, improve your performance. If you are an overweight executive or stay-at-home-mom, take control of your weight and your health by replacing old standbys like fast food with nutrient rich shakes. Young and vibrant? Protect your body for the future with a Xoçai beverage once a day to strengthen your body's defenses against free radicals that seek to destroy your health.

If you are ready to eat chocolate to improve your health, or you want to learn more about Xoçai products, I want to show you how to feel energized, look better and lose weight. These products are not too good to be true; they are too good not to try. Look for Xoçai products at: www.winningthebodybattle.com.

About Bernard

Dr. Bernard Press was born and educated in Philadelphia, PA. He graduated from Central High School and enlisted in the Navy in 1944. Upon completion of his training in radio, radar and sonar, he was selected to teach the program at the Naval Base in Monterey, California. He was honorably discharged from the Navy in 1946.

Upon his discharge from the Navy, he enrolled at UCLA in the pre-optometry program and then entered Optometry School at the University of California. Upon graduation, he opened an office in Solana Beach, CA and then moved his office to Encinitas, CA. His first location was on Highway 101 in Encinitas and he then moved to Second Street and ultimately built a new office with partners on Encinitas Blvd.

He sold his office to his Associate in 1981 and retired from the practice of Optometry. His next venture was to qualify as a real estate broker in business sales. He devoted his time to helping doctors sell their practices. He sold the business to an associate and started a business with the goal of developing an eye implant that would lower eye pressure and help to prevent blindness in people who are suffering with glaucoma.

This business, OcumatRx, has been working to develop the implant. It was discovered that the implant as designed could not be manufactured using present technology. With new technology the possibility now exists by using 3D printing. If a prototype can be made and tested, it will be necessary to procure financing for manufacture and clinical trials.

During his time in the practice, Dr. Press was appointed to the Board of Directors of California Vision Services. As President, he was able to bring in better management and create a thriving business. The name was subsequently changed to Vision Service Plan, the largest pre-paid vision plan in the United States.

While in practice, Dr. Press became a member of Rotary International and served the Encinitas Rotary Club twice as President. He also was appointed to the Encinitas School Board and then elected for an additional 4-year term and served as president.

At present, he is semi-retired and doing some writing. His first book will be called *Meatloaf Marketing* which is ready for publishing. His second book will be *Brown Spots* designed for teenage children.

CHAPTER 17

26 QUESTIONS TO ASK YOUR INVESTMENT ADVISOR NOW

BY BOB ROARK

If you asked me this question, "I am trying to find an advisor to manage my money, what would you ask a prospective manager, knowing what you know now after all these years, if you were me?" There are many things that you could ask. The challenge is asking an insightful question, understanding the answer and putting together a process to find an advisor.

Sometimes it is difficult to know what question to ask. It can be intimidating, embarrassing or both. We have all been in that situation at one point or another. I remember when I first started as an advisor in 1987 I really did not understand the municipal bond market referred to by the old hands as "munis". Municipal bonds, certainly I studied about them for the security license but that really didn't paint the picture for me. So what to do? I went to the resident bond expert, Frank, in our office and asked, he was the muni maven. It was very easy for him to determine how inexperienced I was by the nature of my questions. I asked many questions, he answered in depth and answered some questions I did not even know to ask. His help and patience were so important the experience stayed with me all these years. There is an abundance of information now available on the Internet that will help you form questions, but does the information really answer the question in your mind?

This is meant for the person that is tasked with the challenge of finding an advisor that suits their needs without the benefit of an experienced friend or relative, or perhaps you are tasked with a manager search for a pool of investments. Other than a beauty contest and a nice office, how might you determine if this person is knowledgeable or competent? We have all seen a circumstance where the respondent is nervous or defensive when a particular question is posed, or the answer to a question is ignored or not answered at all; much can be determined by the behavior of the respondent. Are they nervous, overbearing, condescending or earnest and interested?

After setting the appointment, perhaps these series of questions might serve as a starting point and may help you find an appropriate portfolio manager that suits your needs. These are the questions I would ask. It may be that you might not understand all the answers but sometimes that is telling as well, will the prospective manager/advisor take the time to answer until you do understand; does the candidate answer in a manner that is not defensive? Is the answer simplified to the point where the answer is useful? These are some of the questions I would ask:

1. What is your buy discipline? What causes you to add a security or position? If this is part of your strategy, *why do you believe that this is a successful strategy?* Do you have any method of testing what you're talking about in your buy discipline? Is the buy discipline rooted in any academic work? When you add a security is it based on specific criteria, or is it 'get a hunch and bet a bunch'? What makes you think this is a successful strategy in this current market condition? Do you have a disciplined method to describe the market condition you are? In what market condition is your discipline not rewarded?

2. What is your sell discipline? What *would cause you ever to lower your allocation exposure to a particular asset class or market?* Can you describe your sell discipline? Would you ever lower or eliminate your allocation exposure to any asset class? Do you do any work to determine broad trends in the market? For example, do you believe that buying bonds and holding to maturity makes a difference or would you lower your exposure to long-dated maturities if interest rates were rising? At what point in time would you increase or delete a particular asset class?

3. How do you get paid? *If you can understand how an advisor is compensated there are few surprises. Do they charge a flat fee based upon the underlying assets? Does it include trading costs? Are there any other fees or revenue received by the advisor for making a recommendation or using a particular security?* This information would also allow you an opportunity to discuss the potential fees with your tax professional. How specifically do you get paid? What are your fees that I can see, and are there any hidden fees? As with any instrument, there's a cost associated, whether it's the markup in a municipal bond, whether it's an internal management fee or mortality expenses involved with annuity products, it's useful to understand all of the fees associated with any instrument that you might use in order to understand the total cost of portfolio management.

4. How does your investment strategy/strategies fit in with my risk tolerance level? Are you taking more risk than I can tolerate? How do you determine my risk tolerance? There are many different strategies to approach in attempting to achieve a particular rate of return in the marketplace. If you are a conservative investor and you invest in a portfolio that has more volatility than you can stomach, or sleep at night with, then it's unlikely that you will stay in that particular strategy. It's much like going off-shore deep sea fishing. You know that you will leave from a particular port, and will return to that same port at the end of the day. It may be like fishing in 10 foot seas; you're nauseous during the trip and at the end of the day you are back at the same port you started from with nothing to show but a nauseating boat ride. It is important to adopt a strategy that's consistent with what you can tolerate so your odds of staying in the strategy are enhanced.

5. How does your investment strategy contribute toward helping me pursue my goals? *For example, if you are an income investor do you own instruments that are income-oriented?* For example, if you are an income investor, when do the instruments pay? Monthly, quarterly, annually? When do they mature? Rather simple in thought, but necessary if you need a particular rate of return or cash flow to meet budget. What if bond interest rates happen to be extremely low, in the 1% to 2% arena, and you need a 3% or 4% income target, how is it that a particular strategy deployed going

to achieve the income requirements? What is the maturity of my portfolio in order to pursue my goals?

6. How does your investment strategy function in up markets? *Do you overweight or underweight a security or sector based upon your strategy and the market condition?* In an up market condition, what discipline in particular do you use to determine to overweight, underweight or avoid a particular security or sector? Does your strategy utilize position sizing? (Position sizing basically refers to the size of a position within a particular portfolio, or the dollar amount that an investor is going to trade.) Can the advisor explain position sizing as it relates to the strategy?

7. How does your investment strategy function in down markets? *Do you add to money market positions, hedge, short, rebalance or some other strategy?* If you are adding or rebalancing why does this make sense and in what condition would you change your strategy? For this discussion, how does the advisor identify a down market condition for the security or strategy deployed? What's the duration of the strategy? What are the characteristics? Can you describe a down or up-market condition? What research have you conducted to influence your beliefs and confidence in your discipline?

8. What asset classes do you invest in? *Stocks, bonds, commodities, international, REITs, junk bonds or some other asset class.* It may be that there are some sectors or securities that you are uncomfortable owning or are prohibited from owning. There are many tools to use, so it is useful to discuss which instruments your advisor will utilize.

9. What is the best book you have read recently that has influenced your thought process? *It might offer insight whether the advisor is well read or has a passion for his profession. Who wrote it and what did you learn from it? Does the advisor follow his firm's research? If so, which analyst and why? Do you have any books that you might recommend I read for instance to broaden my understanding.*

10. What are the top five books or publications that I should read as an investor? *What has the advisor read, studied or attended that hones their skills on your behalf. You may gain an insight as to how they think. It might even be useful to see if they have a method to test*

their strategy, when it works, when it fails and in what condition.

11. Does your investment strategy reallocate based upon the market condition or rebalance to a buy and hold allocation model? *Is it passive asset allocation, relative strength based, sector rotation or some other underlying concept? Can the advisor describe it?*

12. How frequently do you report performance? *Quarterly, bi-annual, annual? Do you have a copy of a sample performance report? How can you see if you are meeting your goals if you don't receive a report card? It is important to know your requirements. Comparing your returns to a specific index might be interesting but only to the extent that that index return mirrors your goals and risk tolerance. Can you tell from the performance report if you are up or down in dollar terms as well as percentage?*

13. How frequently do I get a statement? *A good method of monitoring activity and balances. If you can't read the statement, who do I talk to in your organization that will help me understand my statement? At a minimum you should be able to tell whether you are up or down and where your fees are reflected.*

14. Can I see my statement online? *Useful but can be counterproductive if monitored too frequently, very useful at tax time. Who in your organization will help me log on and set up my online access?*

15. What type of instruments do you use in your model? *Stocks, bonds, UITs, ETFs, Limited Partnership, or other asset classes? If you have a particular restriction with respect to the types of instruments you are comfortable with, now would be the time to understand what is used.*

16. What software do you use to test your investment strategies? *Does the advisor use software to research their strategies. It may be insightful to determine how the advisor thinks and whether the advisor is organized and disciplined.*

17. What percentage of the time do the strategies win/fail? *Most if not all strategies have periods of time where they are not rewarded as well as other strategies. It is useful if the advisor is familiar with this information.*

18. How many instruments do you typically hold? Why? *5, 10, 20, 100? How many positions can I expect to see on my statement and*

what causes the advisor to hold the quantity they indicate? Do you use position sizing? This can be so important to the potential outcome, this is the second mention.

19. What is your typical portfolio turnover rate? *10%, 20%, 100%? The advisor should know their expected turnover. It could be very important in taxable accounts to manage tax liability.*

20. Is your strategy tax efficient (for taxable accounts)? *Fairly simple, yes or no. If yes, how do you accomplish the tax efficiency?*

21. How does your strategy change if interest rates go up or down? *Will they increase or decrease the average maturity of the portfolio based upon interest rates. Why or why not. Do you stay within a certain credit rating quality?*

22. If I called to sell now, how fast would my funds be available? *At what cost? How liquid, is there a 'get out' fee, is it prorated, if not, when does the 'get out' fee cease? If I called to sell out for an emergency, how fast can you issue me a check?*

23. How realistic are my goals? *You should expect a cogent discussion* that is constructive. There should be some basis to the answer provided.

24. How do you determine how much I need in retirement? *There should be some discussion of how much you have to invest, how long you will work, how much you will save and how much you spend now. Those factors at a minimum would be useful to attempt to arrive at your specific return benchmark.*

25. What rate of return is required to help me pursue my goals? *How much you need in the future, how much you have now, plus how much you are going to add each year, the rate of return each year, less any funds taken out along the way is a good start. How long you plan on adding and at what frequency before you start to distribute is critical to the discussion. A spreadsheet is a very useful tool to visualize the process.*

26. Did you tell me what I wanted to hear or what I needed to hear? *If my risk tolerance is incompatible with my rate of return need, will you tell me if I'm being too optimistic?*

Let's assume that you have interviewed more than one candidate and you have compiled a list of the responses that you thought were useful.

What to do now? If the decision is not clear back off the decision process and let the information perk for a while. Many feel there is a need for an immediate decision. There is a greater need for an informed deliberate decision that meets your needs. If the decision is not clear, interview more candidates and take your time.

There are many different portfolio disciplines, most if not all have periods of time where the discipline is not rewarded by the market condition. It may be useful to explore what course of action you would consider for those periods where the portfolio strategy is not being rewarded. There are qualified portfolio managers that are disciplined, thoughtful and can communicate effectively. Hopefully, the above series of questions will function as a reasonable starting point in your research. It is how I would answer, "What would you ask a prospective manager, knowing what you know now after all these years, if you were me?"

For further insight "The Market for Financial Advice: An Audit Study" was published in March of 2012 by the National Bureau of Economic Research. http://www.nber.org/papers/w17929.pdf?new_window=1 A study was conducted to determine whether advisors did or did not reinforce a prospective clients behavioral bias or misconceptions.

Investing involves risks in regards to all of the investment products mentioned on this page. Any expressed or implied recommendation contained within, are made without regard of investors objectives. Consult your advisor. Bob Roark is a registered representative with LPL Financial, Member FINRA/SIPC.

About Bob

Bob Roark is CEO and co-founder of RS Asset Management, LLC. Born in Naples, Italy on a US Naval Base, Bob subsequently grew up in multiple locations in the southeast. Integrity, responsibility and hard work were the core values instilled by his mother and Navy Chief Petty Officer father. Hunting, fishing and water sports were the chief pursuits where the love of the outdoors and sense of capability were explored. Bob graduated from Middle Tennessee State University and was subsequently commissioned in the US Army as a Second Lieutenant. Stationed at Ft Carson in Colorado Springs after Intelligence and Airborne School were completed; leadership, responsibility and accountability were honed.

As a 27-year veteran of the financial services industry, Bob has held positions with prominent Wall Street firms including Merrill Lynch as well as Morgan Stanley. As a top financial advisor in Colorado Springs at both previous firms, a deliberate decision was made to better serve the client interests by establishing RS Asset Management. Bob serves clients throughout much of the United States in the areas of portfolio management, retirement planning and estate planning. Bob is committed to understanding the client's needs, risk tolerances and pursuing an appropriate, rules-based investment discipline based upon the client's objectives. Bob also works with business owners from agriculture, transportation, energy and retail in pre- and post-business sale strategies to preserve and protect their family legacy. Bob maintains a farm in Middle Tennessee where the values instilled while young a man, was shared with his wife of 30 years and his two children.

Bob is a fierce advocate for the best interest of his clients in helping them accumulate, manage and pass their family legacy on to the next generation or charity. Bob has been a resident of Colorado Springs for 37 years.

Contact Bob at: bob@rsassetmanagement.com

Securities offered through LPL Financial, Member FINRA?SIPC. Investment advice offered through RS Asset Management, a Registered Investment Advisor and separate entity from LPL Financial.

CHAPTER 18

THREE ATTRIBUTES TO IGNITE THE LEADER WITHIN

BY CATHERINE ROCHELEAU

The popularity of leadership in today's business environment is justified, given its impact on success or failure of any organization, and the engagement of employees and supporters.

Leadership has an impact when you are in a structured organization like a corporation, on a committee with a mandate or even in an informal special interest group. Recognizing who is a true leader, and leveraging their abilities to influence the future, drive change, foster and empower followers, leads to a more successful path to the stated goal.

In my experience, there are three key attributes a leader must learn to be more responsive to enjoy the success they are destined to achieve.

1. DELEGATE

If leadership is based on the premise that leaders are very passionate about their vision and able to attract followers who share this passion and want to be a part a winning team, then is it not prudent to ensure wider involvement by those committed to the goal?

Let's look at delegation and its importance in leadership. Delegation is commonly referred to as the act of passing a task or responsibility along to others, most commonly to people who are below you on the totem pole. This interpretation assumes the leader is in a senior position or has someone to delegate to. What happens when you are in business for yourself or when the leader is on a low rung of the corporate ladder?

Delegation offers every leader an opportunity to share the workload and responsibilities to reach their vision. I cannot count how many times I have joined a committee or volunteered for a project only to become frustrated and disillusioned when team members are little more than figureheads. What's worse is being asked to do something, only for it to be completely changed later—not because it was wrong, but because the Chair wanted it done their way.

A strong leader shares the full scope of their vision and mandate with team members. This requires them to leave their ego at the door so they are better able to recognize what's happening today and where they want to go. The same goes for every member of the team. Success is achieved when you focus on the good of the whole instead of individual personal gain. The saying, 1+1 = 3 (the sum of the whole system is greater than the sum of its parts), reflects the synergy and cumulative results possible from a group in comparison to the results which could be achieved by one member working alone.

Delegation also doesn't mean giving away the unpopular tasks. As a leader you gain more respect, foster more engagement and collectively you achieve stronger results, when team members are able to take on a wider range of tasks and responsibilities.

Delegation happens in all directions - up, down and outside of the organization. For example, an entrepreneur may have to delegate to a sub-contractor, a virtual assistant, or a specialist. In a much larger organization, different departments may have to collaborate on a common goal.

If we assume that leaders exist at all levels of an organization, and these leaders are passionate change agents who possess the ability to have others follow their lead, why is it most organizations do little to leverage the leaders within? Take for example a new employee who joins your company. They are excited, motivated and most importantly offer a new perspective on the systems you have in place. As a leader, why not harness the passion of the new employee, develop their engagement quickly and involve them in your change initiative?

New ideas and concepts from the rank and file can also be a driving force within an organization and alter the trajectory of your success. Corporate Social Responsibility (CSR) is a prime example where change and action have been driven from the bottom up. An employee who is passionate about the environment can spearhead a green team and spark innovations within your organization. Today's employees and consumers connect with organizations that embrace similar values and act on those values. Green initiatives and giving back to the local community are recognized as strong attractors for recruitment and consumer loyalty.

Delegation can also reflect how a leader leads. Many leaders are encouraged to lead in and take charge to be noticed and recognized for their efforts. In contrast, leaders can lean back and use their natural strengths and keen skills of observation, relationship building and motivation to influence others. When you lean back, you allow others to step forward and lead and achieve more.

It takes confidence and a clear vision to delegate successfully. Delegation doesn't mean abdication. You continue to hold the overall responsibility. Confident leaders know how to delegate the right task or responsibility to the right person at the right time so that they utilize each and every resource available to them to fulfill their mission.

2. COMMUNICATE

It always amazes me how many people have blind spots when it comes to communicating. We all have our own challenges, but when your team is unmotivated or complaining, and results are less than stellar, what steps do you have to take to lead a change? A keen look at how people are communicating should one of the first steps you take.

This case study highlights how miscommunication can drive a wedge between skilled and engaged members of your team. It also demonstrates how fundamental communication is to effective leadership. Directing is not leading and it definitely doesn't foster collaboration.

Dave, Hank and Larry are three senior managers who must work together to deliver the high quality services customers have become accustomed to. Recent complaints revealed some telling challenges between the three managers.

Communication was at the core of these challenges. Dave was perceived as having unrealistic expectations and his colleagues believed he was never satisfied with the work they were doing. The three also disagreed on the kind and frequency of communication between them. Hank and Larry believed they were communicating sufficiently, keeping Dave in the loop. In contrast, Dave expressed his desire to have confidence in Hank and Larry and their team. He wanted to know they were monitoring staff and ensuring things were completed properly.

These differences were creating a growing crevice between them. Larry was ready to walk away from his job due to frustration. He just wanted to do a good job, but rather than face conflict, he avoided communicating with other managers and just focused on his team. When communication rifts were identified, each manager was interviewed. Interestingly enough, they all wanted the same thing; a positive working relationship based on trust, clear expectations, and high quality customer service.

The first step was designed to rebuild trust and re-establish communication. Short daily meetings, 10-15 minutes in duration were set up; short enough to fit into their day, yet long enough to be productive. Ground rules were also established which included the ability for each manager to talk openly, without fear of reprisal. The topics would include the challenges, frustrations and gaps they have identified and on brainstorming solutions. Together they would set priorities and action plans.

After a rocky start, the three managers were able to establish solid lines of communication, realistic goals and action plans which led to considerable service improvements in only three weeks. With a common goal and purpose, they worked together, gradually rebuilding trust.

This situation went from catastrophe to success in a very short term because of communication improvement that identified these three critical factors:

1) Recognition of a common goal and deliverables.

2) Clear expectations and follow-through (which fostered trust).

3) A desire to do a good job consistently.

As a change agent, a leader recognizes they will upset the *status quo* and therefore can never underestimate the impact that communication can make to the outcome. How others react to change will be guided by the communication skills of the leader. Sub-standard or non-existent messages, or those delivered in the wrong way can increase resistance from naysayers and can quickly cause an about-face by supporters. No matter how small the change, how exciting the initiative, or how insignificant the resistance, a leader's message must be clear and informative and delivered with sincerity to obtain positive results.

Messages must address the issues raised, clarify what will happen and who is doing what. By doing so, a leader can help others to get onside, better understand the process and move through the changes effectively and positively.

Here is my **SPARK** **Framework for Communication**

S—SAY It Clearly – Communicating clearly will maximize employer and employee satisfaction.

P—PLUS – Strong communication is a value add – increased employee understanding and feelings of being valued, improved staff morale, improved employee retention, loyal customers.

A—Actively Listen – Communication includes listening – this skill cannot be overemphasized! "Good listeners are often equally good at getting people to feel understood and this helps build trust and a happier workplace."

R—Recognize non-verbal cues and what they are telling you.

K—Keep It Simple

Remember, communication reflects who you are and the character you bring to the situation. It will help you move mountains or it can close doors forever!

3. CALCULATE

Leadership involves a process of on-going interpretation, decision-making, adjustments, and reflection. An effective leader must lead know and understand their numbers to make the right decisions. It saddens me as a Coach and consultant when I meet intelligent business people struggling to grow their business, secure a promotion or lead a transformation – who are unaware of the value of the information at their disposal.

When you know your numbers, you have a unique method of measuring your own success, and the effectiveness of the methodologies you have in place. Key Performance Indicators (KPI's) allow you to better understand how well the systems deliver the results you want to achieve. KPI's can measure productivity, customer service satisfaction, customer acquisition, employee turnover, inventory levels, delivery times, error rates, organizational gains or losses and more. Choosing the right KPI is important. Each KPI should reflect what is important to your organization.

Financial numbers are probably the most obvious numbers in a business. They may include the budget, cash flow, cost of goods sold, revenues and expenses, or they may include revenues per customer. It is critical to have a sound understanding of what these numbers tell you. Most importantly review your numbers regularly and use the data to help make sound decisions that move you in the right direction.

Another key metric is your risk tolerance and the risk involved with every decision you undertake. Risk management offers leaders a unique perspective that can impact your decisions and the success you achieve. Failing to know your numbers can inhibit your ability to grow and adapt to your surroundings in a timely manner.

Sherrie is a physiotherapist who was hit hard by the economic down turn. She had two therapists working with her, yet she could barely meet her financial obligations. An evaluation of her practice revealed she did not know her numbers. She had not considered how many appointments were needed each month to break even financially, nor did she know the number of active patients, the average number of return visits by therapist, the cost of supplies for specific treatment modalities and so on. Sherrie also failed to recognize how a cash flow projection could help her make better decisions to re-grow her business.

By identifying the KPI's for her business and creating a tracking system, Sherry began to turn her business around. She enrolled in a basic accounting course to understand her financial records and worked with a business coach to ensure the efforts she was taking could be sustainable. Profitability became a reality within four months.

As a leader, when you delegate, communicate and calculate, you create a culture that fosters engagement, collaboration, innovation and the ability to adapt. Don't forget to integrate your own lifelong learning and a willingness to take some risks to enhance your leadership skills so you achieve the results you envision.

About Catherine

For Catherine Rocheleau, corporate leadership is about vision and its effective actualization. She believes leaders exist at all tiers of an organization and are vital allies that smart management aligns with, to drive transition or change. Working with management to identify, nurture and achieve buy-in from these all-important change agents is an important step in manifesting dynamic growth objectives. Growing up as a navy brat, Catherine's family moved almost every year. New schools, new friends, and sometimes a new culture, Catherine learned from an early age how to harness her own leadership skills to navigate differing circumstances. It didn't take her long to figure out change could be challenging, but it was exciting too.

A lifelong learner, Catherine brings the skills of coach, strategic planner, consultant, project manager and trainer to each assignment, enabling her to adjust her focus as the circumstance requires: to business leaders, the organization and all its stakeholders, and/or the functional objective at hand. Early in her career she enjoyed notable success in the food and nutrition industry—including Food Executive of the Year for Western Canada, an award that recognized her forward-thinking and people-oriented management style. Successes—as well as a few inevitable setbacks—inspired Catherine to continue to align her work with her passion for business excellence. As a result, she deepened her practical business expertise with a Masters in Business Administration in Management Leadership and a Diploma in Project Management. Certification as an Executive Coach, Business Coach and Master Certified Coach Trainer followed, sharpening her perceptual and motivational skills.

For more than twenty years, as Ignite Leadership International™, she has enjoyed a thriving professional practice that has included servicing multiple small and medium sized organizations, working with executives and employees to hone their business skills, reduce costs, grow the business and increase revenues. Her extensive on-the-ground involvement and plainspoken, pragmatic approach together with high professional standards make her highly sought after by a broad range of clients. Catherine was recently seconded to act as Executive Director, charged with diversifying a not-for-profit organization in the food sector, and as a direct result of her efforts overseeing the organizational team, succeeded in increasing revenues sevenfold over the course of 24 months.

Asked what motivates her, Catherine will cite an insatiable curiosity and personal desire to learn. She takes pride in being light on her feet, and responding to a diverse array of client needs as they arise. But more than anything, Catherine is driven by a strong desire to see other people succeed and the immense personal satisfaction she gets, knowing she has helped put the wheels in motion.

You can connect with Catherine at:
catherine@igniteleaders.com www.igniteleaders.com/
www.facebook.com/Igniteleadershipinternational
www.twitter.com/ignitesolutionz

CHAPTER 19

THE ART OF REINVENTING YOURSELF — IN ANY ECONOMY, AT ANY AGE

BY DR. DIYARI ABDAH

Being a child is great. Children grow and learn new things every day, many times through trial and error. They are also very proud when asked about their age. "I am five-and-a-half," "I am 7 and 8 months," they answer. This used to put a smile on my face every time I asked one of my younger patients. First, because of the utter innocence in the nature of the answer but more importantly the pride in their tone of voice, *five-and-a-half!* Not five, not nearly six or five-and-a-bit. No, it has to be *five-and-a-half*, proudly! I even heard answers like "I am 8 and 11 months-and-a-half!"

What they mean is that they are growing and they should not be treated like a four-and-a-half-year-old when they are five. They are more experienced now!

Children have the ability to reinvent themselves every time they come across an obstacle, always figuring out ways to do things. It is part of the learning experience and growing.

So why we do stop all that as adults? Is it pride, is it ego or just simply a lack of imagination and creativity. Adults, by contrast, feel they are

179

stuck. With no way out, this is it and we have to put up with our jobs, careers, location, and relationships. Time after time we hear the phrase, " It is too late to do that!" or "At My Age? Are You Serious?"

Today the average human being lives much longer than their ancestors, and for some to go well into their nineties is not so uncommon, so why not live it fully?

However, the flip side of that is that today we also hear more incidents of people getting very ill, with cancer for example, which is becoming more and more common unfortunately. This could be due to many factors, but among the common factors are lifestyle choices; including daily stress and bad habits.

As a health professional who is part of the Anti-Ageing movement and working closely with scientists and other professionals in Anti-Ageing medicine, I feel it is our, in fact everyone's, obligation to be aware of our environment and what causes imbalance in our lives and bodies. Until we realize where we are and where we want to be, we cannot draw a roadmap that leads us to freedom from bad habits, stress and the insults to our bodies that cause irreversible damage.

It is up to us what we do next. Success comes to people who adapt quickly to new situations and act promptly upon them.

In my young life of just over half a century, I have been through lots of ups and downs, like most people, and every time, a lesson – or many lessons – have been learnt and sometimes new directions had to be adopted, not just to survive, but also to be propelled into new life dimensions. Without having faith in myself and that there are always better and bigger opportunities out there awaiting us, I would not have made those changes and things would have been the same or maybe worse. Every adversity is an opportunity to grow and to change what does not work.

"We cannot solve our problems with the same thinking we used when we created them."
~ Albert Einstein

Ten years ago, I got to the stage of burning out professionally. Because I was so passionate about my profession, I had to analyse the situation very rapidly and see whether it was my profession that was the problem or if running that model of business was the problem. You see, we get out of dental-medical school with almost no knowledge on how to run a successful business, and if not careful, it will eventually get to you.

My decision was clear.

I had to get rid of that business model because that is all I knew then, and I'm glad I did, because I got my life back and this gave me time to re-assess everything. I took a year out to execute a very successful comeback. Not only did it give me the ability to practice what I am passionate about, i.e., dentistry, but also a successful business model that gave me that perfect balance between work and family life.

As a result, my patients are no longer patients or clients, but friends and family. I get invitations to many scientific meetings, travel the world and make new friends who add value to my life, in addition to helping my colleagues who need and want help with running a successful clinic by coaching them.

Here are my 5 steps to reinventing your life and business when you are faced with making that decision:

1) Don't Be Afraid Of Change
As long as change doesn't put your life or the lives of your loved ones in danger, then don't be afraid of it.

> *"I learned that courage was not the absence of fear, but the triumph over it. The brave man is not he who does not feel afraid, but he who conquers that fear."*
> ~ Nelson Mandela

Always ask yourself, what is the worst that can happen? Then ask, "What if this change I want to make works out?" Just think how many opportunities you have missed because you never asked yourself, "What If I Did That?" More than once in my life I had to start from zero, and once below zero and it still worked out and I was happy until I reached a "glass ceiling" and I had to either decide to accept it for the rest of my life or change something (reinvent), in order to see what is next.

Being able to make small, sometimes uncomfortable changes can help you make a big change for the better.

2) Change Starts From Within

Many times when we talk about reinventing ourselves, people assume that we talk about reinventing our business or career, which can be true most of the time. However, here we are talking about one of the most challenging and yet very rewarding changes, and that is reinventing Yourself by reinventing a New You – by understanding what goes on in your own body and mind and working towards peak performance in order to live life fully.

Change your mindset! I was reminded of this as I was recently among a few people who attended an award given to the bodybuilding icon, action hero, the politician and philanthropist Governor Arnold Schwarzenegger for his commitment to health and wellness.

Gov. Schwarzenegger is a living example of change and adaptation. In his autobiography he admits coming to America with no money, only a passion for bodybuilding in California. But through focused hard work both on his body and his mind, he achieved tremendous feats, becoming a true living example of a man who keeps reinventing himself all the time.

Keeping a healthy body will definitely improve our mental status, making better judgment of our environment leading to better decision-making. A health misfortune, unless terminal, does not have to be an obstacle to improve our overall health. To reinvent yourself, exercise and diet should be top of your agenda.

It all starts from small changes on a daily, weekly and monthly basis to our habits to look after our health in the best possible way to ensure we are in the best possible shape physically and mentally. In the beginning, this could mean losing a few pounds and avoiding certain foods. That's a change, however small, but it is a change and multiple small changes can lead to a bigger change.

Once you start, you'll never want to stop.

3) Conquer Your "Fire-Walk"

Whenever you make a drastic change, there can be episodes of pain that you cannot ignore. These can be fear of the unknown or what others might say. These are a few examples of pain we may experience. But the secret to success, as Tony Robbins describes, is to use pain and pleasure to your advantage instead of letting pain take over.

I suggest that, from the outset, if you make a list of all the pain that you may feel during this process, and in contrast, if you make a list of all the pleasure you will gain from your change, you will soon see that pleasure outweighs pain. Our brains are wired in such a way that we can tolerate and accept momentary pain in order to gain pleasure. Just remember that if others can do it, you can too.

Years ago I was faced with the situation of walking on fire as part of my personal development.

Now some may say that in some parts of the world, some tribes walk on fire as a game to pass time. Well, not in my tribe! For me, just the thought of it was paralyzing enough let alone walking of it. The same way some people are afraid of flying, needles or spiders! After some intense internal dialogue, I did it with my son Dilan in London (twice!) and the reward for my "little and short" adventure was indescribable at the time.

A few months went by and I had to go through a painful surgical procedure to my nose (nothing to do with the fire walk!) and part of the after-care meant that I had to have dressings changed several times during the day without any pain relief. The process was very painful to the extent that sometimes I used to hide before changing the dressing just to avoid it.

Until I remembered my "Fire-Walk." YES, my silly " Fire-Walk."

I was shocked afterwards to realise how easy and manageable these dressing changes became when I focused entirely on the fire walk and how I conquered my fears and the pain. Even today, after nearly 10 years later, I still use the fire walk as a metaphor to get me through temporary pain, physical and mental.

You don't have to walk on fire to be able to use this method! Just dig deep and think what were the situations in which you conquered your fears in the past and make a list of them. Pick up the most vivid one and make it "Your Fire-Walk".

4) Your Life And Career

Once you change your mindset regarding pain and pleasure when making a change, and being an advocate for healthier living, you will notice a different level of self-esteem and decision-making. I have never come across anyone who lives a good, balanced healthy life while depressed. Even those without much money or a good career are not depressed.

We are living in a very strange economy now. Nothing seems to be certain like it used to be. Despite signs of global recovery, people are still worried generally, and spending patterns and rationales have changed. Businesses need to adapt and change rapidly and careers have to be re-evaluated so we become mindful of what the future might bring.

Therefore we always need to be ready to change, shift and adapt our careers and businesses – so that we not only survive the different economic patterns, but also thrive in them. Every business should visualize and plan how they will grow and expand. Make a plan as to where you want to be in three to five years if the economy stays the same. However, have contingency plans to shift and change direction quickly so you do not become the captain of "Your own Titanic!"

Not everyone needs to reinvent themselves all the time, but the ability to change quickly when the time comes will determine your future success.

> *"Intelligence is the ability to adapt to change"*
> ~ Stephen Hawking

Make plans all the time, revisit these plans and look in your industry and ask what else you can bring to the table. This will satisfy your customers and clients so that they do not go elsewhere. For some time we have done this, and let me tell you, it has helped us survive and grow in this so-called economy. Do your marketing properly and add services and value to what you do. Observe other successful businesses and learn how they do things. Don't let your ego stop you from observing and learning from competitors. Most importantly, treat your customers like friends and family.

5) Planning For Something New

Sometimes you never know where the wind will blow, as they say. I had my fair share of wind blowing me in directions that was never planned in the first place, but I made it anyhow, by believing in myself that I can do it, no matter what.

Always Be Prepared.

Preparation comes from adding many layers to your existing skills, and on top of that adding totally new and different layers. I recently decided to become a student again and started an MBA while at the same time offering my experience and skills in dentistry (Dental Implants) to mentor other colleagues and create life-long friendships and a wider scientific community for the benefit of our patients.

As a successful health professional for over 25 years, together with my team, I always take pride in the way we help our patients and it's that and the appreciation of our patients that keeps us going stronger everyday. Helping others has always been my passion and ultimate goal.

As the legendary Zig Ziglar said;

If you help enough people to get what they want, you will get what you want.

This has been my motto for life:

Helping patients to get what they want and deserve, helping colleagues achieve what they desire and deserve, and helping You achieve the best that you deserve in your businesses and life through planning and being ready for change; these are my ultimate goals.

If we all do above and beyond for each other, we will all have a better life and we will be looking forward to every sunrise – just by asking ourselves "whom do we help today?"

About Diyari

Dr. Diyari Abdah is a Dentist, International Speaker, Author, Educator and Business Coach. He holds two dental degrees. In addition, in 2006 he was awarded a Master of Science Degree – M.Sc. – in the field of Implant Dentistry (UK).

Dr. Abdah is a member of several international Dental and Scientific Associations. He is also a member of the American Academy of Anti-Ageing medicine. In 2013, he was awarded the prestigious America's PremierExpert® status. He is a visiting academic at two universities and on the editorial board of several publications.

Dr. Diyari Abdah is passionate about helping others achieve their goals in balancing life and business or career. He currently practices three days a week in his office in Cambridge, UK and spends the rest of the time writing, teaching and coaching other dentists to achieve success by utilizing his business and marketing blueprints.

He resides in Hertfordshire, UK with his wife Afrah and their two sons, Dilan and Alan. He continues travelling the world, especially the USA, sharing his knowledge with other colleagues through his teaching programs. Currently he is working on an MBA degree in Cambridge.

Dr. Abdah can be reached at: diyari.abdah@yahoo.com

CHAPTER 20

WINNING ONLINE – GIVING YOUR WAY TO SUCCESS

BY LINDSAY DICKS

Even if you have been in business for only a short time, no doubt you have come across the concept of "reciprocity." In fact, life itself educates us on the "law of reciprocity." Reciprocity is simply the expectation that people will respond to general or specific acts by returning the act in a similar fashion. In other words, when someone does something nice for you, it is natural to want to do something nice for them. Even as children we are taught "do unto others as you would have them do unto you."

Businesses often capitalize on this concept and will offer give-aways, or have generous return policies, or go out of their way to exceed their customers' expectations. There is a method to these acts of kindness. Businesses believe if they are kind to their customers, their customers will be kind to them and purchase goods or services from them.

The law of reciprocity has also been applied to online businesses and it's interesting to watch how this thought plays out in the online marketing world. We've all seen it, and possibly even been a victim of it (I know I have), where online marketers hold their "good stuff" at arm's length from their potential customer. They most often will entice a potential buyer to believe they have a revolutionary product that will dramatically change the life of anyone who participates, the *magic pill* if you will. These techniques prey upon the person that is struggling to make ends meet and who is looking for that *magic pill* that will bring them wealth and prosperity. All they have to do is sign up for the live webinar and their life will change forever.

Sadly, a lot of Internet marketing has become this way and it has created a bad name for "Internet marketers." Unfortunately, many now look at Internet marketers as the stereotypical, sleazy, used car salesman.

Here is the secret to winning online. Don't be "that guy." Don't be afraid to give good, valuable content away for free. Although yes, some Internet marketers make a very good living by *selling* their content as "info products," the successful ones still offer something of significant value without giving away the entire store. And better yet, one of the things I have learned over the years is even if you do give away your BEST piece of information, people:

(a). Don't know how to implement it;

(b). Don't have time; and/or

(c). Wind up just wanting to hire you because "if you gave away THAT piece of information for FREE, imagine if they pay you what you can do for them."

To quote Dan Kennedy, "People are much less interested in learning how to do things for themselves than they are in just learning *about* things so they can have those things done for them." Even if you were to sell your greatest piece of information, your greatest profit will always come from doing it for them.

When we decided to publish our first collaborative book a number of years ago, we brought together our top twenty clients and told them about a book we wanted to publish called *Big Ideas for Your Business*. Each of the twenty clients were asked to contribute one chapter of the best knowledge they had to the book, their "$10,000 Secret." Why did we call it their "$10,000 Secret?" Because it should be a piece of information that they would normally charge somebody $10,000 to receive from them. The clients agreed and *Big Ideas for Your Business* became the first of many collaborative books we would publish. That book quickly hit several bestseller lists and twenty people instantly became bestselling authors as a result. These twenty collaborative authors weren't stingy with their information. They contributed good, solid, valuable information that would be beneficial to the reader and it paid off for them in a big way.

Here is a simple formula for winning online. First, be a "Giver." Don't worry about getting anything in return. If you believe in the philosophy that "people buy people" and that the only way a person buys from you is to buy into "you," then you must first get them to know you, to like you and to trust you. Giving away great content is one of the best ways to do that. Not only that, but good, valuable content also builds credibility. You may consider yourself an authority in your niche market, but until others perceive you as the authority you are, you will not be credible in their eyes. Giving away your knowledge in bits of well- organized and useful information is one of the best ways to position yourself as a credible source. This can be done through blogs, e-books, e-mail, newsletters, audio files, or downloadable video files. I would suggest using a combination of all of these mediums to drive content to your audience.

In our publishing company, we have helped over thirteen-hundred people become best-selling authors. But, most people don't make money by *selling* books. They make money by *having* books. A book gives you credibility. It establishes you as an expert in your field. In a book, a blog, a newsletter, or in a social media venue, when you give people solid and useable information you establish yourself as an expert. Ask yourself this question, "Will the information I am giving people cause them to view me as an expert in my field and will it cause them to want to come back to me for more information?" Providing quality information is part of the process of creating a loyal readership base. Your readers will become your customers and they will also become your best advocate. A satisfied and impressed reader will promote your information and your business to their friends and colleagues. When your readers promote and recommend you to their associates you can see how that will exponentially attract more customers to you as a leading expert in your field. This is business you may never have been able to reach otherwise.

Second, be "Genuine" in your purpose and in the information you offer. Develop a genuine desire to be a giver without expecting anything in return. If you have a blog or newsletter or post information on your website, make it genuinely important and content rich. Give people something of value, something that will help them in their business, in their relationships and in their life. Don't give them bits and pieces and hold back your "best stuff." Give them something they can use and something that will genuinely benefit them.

Third, be "Generous" with what you give. If you're generous with what you give, people can't help but come back for more. The most read blogs are blogs that generously give useful information. When you provide information, ask yourself, "Is it enough? Will this information cause readers to want to come back to my site? Is this information something my readers will find valuable enough to pass on to their friends or business associates? Is it meeting a need for my readers?" Once you have established that you are providing the right content, another important factor to consider is that your content flow needs to be consistent. Providing the right content on a consistent basis is a powerful combination that can eventually turn into income opportunities. Giving your audience good content once every six months is not going to establish you as a credible authority, but giving information in shorter, consistent intervals will help others perceive you as an expert. I would recommend communicating solid content to your audience at least weekly if you want to establish yourself as the 'go to' person in your niche market. I also recommend making a schedule for your information sharing and adhere to your schedule to maintain consistency. If you don't make information sharing a scheduled priority, it will become very easy for other things to get in the way and prevent you from consistent content generation. Keep in mind that this process is more of a marathon than it is a sprint. It will take time for your message to resonate with your readership and expand beyond your current borders. That's why sending useful information to your readers consistently and over a long period of time is so important.

Fourth, be "Gregarious" in your online presence. Be interactive and outgoing when it comes to engaging your audience. When someone submits a question by e-mail or responds to your blog or comments on your Facebook post, gregariously interact with them and let them know you are reachable and you desire to help them. Now, it's obvious you can't be all things to all people and you may get to a point that you can't respond to each inquiry individually. But, you can cluster questions and inquiries and address them in future blogs or writings. You may want to hold a free webinar to discuss your readers' concerns or questions. However, in some way, let your readers know you received their inquiry and how you will be addressing it. Remember, "People buy people."

Lastly, be "Gravitational." As you put into practice the previous four principles of being a Giver, being Genuine, being Generous, and being Gregarious, you will become Gravitational. People will gravitate toward you because you have built a relationship of trust with them. People will always gravitate toward someone they trust. Trust is often difficult to create and it can be damaged very easily. Trust is much like a savings account, the more deposits you make, the more stable the relationship becomes. If you continue to make deposits of good, solid, valuable information that people find useful, you will build a strong relationship with your audience, you will be viewed as a credible resource, and you will become like a magnet to which people will gravitate.

Whether you are blogging, writing an online newsletter, or interacting via a social media platform such as Facebook or Twitter, what you say is a reflection of who you are. Choose your words and your content wisely. Don't be frivolous in your communication just so you can say you are socially and virtually interactive. Make sure your content is deliberate, purposeful, helpful, and useful. Be a Giver!

About Lindsay

Lindsay Dicks helps her clients tell their stories in the online world. Being brought up around a family of marketers, but a product of Generation Y, Lindsay naturally gravitated to the new world of on-line marketing. Lindsay began freelance writing in 2000 and soon after launched her own PR firm that thrived by offering an in-your-face "Guaranteed PR" that was one of the first of its type in the nation.

Lindsay's new media career is centered on her philosophy that "people buy people." Her goal is to help her clients build a relationship with their prospects and customers. Once that relationship is built and they learn to trust them as the expert in their field, then they will do business with them. Lindsay also built a proprietary process that utilizes social media marketing, content marketing and search engine optimization to create online "buzz" for her clients that helps them to convey their business and personal story. Lindsay's clientele span the entire business map and range from doctors and small business owners to Inc. 500 CEOs.

Lindsay is a graduate of the University of Florida. She is the CEO of CelebritySites™, an online marketing company specializing in social media and online personal branding. Lindsay is recognized as one of the top online marketing experts in the world and has co-authored more than 25 best-selling books alongside authors such as Brian Tracy, Jack Canfield (creator of the *Chicken Soup for the Soul* series), Dan Kennedy, Robert Allen, Dr. Ivan Misner (founder of BNI), Jay Conrad Levinson (author of the "Guerilla Marketing" series), Leigh Steinberg and many others, including the breakthrough hit *Celebrity Branding You!*

She was also selected as one of America's PremierExperts™ and has been quoted in *Newsweek*, the *Wall Street Journal*, *USA Today*, and *Inc.* magazine as well as featured on NBC, ABC, and CBS television affiliates speaking on social media, search engine optimization and making more money online. Lindsay was also recently brought on FOX 35 News as their Online Marketing Expert.

Lindsay, a national speaker, has shared the stage with some of the top speakers in the world, such as Brian Tracy, Lee Milteer, Ron LeGrand, Arielle Ford, David Bullock, Brian Horn, Peter Shankman and many others. Lindsay was also a Producer on the Emmy-winning film Jacob's Turn.

You can connect with Lindsay at:
Lindsay@CelebritySites.com
www.twitter.com/LindsayMDicks
www.facebook.com/LindsayDicks

CHAPTER 21

THE FIFTH DECADE OF SELLING: THE ERA OF THE "VALUE CREATOR"

BY BILL WALTON

The thought of co-authoring a book with Brian Tracy brought back many memories of starting my career in the world of sales. I had some of the best training and coaching as a field rep and unit manager in the Consumer Products industry. But I always wanted more. Just a few years later I started to become a student of selling. It was in the mid-nineties when I turned to Brian and his work. I can still hear his voice on cassette as I listened to "Advanced Selling Strategies" on my way to my major accounts. It was inspiration when I needed it.

Years later, after many successful sales positions and a career in management consulting, I had finally realized my goal – to run my own sales training and executive coaching firm, ProDirect. I completed Brian's bright blue workbook, "The Psychology of Selling - The Art of Closing Sales" while on vacation just a few years ago. I still have the CDs and the companion workbook! All of these experiences have led me to the strategies that I recommend to my clients to help them create greater value than their competition.

I found that most of my answers to Brian Tracy's workbook questions all had a common theme...that I wanted to be able to HELP the client

- educate them, solve their business problem, alleviate stress, and positively affect their bottom line. My product was almost secondary. But I wanted to do this in a way that set me apart – a way that made my customers feel comfortable relying on me. This outlook is now what I call Value Creation and it's woven into all the work that I do.

Value Creation is my firm's "Winning Way." It is about being in a position to help someone in business. Thanks to my dear friend and sales coach John Orvos, my firm lives by "a giving hand is always full" motto and we've woven that thinking into our training and coaching programs. It's amazing what happens when your focus turns to getting your clients what they want in a way that validates and affirms *them*. But to adopt this winning way for your business, it's important to look back on the history of selling and client development.

SELLING EVOLUTION

The 70s
To forge a path forward in sales it's important to know where we've been. Over the past 40 years there have been four seismic shifts in selling. In the 1970s, it was simply about selling what you made. "Salesmen" were simply a distribution arm getting the product out the door. "Stack it high and watch it fly" was a popular saying in the Consumer Products industry – an industry I joined and worked in for 12 years. The goal was to get the buyer to say "yes" at all costs - the sales approach was pushy and manipulative. But the reward at the end was the three-martini lunch that cemented the relationship – at least until the next negotiation! And yes, buyers and sellers were probably wearing bell-bottom pants.

The 80s
The 80s brought us Duran Duran, Yuppies and the cell phone. You know, the ones the size of an army field radio. It was also the era of the features and benefits sale – a formulaic selling approach that assumed more information was *more*. I remember my days at Nestle Foods selling CRUNCH® and Toll House® Morsels. Our sales call "formula" was *SIERA*:

S - *Summarize the situation,*

I - *Share an idea,*

E - *Explain how it works,*

R - *Review the benefits* and

A - *Ask for the order.*

It wasn't a bad model but you had to have a real gift for the gab to pull it off, and be able to do so in five minutes or less. But the real issue was little or no buyer engagement. The only possible replies were yes, no, or maybe next week.

The 90s

The pendulum swung the other way in the 90s. Rather than bombard customers with laundry lists of features and benefits hoping something would stick, salespeople did the opposite. They left their presentations at home and showed up with a simple pad and pen. In a way it was refreshing for both buyer *and* seller. Buyers didn't have to brace for a pitch and sellers could relax and just listen for a change. Sounds like sales nirvana, right? Well, not exactly.

While consultative in intent, sales calls turned into clever Q & A's where the salesperson impressed with the nature of their inquiry. This worked for a while but buyers realized that they were spending too much time educating sales reps while still receiving a product recommendation in the end. This approach featured very little engagement around the problems buyers were facing and solutions were still grounded in what the seller wanted to sell. Add to this the advent of the Internet and buyers started relying less on salespeople for information and product specs.

The year 2000

The last 10 years in selling brought salespeople to a better place in that the dialogue had become focused more on solutions vs. product. Account teams were formed to penetrate high value customers, and marketing started creating what the customer actually wanted. For small businesses, social media and easy-to-execute email marketing programs made them less reliant on couponing and price reductions. In the big firms, Sales and Marketing organizations started to leverage the mountains of data they had collected on their customers and began to communicate with them more personally. Blogs, e-Zines and other social media opinion sites democratized the process of sharing feedback, which further emboldened the customer with a voice.

THE FIFTH DECADE OF SELLING – THE VALUE CREATORS

So as we sit in the second decade of the millennium, it's actually our fifth decade of selling along our timeline. The fifth decade of selling will be different for several reasons. First, customers have so much information at their fingertips they don't need salespeople as an information source anymore. According to the Harvard Business Review article "The End of Solution Sales"(July, 2012), nearly 65% of client's requirements are satisfied before they even engage a salesperson.

Second, the recession of 2008 – 2011 had a cleansing effect on many markets. We all know how the housing market was impacted, but other industries were affected in different and unique ways. The companies that had committed capital to reserves used those funds to take waste out of their system and to train their best people. Other organizations questioned themselves as to just what business they were really in and sharpened their focus and value proposition. Others put their neck brace on and asked their customers for honest feedback and shaped their offering with those valuable insights.

So why is this relevant? In my talks I speak about the fact that any company you're selling against has a good product, talented people, and the right technology to deliver value pre- and post-sale. The competition in most industries, even down to your local family dining establishment is fierce and formidable. So what do we do when every competitor for example, has a good car, an effective pill, a feature-laden wrench, or an engaging social media presence? As sellers we need to adjust our approach: *We need to create customer value*.

STRATEGIES TO WIN IN THE FIFTH DECADE OF SELLING

The essence of selling in the fifth decade is all about leading with insights vs. leading with the virtues of your product or service. Clients can spec out your product with the click of a mouse, so there has to be something more. The training clients we work with at my firm, ProDirect, often honor us with the opportunity to speak to *their* clients and we relay valuable feedback to them.

Over the last 20 years, sales reps have gotten better at discovering customer needs and thus creating better solutions. Much of this success was a result of the fact that customers didn't really understand their true need and the salesperson played a valuable conduit to solving problems. But in the fifth decade of selling, customers not only know their problem, but also have a few solutions lined up proactively to potentially solve it. What they need now is a *thinking partner* – someone to bring them insights their due diligence might have missed or their Business Intelligence group failed to uncover. Every decision your customers are making today comes with it a career implication – *customers can't afford to be wrong*.

People still want to be sold, they just want to think and feel differently about buying.

For small businesses, this same dynamic holds true. Your customers are coming into your business armed with information and a point of view. In the era of value creation it will be important for you to validate these customers. Ask them about the research they've done and mention early on that you want to help them make their best decision. People still want to be sold, they just want to think and feel differently about buying. For example, I work with several well-known retail chains. We tell their senior leaders and store managers to help customers with their biggest fear – the fear of being wrong or making a poor decision. So the winning way in the era of value creation is helping the customer *be right* by working with them in the manner in which they like to buy.

So lets talk about how to get yourself in the position to add greater value to your customers. Here are seven strategies to ensure that you are meaning more to your clients and adding value in a manner that they expect:

1. **Talk to your best customers**. And then really *listen* to them. I've done this for several of our corporate clients and the data is invaluable. Customers want a great experience with you and most often are willing to help you shape it. Customers can be the greatest source of inspiration for your capabilities and services.

2. **Invest in your messaging**. You might think this is a good idea as you pursue new business. This is true, but the folks who really need your messaging and the proper way to deliver it are *your referral sources*. In business, your most profitable customer is the repeat customer or the one that was referred to you by a raving fan. So help your fans get the story out – they are your *de facto* sales force

after all! Ensure your messaging speaks to why other customers have chosen you and why specific prospects should be interested in learning more.

3. **Lead with insights vs. your product.** Everyone who competes in your space who has survived the recent economic downturn has good product. They've invested in quality, the needs their solution addresses, and support for their solution well past the sale. While customers are armed to the teeth with data, bring them insights about their business, such as competitive threats and available technologies to help them be successful while reinforcing the value you and your product can support. If you are in corporate sales, help your customers motivate their teams, or achieve personal career success. You can do this by bringing them ideas for personal and professional growth – we all want that killer book or blog entry that can give us inspiration or a leg up on our peers. For small business, think about related uses of your product or service and keep your customers apprised of trends. *Help them be right!*

4. **Diagnose "like a doctor."** When working with customers, go beyond your typical Q & A to determine issues worth solving and to prescribe the right solution. Ask a shorter list of questions and focus on the *answers* you want. Customers love to "hear their name in lights" so play back what you heard. Use these spoken words when recommending your final solution. It's how *you* buy, so why do anything differently? A great focus to think about is where your customer is as opposed to his or her view of perfection. *Ask what's standing in the way and help them remove the pebble in their shoe to get to their goal.* They'll want to talk about that!

5. **Forget the money**...**for now**. In corporate sales, it's tempting to respond when the prospect asks you to send them a proposal ASAP. We've all done it. We've agonized over every word, added the most eye-catching graphics and listed feature after feature along with their benefits. It felt great to hit send when emailing the proposal to the prospect on time. But then what happened? Often we received no response. This is because there was no engagement in the creation of the approach. People buy in to what they have a hand in creating. Involve your prospect in what you're recommending and unless they threaten to never speak to you again, never put dollars in the your initial proposal – it will always

be too expensive. Instead, *agree to review your approach with your prospect, secure their input and agree to review a final proposal* (with the investment) *together.*

6. **Know whom you're selling to.** A prospect is not a prospect is not a prospect. In the spirit of value creation, value is role and industry specific. A CFO in Aerospace and Defense cares about different things than a CFO of a large consulting firm. They use cash differently and manage risk in a manner consistent with the business they are in. For local businesses, your customers are members of your community. *So know what's trending in schools and across other businesses to align with the heartbeat of where you operate.*

7. **Ideas are currency**. In tandem with value creation tactic #3, your clients will never shoo you away from feeding them an authentic idea. Some of the best relationship managers we work with approach their role with genuine curiosity. They have a way of turning themselves inside out to really connect to the business and culture of their customer. I call it a joy of helping. Customers can feel this and will always appreciate that you're looking out for them. Small businesses are using social media and other customer relationship management strategies *to make recommendations based on prior purchases and search trends.*

CONCLUSION

Selling in the business-to-business and small market arenas is hard. Sales cycles are chaotic and getting ever longer. It is impossible to predict when opportunities will close and to plan for the future. More and more existing relationships are going out to bid since customer satisfaction rates are dropping, and relationships are not expanding. But there is a way to succeed in this fifth decade of selling.

Building customer relationships today has to be one of exchanging insights, insights that the customer's own staff are not providing. High-performing salespeople are improving their business acumen to truly understand the markets in which their customers operate and are using this knowledge to delicately challenge the status quo.

Thus value creation is about doing what the average salesperson doesn't do. It's a belief that anything worth doing is worth overdoing. It's a credo that holds as its highest principle that mediocrity is not an option. And it's an ego drive that pushes you to make yourself indispensable to your customers – customers that are looking to create value for *their* customers.

I hope you found these value creation strategies helpful. They have helped me find my winning way – I wish the same for you.

Good luck and good selling!

©2014 ProDirect LLC, All Rights Reserved.

About Bill Walton

Bill Walton is a nationally-recognized sales trainer and coach with more than twenty-four years of experience helping individuals and teams add value to customers. He is known for his cutting-edge sales training and value proposition work with prominent Fortune 500 companies such as Avis Budget Rental Car, American Express, and Merrill Lynch. Bill's approach has helped his clients retain their most coveted accounts and win business back from the grasp of the competition.

Prior to founding ProDirect, Bill worked for two prominent professional services firms selling large-scale sales training and consulting projects. His clients included CIGNA, Stanley Tools, and Unilever. During this time, he formulated his value-creation philosophy by learning what it took to sell to and serve clients with extremely high expectations. Bill also spent ten years in sales and marketing within the consumer products industry, learning the value of delivering on a brand promise. These experiences have all served to provide the inspiration for his work with salespeople today.

As a noted speaker, Bill is asked to deliver engaging talks on such topics as *Bullet-proofing relationships, Making your story make the difference* and *Sales process as product.* Bill recently published *Taming the Four-Headed Dragon,* a value creation playbook to help professionals get the sales growth they need and attract the clients they want, all on a limited time budget. Bill was recently acknowledged by America's PremierExperts® as one of the leading experts in his field.

Bill publishes the Value Creation sales blog and has been a featured guest on CNN. He's worked as an adjunct professor at New York University and has been a featured contributor to *Human Resource Executive* magazine. Bill is an active member in the Professional Society of Sales and Marketing Trainers, and the Greater Philadelphia Senior Executive Group (GPSEG) and currently sits on the board of the Juvenile Diabetes Research Foundation.

Bill graduated *magna cum laude* from Connecticut State University with a degree in Business Administration and received a Master's degree in Human Resource Education from Fordham University.

Bill lives in Lawrenceville, NJ, and spends his spare time playing tennis and rooting for the New York Jets with his wife Amy and daughter Juliet.

For information on Bill and his results-producing programs, books and speaking topics, visit:
www.BillWaltonSalesTraining.com.
http://www.facebook.com/billwaltonsalestraining
http://www.linkedin.com/in/billwaltonsalestraining/
https://twitter.com/bwaltonSTrain

CHAPTER 22

CONNECTING FOR THE WIN!

BY BRENDA F. WISE

Imagine that you are in a bustling metropolitan or urban area. Now, imagine that you are riding the subway. You have stepped onto a crowded railcar. You notice that as people are getting on and off... more than likely, a great number of them, will have this one thing in common...they each have some type of electronic device such as an iPod, an iPhone, a Kindle or other eReader to which they seem to be tethered.

Why is nearly everyone tethered? Maybe they fear missing out on some earth-shattering event that would change the course of history at any moment. Maybe the marketing of these devices is just so great that everyone absolutely has to have one. Maybe this is a grand exhibition of "herd mentality." If you venture to ask them why, their response... if you get one...might be something like, "I like being connected." Absolutely, these devices can readily provide you with untold amounts of information with a click or two—no question. But I say they are tethered because it's easy. These devices don't criticize or challenge you personally. They don't question your motives. You don't have to look them in the eye or tell them how you feel. There's no actual or perceived rejection to experience.

Most people are uncomfortable making face-to-face interpersonal connections. Most people will not attempt to make a connection unless it is absolutely necessary. When they do reach out, their anxiety increases, which makes reaching out even more uncomfortable. There seems to be a loss of the ability and the willingness to connect in person, so these devices become an escape or a conduit for communication. These days our business life is so connected to our personal life. In order to succeed, we simply cannot afford to be schizophrenic and compartmentalize how, when, and with whom we connect. If we adopt habits that are genuine, respectful, interactive and responsive, then these habits become second nature. This allows us to grow our network, which opens the door to greater achievements as we make positive connections. No matter what your profession, success is not achieved in a bubble. Success personally and professionally is directly related to the positive connections you make with other people. Over the years, I have learned to interact with people in order to achieve excellent customer satisfaction. Having been employed in the retail, service, and financial industries as well as the public sector, I have established many winning connections.

In the current marketing and sales environment, the electronic devices we spoke of earlier are so readily available and because potential customers are so connected to these devices, people become inundated with sales offers. Often, these sales offers come in the form of an email or advertisement with a direct call to action. A customer should not be a meal ticket. A customer should be respected and "courted." Time and effort should be taken to build genuine connections, which will assist in your reaching the ultimate goal of long-term positive relationships.

Anything we achieve in life, we achieve with the help or assistance either directly or indirectly of others. You have no doubt heard the expression that "no man is an island" taken from the poem of the same name by John Donne. It's true, we are all connected. This connection means that we have to be able to communicate effectively in order to realize our dreams or goals and be successful in life. Communication can be verbal or nonverbal and both forms are equally valid and equally effective. It requires at least two interacting parties and is predicated upon active listening, processing of the information received, and subsequently, the formulation and transmission of proper responses. Effective, positive communication typically results in successful interactions—which creates the basis for all winning connections.

Not every customer is a happy one. When they enter your domain, they bring along with them their personal baggage. It may be difficult at times, but it is our job to show up with the smiles and the excellent customer service regardless of how we are being treated. We are charged with affording each customer dignity and respect. Our feelings are irrelevant. You cannot bring along your baggage or you lose the potential for reaching clients and increasing your customer base, which directly affects your bottom line. If you are a professional, a consultant, or an entrepreneur, then reaching those clients and making those connections with them no matter what's going on in their lives (or yours) is especially important. It is incumbent upon you to break through that individual's disposition and provide the service that we have been tasked with providing. You can be sure that none of this will happen without making positive connections.

One evening last year, my family and I were celebrating my birthday at a local restaurant. A cake was brought along to share after dinner. It was a very busy night. As it happened, another server bumped into our server as she was delivering the meal to a nearby table…food was spilled, trays were dropped, and glasses were broken as they fell to the floor. Though both the servers apologized to the family, unnecessary words were directed toward the servers, which drew the attention of quite a few patrons. There was broken glass on the floor around one side of our table. Clearly flustered, our server returned to inform us that she would clean up the glass immediately. Upon her return to our table, she brought dessert plates and a serving knife so that we could serve the cake. That night there were ten of us so the server was already going to get a large tip. This was without question.

Sometimes money isn't the problem. People need to feel appreciated. That feeling of being appreciated and expressing appreciation has great personal value because it affects the psyche, increases self-esteem and influences future behavior. This reinforces the positive connection, which presents enormous returns personally and professionally. I wanted to show appreciation to my server along with the server who assisted her with the cleanup. Each of them received a slice of birthday cake. I wish you could have seen the smiles on their faces and the look of appreciation they expressed for this simple gesture of inclusion. While I am sure that receipt of a slice of cake that night had made no real world change in the broad scheme of things; I am sure that my server's last memory of that evenings work was not the accidental spill, the unkind words, or even the large tip. Instead, I am sure the last memory of that evening was of a sweet gesture on the part of a customer making a happen-stance connection. She knew she mattered and it was evident she was appreciative.

We need to feel accepted, respected and appreciated. It really doesn't matter if the person you are connecting with is a janitor, a neurosurgeon, or a millionaire; we all need to feel valued. We all need to feel that we matter and that our existence makes a difference. There is great power in being able to affect the lives of people on this level. You establish trust, build credibility, and create and sustain winning relationships by treating all your connections in a dignified respectful manner. We do this by recognizing that every person, regardless of their station or occupation, has value...human value! You must recognize that we all have the same right to be treated ethically, morally, civilly, and equally. No one person has more human value than the next. One person may have more money, more knowledge, or more fame than the next. No one person, however, has more human value than the next. Treating each of them with dignity and respect will open a lot more doors—which can provide you with more opportunities to network and connect.

You must first establish a connection in order to build a relationship. The following lists eight key factors which have helped me to establish many powerful positive connections both professionally and personally:

1. **It's not about you.** The interaction should never be about you. When you are providing a service or giving your attention to someone in a conversation, give them your full attention. Ask probing questions to demonstrate that you are paying attention. Tailor your response to their specific issue. Time is one of the most precious things that you can give to another person. I found that people will almost instinctively want to give you some of their time in return. On occasion, clients have phoned me...not because they had an issue or needed something...but simply to inquire about me personally which is a really great feeling.

2. **Be in the moment.** We all have a million things going on at once. When we are busy with texts, emails, meetings and phone calls, it is really easy to start multi-tasking inside one's head to stay abreast of all the daily tasks. However, it is really important to stay focused

and be present especially during a face-to-face meeting or phone call. You cannot be responsive and provide an effective solution if you fail to capture the problem.

3. **Really listen.** One of my grade school teachers used to say that there is a big difference between hearing and listening. I might not have gotten it then, but I certainly get it now. Hearing is perceived sound. Hearing is the function of the ear for the intake of sound created by vibrations. Listening involves taking what you have heard…analyzing it and interpreting it. It is an active process. Listening gives you the ability to generate and offer effective solutions.

4. **Discover the value.** All too often, when we encounter someone, our thoughts fall to the negative. Negative thoughts reflect low self-esteem and scarcity thinking whereby we feel the need to subtract from one another so that we can feel better about ourselves. Positive thoughts and actions increase self-esteem and are transformational. Focus on something positive about the encounter. Everyone has value. Find the value and express it. Showing appreciation for that value is empowering and leaves no room for scarcity thinking.

5. **It costs you little, if anything.** In the study of economics, there is a theory called "opportunity cost." The theory states that you may risk losing potential gain from one source if a different source is selected and utilized instead. These connections that you will be making cost you little time and effort, however, the benefits far outweigh any "perceived" costs. The goal is to create winning connections and build mutually beneficial long-term relationships.

6. **Actions can be contagious.** Most people are good, decent, honest human beings. We want to do right by our fellow human beings, but sometimes we let circumstances force us to make ourselves the priority. Our outward actions appear rude and insensitive when we are really just kind of caught up in our own little world. Recognize that you are not in a bubble and your actions, good or bad, can influence others. Acts of decency and kindness can spread like wildfire.

7. **Focus on making the connection.** Focusing on the fact that this person may be a prospect is a mistake. Give…then receive. People know when you are disingenuous. They know when they are being

used. Approach all connections from a "What can I do for you?" perspective. Your actions will be reciprocated.

8. **Create a memory.** Give your connections an experience which goes above and beyond what is expected. Always, always give them more than they hoped for. Make every moment they spend with you seem extraordinary. Give them an opportunity to feel that you are invested in the best possible outcome for them. Be helpful, courteous, responsive, sharing and caring. Be genuine.

Not everyone will be receptive to these techniques, but most will. It is crucial to remember that you are not making a sale; you are making connections in order to build better, sustainable relationships. These types of relationships attract clients and make sales. There is an empathy deficit where the natural connections between members of society are being lost to a large degree. Reestablishing these connections is vital to facilitating personal and business success. On a much grander scale, reestablishing how we connect is also vital to a successful society.

About Brenda

Brenda Wise builds winning relationships that foster ongoing communication and effective problem resolution. She currently manages a $57 million federal award fund assisting rural farmers all across the nation. The fund is expected to increase by $40 million over the next four years. Brenda also serves on a federal communications team which publishes a quarterly newsletter highlighting the work of the farming community and the benefits of agriculture. Her clients are especially receptive to what they identify as her "southern voice" or her effortless way of making them feel special and connected. Clients often make requests for Brenda to attend and speak at events held by their organizations. She began public speaking at the age of six in Sunday school and has transitioned into speaking to groups of up to 400—addressing the benefits of a healthy diet.

Growing up in southern Louisiana, she was surrounded by friends and family. That great spirit of southern hospitality has stayed with her. She purposefully imparts this goodwill upon whomever she meets. Brenda's well-honed interpersonal communications skills illustrate how forming great relationships are the absolute key to success in any avenue of life—whether personally or professionally.

Brenda moved to the Northern Virginia area in the early 1980s. She began a 30-year stint in the financial services arena working with such companies as Ameriprise Financial, Mortgage Guaranty Insurance Corporation (MGIC), the First National Bank of Arizona and Ivanhoe Financial.

Brenda started Wise AcQuisitions, a real estate investment and consulting business, in 2005. The company assists homebuyers not served by conventional banking methods to obtain both home ownership and increased personal wealth through other non-conventional methods. Wise AcQuisitions has expanded to incorporate consumer advocacy and became actively involved in protecting consumer rights with regards to the Fair Debt Collection Practices Act or FCDPA.

Earlier in her writing career, Brenda had been published in several poetry anthologies. Her forthcoming books entitled, *How to Make Winning Connections in 8 Easy Steps* and *How to Grow a 7-Figure IRA in 7 Easy Steps* will enable her to help many more people reach their interpersonal and financial goals.

Future plans include the establishment of a non-profit organization that will reach out to service the needy. The organization will seek to provide acts of service and good deeds throughout communities in order to reconnect members of society and build a stronger sense of community. She hopes to create chapters across the nation which will work with other existing organizations to bring action against American poverty, and to affect change by making a grassroots societal push towards a substantive democracy—calling for the eradication of economic and social inequalities.

You can connect with Brenda at:
Brenda@BrendaFayeWise.com
www.FaceBook.com/BrendaFayeWise

CHAPTER 23

CHANGE YOUR PERSPECTIVE – CHANGE YOUR LIFE!

BY CHERYL CATCHINGS, PhD

Have you ever been happy to be left behind? Well, I was super-excited when my mom said she was leaving me behind while she, my godmother and our friend's mother from across the street all went to the grocery store. My two friends and I were happy to play on a Saturday morning freely without needing a babysitter; I was in the fourth grade, for goodness sake. Well, my god sister was there, but that didn't count as a babysitter because she was inside and upstairs.

We'd been told to have lunch at my godmother's house, which added to my joy because she always gave me two slices of cheese where my mother only allowed one. After a great time ripping and running between three houses, we decided to take a break and eat. We built our sandwiches and were ready to toast them in the cast iron skillet as usual when the gas stove didn't light up. However, this wasn't a daily occurrence, and I'd been taught how to light the pilot and had done so many times. I turned the knob off and went to get the newspaper to twist, and then ignite the pilot light.

I returned with the twisted lit paper, opened the oven door and there was a BIG BLINDING FLASH in my face. We were all startled and couldn't understand why the twisted paper was out and the pilot light was still out too. I turned around to tell my two younger friends not to worry about lunch, we would still eat our sandwiches – when my youngest friend screamed and the oldest one pointed at me. I went into the bathroom to see what they were pointing at, and saw I had no eyebrows and no eyelashes!

We ran upstairs to tell my godsister what happened. As I shook her to wake her, she opened her eyes and kept rubbing them in disbelief when she saw my face. There were no cell phones, so she had to call the grocery store directly, and told everyone what happened. The grocery store was downtown. However, I do believe they ran a few traffic lights in making it back to my godmother's house in record time. By the time they arrived, my face had begun to tingle and my eyelids seemed heavier than usual. My mother immediately called the Doctor asking him to hurry right over; yes he did a house call. The doctor explained what we experienced was a "flash burn" from the gas filling the kitchen. I couldn't understand how that could be true until my friend explained; when I left to go get the twisted newspaper, she tried again to turn the stove on. So of course when I lit the twisted paper and opened the oven door it was completely filled with gas which ignited causing the flash burn. Since I was closest to the oven, I suffered second and third degree burns from the waist up; whereas my two friends only had minor ones. The doctor took me to his office and prescribed a new ointment on the market for burns and said I'd be uncomfortable for the next few hours, as the heat trapped inside the tissue was released. We still needed groceries, so everyone left the doctor's office and returned to the store to complete our parents shopping.

As I walked around the store helping my mother, I noticed my face was beginning to feel funny, kinda tingly all over. I began to feel a little warm, even hot, and it moved to hot burn quickly all over my face. I reached into the freezer for the frozen vegetables and realized my arm and face felt cooler. My face felt like it was on fire and I kept sticking my whole face down in the ice cream section trying to cool off and every time I raised up it the burning came right back. I began trying to tell my mother what I was feeling, but because I'd never felt anything like this before, all I could do was cry harder.

My days were spent confused, trying to understand as a fourth grader and process my physical pain, mental hurts and my fear. This was a life-changing event and I was so scared. The doctor told me the old "burned" skin would slough off and that was a good thing because it meant my body was healing. He didn't tell me it would be painful as old skin came off and the new skin was exposed to the open air. I remember one day looking in the mirror checking out my healing and the entire side of my face peeled off. I was terrified looking at the reflection of a black girl who now had a white face!

I was home for another week and then I had to go back to school, a day I dreaded. It was the fall, so in Michigan we were already wearing warm coats. At the time there was a coat everyone wanted called the "triple fat goose" which of course was the fashion rage; they were very warm, expensive and everyone wanted one. I was no different and I wanted one before the burn. However, afterwards I <u>really</u> wanted one, because one of the features besides being super warm, was that they had a hood that you could pull the drawstring closed and leave a small circle for vision and breathing. I wanted one to hide my face.

That dreaded day came when my Mom said I had to return to school. Well, of course in my young mind, I thought everyone in my town knew what happened to me, blamed me and wanted to see the "little burned girl." I was scared of my reflection, scared to go outside, scared to go to school and doubly scared of what the other kids would think or say. We all know kids can be brutally honest and often cruel; well, that hasn't changed throughout the years. My mother very carefully wrapped my face for warmth, but not so close as to rub me, which would've caused pain just from the touching of the coat and scarf on my face and neck. I put my coat on (not a triple fat goose), and pulled my hood over the scarf, and we headed out. My two big brothers were my heroes that day on our eight-block walk – which seemed more like a million-mile walk to school. I'd always been an avid reader, so in my imagination I remember comparing it to the prisoners we see on television walking to the gallows. As kids began to notice it was me heading to school, they of course were curious and began to surround me. My brothers became rock stars as they held out their arms, one in front and one in back – making sure no one saw my face.

When we arrived at my school, my teacher met us at the door and walked me to the room. My desk had been moved into the coatroom, so I could see out of the darkness but they couldn't see in. I also ate lunch in the classroom and used the bathroom during recess since I didn't join my class for our daily exercise outside. This went on for a few days, and I finally came out of the coatroom during lunch. One day, I was sitting at my teacher's desk in the front of the room eating lunch when the door suddenly opened and I was exposed! In walked my friend who stopped at the door and just looked at me. After what seemed like a year, she finally said, "I missed you and wanted to see if you are okay." She asked if it still hurt, asked to give me a hug, and stayed for lunch.

My healing was moving along just as the doctor predicted, but it sure wasn't fast enough for me. Ugh! I had to keep the greasy new ointment plastered on my face, neck and arms all the time to decrease the dryness, itching and hopefully decrease the permanent scarring. No one realized the real scars were unseen.

As time went by, I slowly saw my eyebrows return with my eyelashes and I became brown again. Physically I was recovering, but mentally I was a changed, unsure, scarred young girl – which would last for many, many years to come.

Without noticing how or when it happened, I moved into the shadows becoming the behind-the-scenes, second-in-line person, the person willing to settle and compromise. I made choices that were detrimental to my health and wellbeing. Just like in the coatroom, I didn't want to be noticed or call special attention to myself, so I settled for B's when I could have easily earned A's. I was the leader of my friends on that day at my godmother's house when it didn't turn out so well, so it wasn't hard to become a shadow, the assistant, sidekick, vice president, co-captain, junior varsity, nurse versus doctor … you get the picture. I did not take on leadership roles even when I knew I could do a good job. I wanted to blend in unnoticed with everyone, so I allowed others to make decisions that I knew were hurtful and sometimes illegal. Looking back, I see the choices I made were due to my low personal esteem and feelings of unworthiness. I was taught, and still believe, that actions speak louder than words; my choices led me down a path of brokenness, self-sabotage and destruction. I hurt myself, my family, other people, joined a gang and became a single mother.

Becoming a single mother in college was probably the beginning of my self-evaluation and real road to recovery from the inside out. My zeal to be a good mother led me to go back to my love of reading. I started reading everything I could find on parenting, self-development, religion, counseling, transformation, astrology, psychology, spirituality, yoga – you name it and I researched it. My revelation was deep down inside, buried and had begun to surface. I knew I always wanted and thought I deserved more … especially for my daughter.

Mind you, I didn't go into so many specifics regarding the flash-burn to graphically share all my gory and gruesome details as a shock factor for you or for your sympathy. I wanted to share the details, using my physical event as a comparison for my life events and the choices I made; choices we all make knowingly and often unknowingly. I had to accept, acknowledge, relearn to love myself, and be willing to expose myself to the elements of life, in order to completely heal, live and love again.

It's no surprise that I would go into a career of nursing, evolving through counseling and psychology into human services and land as an empowerment coach. My transformation was a long and winding trail on which I had to choose to *take* control of my life, *put* experiences in their proper perspective and *move* forward. Remember actions speak louder than words. As my spiritual life and awareness increased, the realization of life's perspectives continued to come. My life wasn't a continual downer – there was sunshine and happy days I'd forgotten. I knew my life had stages and I was in an ongoing, constant state of transition, and that I had choices regarding how I'd move forward – either in a positive manner, or not. Life has good and bad, ups and downs; I was lacking "perspective."

My great-grandmother, we called her "Big" – short for Big Momma – used to say, "old standing water stagnates and smells stinky" as she hosed down the sidewalk. As a child I couldn't understand the meaning. However, another epiphany moment was my new sense of peace as I chose to look up to the sun with its warmth and light and not down at the ground, shamed and too embarrassed to move, becoming stagnant. I could have settled for the half-empty glass, but I chose for my glass to be half-full, pressed down, shaken together and running over. I chose to give myself a new faith-filled, no longer fear-based, perspective on life. I accepted if others saw good things for me, then I must have some good things in me and YES, I was and am worthy.

Do you remember the Neapolitan ice cream with chocolate, vanilla and strawberry? It was very defined until you mixed it up and it turned into one bowl of brown mush. Well, that was my life, an undefined ball of confusion and indecision. My daughter depended on me and I had to make some choices if I wanted our lives to change.

I realized life has LAYERS. Ever enjoy a multi-layered sundae with whipped cream and cherries on top?

All sundaes have LAYERS:

L—*Listening* is paramount. You've listened to self-doubt, fear, confusion and relived past mistakes and/or opportunities missed. Now it's time to listen to your heart and spirit to hear what you really want. Where do YOU want to go?

A—*Accept* all of you, acknowledge the past mistakes and choose to forgive yourself (and others) so you can move on. Choose to forgive YOU!

Y—*You* are the creator of your future and YOU are worthy of so much more. CHOOSE YOU!

E—*Empower* your new life with whatever you need to get to your next level. Choose to work on YOU!

R—*Respect* yourself. Repair, restore and foster relationships that are supportive. Rejuvenate YOU!

S—*Share* your story – it keeps it real, up front and personal. SHARE YOU!

Life as a sundae means there may be some layers darker than others, however, they don't last forever—some happened and some you may have chosen. However, the best part is that there's always another layer coming, and it gets sweeter as you work through the layers. I came to understand, acknowledge and accept that no one remembers the dark bottom of the glass ... *everyone focuses on the next layer*. You can and must choose to move to your next layer or level of life. You will be your own rock star and champion as your actions will speak volumes. Get to the good stuff. Remember the good stuff – like the whipped cream and the cherry – is on top!

Build your life like a sundae. ☺

About Cheryl

Cheryl R. Catchings, PhD, established the 24-Hour Youth Hotline and was a featured speaker at the National Urban League's Summit, Youth Crime Watch Convention and a true community advocate. She's received the BET Trailblazer of the Decade Award, March of Dimes White Rose Awards, LINKS Founder of the Year Award and the Crystal Reel Award from Florida's Motion Picture and Television Association for producing several public service announcements for her work in the areas of youth and community issues.

Many gravitate to the energetic and dynamic personality of Dr. Catchings, often young people and parents struggling with difficult and challenging experiences are her greatest attractors. She's not afraid to share her experiences as a childhood burn victim, surviving an alcoholic family, a former gang member and single parent challenges – she calmly says it gives her the added ability to relate to and assist with motivating youth, reengaging adults and revitalizing communities where she gratefully and humbly serves as a positive role model. Her global advocacy establishes her as an inspiring, motivational speaker, wellness consultant, empowerment coach and strategist for special interest groups and communities. The quotation above is the hallmark of a life dedicated to serving villages and is the mantra by which she lives. Through her works and efforts it's easy to see why Dr. Catchings has been designated a true millennium "Village Teacher."

Leaving her thumb print across the United States and Europe, she successfully developed programs which include: A+ Parenting, Town Hall Meetings, Advisory Council for Teens and produced two radio shows, further demonstrating her passion and tirelessness for improving village conditions. She gained prominence for creating a unique after-school tutor-mentoring program partnering high-risk urban youth with students from the University of Michigan, and founding the T. G. Mitchell scholarship for single parents. After a brutal hate crime-gang attack, she and her son founded the positive vocal group Chivalry, established the 24-hour, toll free, anonymous *Speakout* hotline program still used as a national model for its success in decreasing gang activity, weapons on campus and neighborhood drugs sales.

Dr. Catchings often focuses speaking engagements and training sessions on the coined phrase "layered prevention." She created, directed and produced award-winning prevention videos, her very own proactive response to violent crime by and against youth. Featured articles highlighting her community advocacy have appeared in *Newsweek, Emerge, Creative Youth,* and *Simply Living.* She also appeared on

CNN's *Talkback Live*. CNBC and her families' positive triumph over a public tragedy is the inspiration for NBC's *How They Changed America* documentary. Dr. Catchings background includes degrees and experience in Nursing, Organizational Management, Counseling, Educational Leadership, Community Psychology and Human Services. She's written an anti-drug activity book for preschool age children and developed a community-based television show for teens – to empower youth as our future leaders.

You may contact Dr. Catchings at:
mscrc74@hotmail.com or 321-591-0144

CHAPTER 24

THE WINNING WAY TO RETIREMENT

BY RICK POSTON

I enter my 19th year as a comprehensive financial advisor with an increased conviction that financial advisors must possess the heart of a steward and the passion of a new school teacher. History proves that the financial markets are more dynamic now than ever and we find ourselves in a complex geopolitical economy with manipulated currencies as the cornerstone for this house of cards. The average investor is growing frustrated because they just don't have the financial education necessary to successfully navigate these economic waters with confidence. Most people learn the principles of investing from the perspective of a specific period in time. As the economic conditions begin to change and the strategy that the average investor has been using effectively for the last decade is no longer yielding successful results, out of sheer frustration, the average investor is likely to panic and make investment decisions from a far-too-emotional state of mind. Panic trading opens the door to history making volatility in the markets and very lazy recovery cycles.

A recent example of my assertion is a recent conversation that I had with a client about the national debt and potential tax increases on the horizon. The fact is, the client that I was speaking to was a very intelligent surgeon. I mentioned that in 2012, the United States collected about $2.4 million dollars in tax revenue and our government spent $3.5 million dollars to run the country. We discussed how the current national debt was $17 trillion dollars and that there are $90 trillion dollars in unfunded liabilities. I could see his eyes glazing over - I had lost him. I walked over to my flip chart and broke the example down to a more realistic format by erasing 8 decimal places and adjusting some commas. It now appeared this way:

$2,400,000,000,000	Tax Revenue/Income	$24,000
$3,500,000,000,000	Expenditures	$35,000
$17,000,000,000,000	Current national debt/ Credit card debt	$170,000
$90,000,000,000,000	Unfunded liabilities	$900,000

I changed my explanation to say: imagine for a minute that you make a salary of $24,000 per year and that your living expenses run $35,000. Consider that the balance on your credit cards is $170,000 and you are committed to paying an upcoming $900,000 in bills. All this on a $24,000 salary. This is why you hear some people refer to this situation as Generational Theft. The generation that will pay back all of this debt has not even been born yet.

Considering the $17 trillion in current national debt and the fact that it could take over 50 years to pay it back, *do you believe that taxes are likely to go up, go down or stay about the same during that 50 year period?* Most people tell me that they believe that taxes will go up, especially if interest rates rise and the debt payments become harder to cover. If tax rates are likely to rise over the next generation, does your investment portfolio reflect these risks? Remember, it's not how much money you make – it's how much you get to keep, that really counts. Let me present you with your options, so you can consider an effective investment income tax strategy moving forward.

There are two primary ways that you can invest money - before income tax or after income tax. Pre-tax investing is usually done through a company-sponsored retirement plan or participating IRA. The money is saved pre-tax, but when the money is withdrawn during retirement, it is all taxed as ordinary income. After-tax investing can have either of two outcomes - the funds can be partially taxed or they can be tax- free. In partially-taxed investing, only the growth of the money is taxed and it is currently taxed at either 15% or 20%, depending on your current tax bracket. Tax free is where simply no taxes are payable. People get in such a hurry to consider the current tax benefits that they rarely take pause to consider the more important point of taxation - which occurs at the time the money is withdrawn for use. Tax-free investments at the time of withdrawal will prove to be extremely valuable - especially if we see income tax rates rising in the years ahead. Again, I will show you the convenient way that I like to display this information when discussing it with a client.

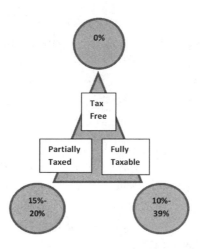

When you retire, your investment income will be created by a mix of the three different tax categories shown above in the Tax Triangle. Take a look at your investment portfolio and categorize your investments into these tax categories. Are you in balance? Do you have tax diversification?

Just like your portfolio needs asset class diversification, I am a strong supporter of tax diversification. If income tax rates rise in this country as a result of the current debt crisis we find ourselves in the middle of, it will be imperative to have a significant portion of your investment savings in a tax free position. Consider this oversimplified example. Let's say you need as much as $140,000/year as retirement income. If you were to take half of it from a fully taxable position and half from tax free, you would stay in the 15% tax bracket throughout retirement.*

You could take between $140,000 and $290,000 and stay in the 25% tax bracket.* Ordinarily, $140,000/year would have you at the upper limit of the 25% bracket, but with tax diversification, you would stay in the 15% bracket.* This is a HUGE difference in the amount of income tax that you would pay. Several of the new taxes associated with the Affordable Care Act are investment income taxes. This means that they are taxes specifically designed to be taken from people as they create income from their investment portfolio. This type of tax has become the new favorite amongst the progressives who are attempting to redistribute wealth from the "haves" to the "have-nots". If you "have" an income-producing investment portfolio, then you just put a target around your neck. Expect to see more of these "taxes-on-the-rich" being directed your way.

Just one generation ago, the foundation of retirement and our financial markets were dramatically different than what we see today. Most people could live comfortably in retirement with the company provided pension plan and a Social Security check. Some say those were the "good ole days."

Pensions have all but disappeared, being replaced by the 401k. This change fundamentally shifts the funding responsibility for retirement savings from the <u>employer</u> to the <u>employee</u>. This new environment that was created has been referred to as "The New Normal". Needless to say, we as a society were not adequately prepared to assume the responsibility for this change.

I will discuss several different strategies and topics that – if properly executed – will help reduce the risk level in your portfolio and provide a safer diversification for your portfolio design than using traditional asset classes alone. The following list of Financial Strategies help you plan a more reliable retirement:

- Don't leave accounts, especially 401k accounts, pensions and company stock plans, behind when you change employers.

- Take advantage of the opportunity to better control the diversification of your money by considering an in-service rollover if you are over the age of 59 ½ years old.

- Now that we are near all-time highs in the stock market indices, it is a good time to consider doing some profit taking or at least protecting your account values with an exit strategy like utilizing a stop-loss sell order.

- Make sure your Asset Allocation is in proper balance. Over time, the percentages of each asset class can grow at different rates and get the overall allocation out of balance.

- Make sure your Asset Allocation has proper hedges against stocks and bonds - such as real estate, loans and commodities (like oil & natural gas). Hedges are asset classes that have a naturally-occurring negative correlation to traditional asset classes, such as stocks and bonds.

- Decide the disposition of your house. If the mortgage is paid-off or close to being paid-off, then you have the value of the equity to consider. If you will be making mortgage payments during retirement, you may want to consider down-sizing or a reverse mortgage.

- Re-assess your protection needs. Most people, who have saved sufficiently for retirement may have reduced their need for life insurance significantly. As you transition from the working years into retirement, you can consider replacing your long term disability insurance with long term care insurance to cover you through the retirement years.

- Consider converting a portion of your IRA money into a Roth IRA. If this portion of your savings could be converted from tax-deferred growth into tax-free growth, it could make a significant impact on your tax obligations during retirement.

- Don't over-react and buy commodities like Gold and Silver out of fear of the stock market. Those of you who listened to the advisors and the never-ending radio and TV commercials have lost over 30% during 2013. This is a perfect example of another traditional safe haven that doesn't work in this economy the way it has in the past.

Finally, put your thoughts, ideas, goals and objectives on paper. The act of putting them on paper turns it into an action plan. You are much more likely to follow through with the implementation of these kind of strategic moves if you have a written plan of action.

During 2008 & 2009, while we were discovering the epic meltdown of the sub-prime mortgage portfolios in the U.S., Europe was finding themselves in a financial crisis of their own - a debt crisis. Since 2008, most of Europe has been on the brink of bankruptcy. Of the seventeen countries that comprise the European Union, five countries have declared bankruptcy with several others not far behind.

The European Central Bank has stepped up and assisted the countries that needed help the most - so far, but how much longer can they make it unless Europe starts some exporting of their goods - quickly. This debt crisis is contagious- all of Europe is suffering because of this crisis. The member nations of the European Union have had many meetings and have put together operating budgets for the countries in trouble to operate under - to keep them from over-spending. If you think that Europe is far away and the European Debt Crisis will not impact you - well, you're wrong. There are 6 key ways that the European Debt Crisis will effect everyday Americans.

1. Dwindling jobs in America- The largest U.S. companies rely heavily on global sales for success. Europe's demand has been cut by double digits - weaker demand means reduced supply or exports from the U.S. Europe represents the 3rd largest export destination for the U.S.

2. U.S. banks have massive loans in Europe - if their money is tied up in potentially bad loans in Europe, they can't loan that money to anyone in the U.S., which could decrease U.S. expansion opportunities. Five of the largest U.S. banks have almost $100 million dollars invested in the most economically stressed nations in the Eurozone.

3. Global 24 hours news cycle - Wall Street reacts negatively to the trouble in Europe. A recession in Europe could pull the U.S. into a recession.

4. Your investments or pension probably contains more European assets than you can imagine- since mutual fund managers believe in widely diversifying their portfolios, many Americans own more European assets than they know - even if they are considered domestic funds. This occurs under the guise of style drift. Some international funds hold as much as 50% of their assets in Europe.

5. The debt crisis makes European goods cheaper - for the people who are looking to buy European goods this is good, especially big ticket items, but it's not good for the American companies who will be losing the business to the cheaper competition.

6. The debt crisis could keep interest rates at record lows- this may be a good sign for the people in the U.S. who are using debt to finance a large purchase, like a car or house, but it is bad news for the retirees who will not be able to make much safe interest income from their retirement savings.

We live in a dynamic time in history. Financial success is earned by learning from the past and applying that knowledge to how we behave in the future. Financial strategies that worked 20 or more years ago simply don't work today. We even find that the Nobel Prize-winning concept of Asset Allocation needs to be significantly modified to remain relevant, as the relationship between asset classes has dramatically changed. As a society, we are not prepared for this change and many people approaching retirement stand to suffer from their lack of preparation. As a financial steward, I have been blessed with the resources to make a difference for you. Making a difference for you and the ensuing peace of mind is my purpose.

*Footnotes

1. 2012 Source Data from the Congressional Budget Office

2. 2012 Source Data from the Congressional Budget Office

3. Assumes taxpayer is filing Married Filing Jointly

4. Assumes taxpayer is filing Married Filing Jointly

5. Assumes taxpayer is filing Married Filing Jointly

6. Assumes taxpayer is filing Married Filing Jointly

About Rick

Rick Poston is a 19-year financial veteran who has helped hundreds of small business owners take their companies to the next level – by helping them grow their personal savings and retirement accounts.

Establishing himself with American Express Financial Advisors for seven-and-a-half years before launching his own company, Poston Financial Services, the Shreveport-born, Dallas-based adviser, has worked with a diverse client base of private practice professionals and many small business owners.

Rick has been chosen by Bloomberg's *Businessweek.com* and *Forbes Magazine* as one of the Top 20 "Game Changing" financial advisors in the country. Rick stays in touch with his fans each week by hosting a most educational hour on talkradio with the *Empowered Wealth* radio show every Saturday morning at 10am on 660 AM, The Answer, and on 100.7 FM, The Word.

Beyond his media presence, Rick continues to work directly with clients in his full-service boutique practice. Rick currently maintains three professional designations: Chartered Financial Consultant (ChFC), Chartered Life Underwriter (CLU) and Chartered Advisor for Senior Living (CASL).

For additional information or to schedule an appointment with Rick, please call 469-361-4020 or go to: www.rickposton.com.

CHAPTER 25

FINDING MY WAY

BY JOHN HAGGERTY

We never know what awaits us. For me, it was the slow progressive loss of vision. The doctors believe it began after accidental trauma around the eyes while serving in the Army. Several army eye doctors suspected my decline in vision was due to an emerging eye disease resulting from injury to the corneas, It was after I was discharged, that I was diagnosed with severe *kerataconus*. By the fall of 1977, I was declared legally blind by the State of New York. For the next three years I was on disability and unable to work. It was a local optometrist that referred me to a cornea specialist in New York. After several unsuccessful attempts to fit me with hard contact lenses, it was determined that surgery was my only option. In the fall of 1978, I had my first cornea transplant. It resulted in fairly good eyesight and I was optimistic about my future. Unfortunately, after a year, my cornea rejected. I fell into a depression. My wife and I separated after two years of marriage as I awaited a new cornea via the New York State Eye Bank. We would reconcile several months later. In April of 1979, I had my second cornea transplant on my left eye. My Father, an amputee, was a tremendous pillar of support for me. Dad lost his left leg in an accident while working for the railroad in 1948. He also advised me that the best approach to dealing with the anger, blame, and depression fallout, was to fight it and move on with my life.

In November of 1980 I hired on with Greenwich Office Supply, in Greenwich CT as a sales manager. My job was marketing business equipment to Southern Connecticut area businesses. I was still struggling big time with my poor eyesight. In March of that year, The Lighthouse called me about a job opportunity with AT&T in data processing. The Lighthouse was a resource agency for individuals with visual impairments. I was extremely excited with equal parts of apprehension. I thought, how can I handle data processing with such poor eyesight. I really enjoyed working at Greenwich Office Supply, but knew that a huge opportunity awaited me at AT&T. I decided to move out of my comfort zone, and in April of 1981 I was working at AT&T in White Plains, New York. My first job was mounting data tapes on large tape drives. I was the slowest on my team as I struggled to find the right volume number in the library. It was humiliating, and my self-esteem plummeted. To compensate, I performed other associated tasks that allowed me to feel that I was contributing to the team. I looked for ways to improve the tape library process and make the job more efficient. Many of my ideas and process improvements were implemented.

By May of 1984, I was promoted to management. My first job assignment was as a night shift supervisor in computer operations. I enjoyed the challenges of working in a large-scale IBM mainframe environment. I provided leadership for a team of three lead technicians and ten data processing associates. While I felt comfortable in this position, I was suffering internally as I struggled again with rapidly declining vision. In the fall, my Ophthalmologist fitted my left eye with a new gas permeable contact lens and my vision improved somewhat. My confidence and quality of work slowly improved as well. I was eager for new challenges. I was offered a new position working on costing out the data centers computing services. This unit cost assignment would prove to be my biggest challenge yet. It was an assignment that would undo me in terms of my confidence and self worth. Within the course of a few weeks, I found myself making critical spreadsheet errors. I had a terrible time discerning the data as my eyesight deteriorated even more. My doctor told me I needed to have a cornea transplant on my right eye. I was devastated. I wondered if this would ever end. As I waited for the eye bank to provide me with a suitable donor, I continued to struggle with the unit cost assignment. I was too proud and too afraid to admit I was suffering. My self worth was at an all time low. In February of 1986, I was notified that a cornea was available and had my third major eye surgery.

The corneal surgery on my right eye was successful, and I returned to work after a three-month disability. My eye doctor was hopeful that

I'd soon be able to tolerate a contact lens on the eye after a few more months of healing. However, that was not to be. We tried every type of lens available and I just could not stand to have it on my eye for more than a few minutes. So, my hope for greatly improved vision was dashed. My only hope was that some new technology would present itself in the near future. In the spring of 1987, we were told that AT&T would be consolidating its data centers and that the White Plains data center was slated to close. Luckily, we had a wonderfully empathetic data center manager, George Hess, who was always thinking of ways to ease the tension and stress associated with this life-changing event. It was before a major managers team function that he would provide all his managers with a book that would change the way I viewed myself, my job and others in a very profound way. He gifted us with *The Empowered Manager* by Peter Block. The book is about organizations moving away from a negative corporate culture to a positive entrepreneurial culture. It suggests that all members of the organization take responsibility for success. In other words, every member of the organization has skin in the game. I was hooked. Block wrote about how managers need to embrace love and trust as elements of true effective leadership. It taught me to look differently at my situation. I began reading everything I could on organizational theory and leadership. I was finding out many new things about myself, as I looked inward. I found that I possessed an inner strength and resilience I thought I was otherwise void of.

In the beginning of 1989, just before the doors would close on the White Plains data center, I was transferred to the Mesa Regional Processing Center in Arizona. My first assignment was in Application Support. I was doing very well, and soon moved into the hardware planning manager role for the centers infrastructure working closely with capacity planning and vendors from IBM, and Storagetek. After a Saturday golf outing, I noticed that the suns glare was extremely painful. I panicked as I sensed what was happening. I made an appointment with a local Ophthalmologist in Phoenix. I was told that I had the Kerataconus return outside the perimeter of the corneal grafts on both eyes. I was extremely angry and frustrated. It was confirmed that I did have the eye disease again. I broke down in tears at the unfairness of it all. As I began to look for options for treatment, I was told my job would be moving to central Florida as AT&T was going to centralize its Information Technology functions. My wife and I relocated to Altamonte Springs,

Florida, with a five-minute drive to the office. While I was still dealing with very poor vision, I felt different. The sense that I could overcome all disappointment and hardship associated with my eye disease coursed through me. I knew I could make a difference. I just didn't know how or where. Things went well for me in my new position. I excelled and was always rated highest in my work group. I was giving a presentation in New Jersey to a group of clients when something unexpected happened. While speaking, my left knee buckled. I had extreme pain in my right leg. I couldn't determine if it was my back or hip. I was in agony. I was being treated for low back pain but never felt any relief.

It was after a transfer back to Arizona in 1993, that I was diagnosed with Avascular Necrosis. The bone at the top of my femur was dying due to the blood supply being cut off. My orthopedist said this condition developed as a result of all the IV anti-rejection drugs I took to fight the corneal rejection in 1979. I was outraged and at my end. A fellow employee that suffered from shrapnel wounds in Vietnam encouraged me to fight. I remembered the advice my dad gave me. I was reenergized and ready to take this new medical issue on. It was in '94 that I had my first of four hip surgeries, a core decompression. The brightest point during this period was the birth of my beautiful daughter Emma. I had never been happier. She gave me reason to face anything and be the best I could be. Before Emma's second birthday, I fell while exercising and fractured the right hip. After surgery to install screws and pins, I went about a year until the next surgery to remove all the hardware. During my surgical rehab, I reread *The Empowered Manager* for the fourth or fifth time. I was determined to read everything that had to do with empowerment, organizational management, leadership, and self-improvement. I was ready to face any challenge. I was going to win my battle.

I was promoted to Regional Manager Western States in support of all IT needs for both the Business and Residential Sales force in twelve states. I loved the challenge. The greatest reward was providing leadership to many technical managers and their associates, and contractual employees. We were the best in terms of service, and meeting or beating service-level objectives. I felt totally engaged, energized, and empowered. I had overcome so much by not giving up, embracing new ideas, incorporating love and trust, and getting on with my life, despite all I had to endure. Others began to recognize it too. Employees would thank me for making a difference in the workplace and in their lives. Many said I was an example of what hard work and a positive attitude can overcome. This was the greatest compliment I ever received on the job. I think my attitude permeated the team. We excelled as a service organization. Our clients presented us with awards. I received several SVP awards. In 1997, I represented AT&T and spoke at a huge benefit in San Francisco right before Mayor Willie Brown addressed the audience. I spoke about technology and its impact on the culture. I received a standing ovation.

In 1999, I moved to New Jersey. I had my right hip replaced in 2000. Shortly after returning with this disability I took an Account Executive - Information Technology Services position in support of AT&T Labs in Middletown, New Jersey. In December of 2004 on the cusp of the AT&T/SBC merge, I took an early retirement as my vision worsened once again. I walked away proud of all I had accomplished in the face of adversity. I left a winner. My dad died in 2005 before I was awarded a service-connected disability from The Veteran's Administration for my eyes. He pushed me for years to file. He would've been pleased. It was the recognition of the service connection he wanted for me. I always thought there were much more deserving servicemen and women who have lost limbs and more. My dad was an example of how to fully live with the difficulty and hardship of a disability. He taught me that it's not about being second best, but about being your best. I miss him dearly.

I owe much thanks to all those who have helped me throughout the years. I now know it's about keeping your heart and mind open, staying positive, and your willingness to learn new things in the face of adversity that allowed me to find my winning way. I know you can too. While I still suffer with the disease today, I accept it as a challenge and not something I feel burdened by. I'd love to hear from other veterans and anyone else who have faced similar challenges and have found their own path to a successful and meaningful life.

Science may have found a cure for most evils, but it has found no remedy for the worst of them all – the apathy of human beings
~ Helen Keller–

About John

John Haggerty is an entrepreneur, speaker, and business executive. John has had over thirty years experience working for AT&T, and IBM. He has been dealing with vision problems for most of his life. He developed a severe eye disease after receiving trauma to his corneas while serving in the Army. John received a service-connected disability from the Veterans Administration in 2005.

He was educated at Baylor University, The Academy of Health & Sciences at Fort Sam Houston, Texas, and University of Phoenix. He has developed a passion for helping those veterans injured in service find ways to reshape their lives. John is interested in mentoring those veterans that want to share their stories of transcending the limitations of disability.

John lives in Scottsdale, AZ and can be reached directly at techieny@live.com

CHAPTER 26

RESISTANCE BREAKTHROUGH

BY JOHN MULDOON

If you are committed to reaching your full potential in life and in business, then you are going to experience something that all successful people do encounter – *RESISTANCE*. That the greater your ambitions, the more resistance you will encounter!

As a young boy, I saw the world as a very exciting place and I used to dream about all the wonderful things I would do and have. I believed all things were possible! My name is John Muldoon and today I have and live an extraordinary life! I own and operate a very successful business, I have great health, I have an incredible relationship with the women I love, I get to travel the world, I get to do creative things, I help others and I have a tremendously rewarding spiritual life. However, this was not always the case. I left home at a very young age, was a high school dropout, had little or no life skills, and I knew nothing about business or business principles. Because of this, I soon began to experience enormous resistance in life and experienced some serious pain along the way. Every successful person I know has encountered enormous resistance and only when they began to learn the "truth" about it, they were then able to make real progress in reaching their potential. When people understand resistance, they can break through it. Unfortunately, people who don't understand it, retreat and turn back to a life of mediocrity. I know that you are someone who is working to reach your full potential, or chances are you wouldn't be reading this book. My goal in this chapter is to provide you with some powerful approaches to break through resistance. So let's move forward and break through!

Are you in a place right now where you are facing enormous resistance? I will guarantee, if you are pursuing anything that is important to you, you will, without fail, meet resistance— and my guess is, I am not telling you anything new. I call it "resistance" because it is like trying to move something out of your way so you can move forward; however, the obstacle in your way is pushing back, resisting all your best applied effort at that time. When this persists for a long period of time without any breakthrough, we soon become frustrated, discouraged and some people give up. This is the tragedy for so many individuals. They meet resistance and give into it. They do so in many cases because they do not understand the real "truth" about resistance and how it works. Resistance is there to help us on our journey in life, to reach our full potential, and to create a life of creative self-expression. As Napoleon Hill said, "Within every adversity, there is a seed of equal or greater benefit." All successful people know the truth about resistance, its source, and its value.

The greatest resistance we experience in anything, almost always comes from within our own consciousness, our own psychology. This belief that we can't overcome resistance or that we don't have the resources to, is the real source of our resistance!

The one thing I have learned in life is this: you cannot argue with the truth. Once you know the truth, you will never argue it! Here is the truth, once you understand that resistance is there to aid you and you have the resources within you to break through it, your whole approach to business and life begin to change significantly for the better. Resistance comes not to defeat us, instead it comes as a signpost to provide us direction as to where to go next. When the resistance is overcome, it will energize and build confidence within us. You will now operate from a different state, one of higher consciousness. Problems become easier to resolve and success is inevitable. **Resistance is only an indicator light on our dashboard saying something needs attention – either our psychology or our physical approach to what we are doing is incorrect.**

It's been said, change your thinking and you change your life. Successful people think differently about resistance than unsuccessful people.

Because they think about it differently, they approach it differently. You will soon discover that resistance is a very important aspect of your success and you will learn how to get resistance working for you instead of against you. Here are four powerful, new ways to approach resistance. These will provide you with an enormous amount of additional leverage in creating the extraordinary breakthroughs you desire, and will help you reach the next level of personal success and happiness.

The next question is: how do you change your approach? Here are some proven methods of how to approach resistance that will give you the leverage you require to break through. Once I began to use this systematic process in dealing with resistance, my thinking began to change dramatically and so did my outcomes.

Here are four steps to create a successful strategy for breaking through resistance. Keep the following in mind when approaching these steps:

Psychological: if your decisions are motivated by fear, anger, resentment, etc., then be clear on this, nothing positive will ever will come when you are operating in this state of mind. Why? Because, these negative emotions affect our state of mind and will lower the consciousness that will be reflected in your law of attraction. Like attracts like.

Physical: this is when the physical approach to systems you are using is incorrect and requires adjustment or change. This is a much easier to change than our psychology, and that is why people tend to look to this first.

STEP 1

First, write down the facts. You will be surprised at the clarity this can provide. You need to ask yourself this question: what is the real source of the resistance I am experiencing right now? This is so important because you can't fix something if you don't know what needs fixing. When you believe you have identified the resistance, ask yourself again, is this the absolute truth? Is this the real source of my resistance or just a symptom? Let me give you a personal example. I had a major client with whom I was doing a large amount of business. Our company continued to experience an enormous amount of resistance in trying to satisfy this client. This client was providing us millions of dollars in business and I wanted to service the hell out of them. However, every adjustment we made was not working. The amount of resistance we were experiencing was massive. Customers were unhappy, we weren't getting paid, bills were piling up and our staff was frustrated. Finally, the truth came into focus for me. There was no satisfying this client's needs. Even though this client was one of the largest in their industry, it became clear that there was a lot of internal chaos in their company operations. This was the source of our resistance. They were continually changing their processes and we could not keep up to their changes.

In addition, I recognized another level of resistance that was even worse, this resistance was coming from a place of fear! What will happen if we lose this client? I could have broken through this resistance a lot sooner had I dealt with the fear rather than changing all these systems. I knew in my own mind we were a great company, because that is what my other clients were telling us. I knew from the onset that the cost of doing business with this client was high. The universe was screaming at me "bad client," but my fear was keeping me from seeing the truth. The answer was to accept the truth, let go of the client and remove the resistance. So I fired the client and soon added a number of new smaller clients. The resistance stopped immediately and we broke through to a new level of success because our clients were happy! Ensure that you are really dialled in to what the source of the resistance is! It will save a lot of time, pain and money!!!

STEP 2

Now that you have the facts, it is time to start the process of getting a creative solution for removing the resistance. This is a mental process and in the mental workings of life, the relaxed approach is always the best. We know that mental effort defeats itself. All successful people know this and apply it when problem solving. I am sure if you do some reflection on your own life, you will agree that some of your best ideas and answers to your biggest problems came to you when your mind was relaxed or quiet. So during this process, take time to quiet yourself, as Albert Einstein stated, "the conscious mind that presents the problem is not the same mind that solves the problem." When you get quiet and are relaxed, ask yourself the question, "What should I do?" Let your subconscious mind do the work. If you can sit quietly long enough, you will be amazed at the answers that will come. This is one of the most powerful problem-solving resources you have available to you.

STEP 3

If you have completed the above steps and are still not completely clear about the source of your resistance and how to resolve it, I want to share with you another approach that will literally change your personal and business life. Whatever the source of your resistance, I can almost guarantee you that someone, somewhere, at some time has faced the same resistance and had success breaking through it. So there is no need for you to go it alone, and rely on yourself for all the answers. Why walk if you can fly? In other words, you can save a lot of time, money and heartache by having someone else tell you how they overcame the same resistance successfully! In today's world, it is so easy to get access to this knowledge. Knowledge is power, by gaining the knowledge from others, you can gain leverage to overcome the resistance...that is power!

So here again is another truth we all need to accept, life is short and time is our most valuable commodity, especially today. Time waits for no man and nothing could be truer than in today's business world. Get the help you need in overcoming the resistance that is holding you back!

Today it is easier than ever before to gain access to the most successful people in all areas of personal and business success. These people will become your personal advisors for less than pennies a day. You will be able to resource these individuals who have already done it, notice I said, "have done it," they have not just read about or studied the subject, but have "Done It!" This is where so many people go wrong. They take advice from people who have no real world experience, only opinions. If you are getting advice from anyone who would not be deemed an authority on the subject, RUN!!! Get to the experts. How is this done? Well, I will assume that many of you already know this, but may not be utilizing it to its full potential. It is vital that you realize what a phenomenal resource this can be to you. This alone is the most powerful factor in my own personal success. These people have all written books, made DVDs, offer courses and training and now they are available even on YouTube. When you are experiencing massive resistance, and you will, if you are wanting to reach your full potential, you better allocate a certain amount of your time each day to meeting with these people, through reading, listening to CDs, watching DVDs and taking their courses.

Identify your resistance and then search out the experts in this area. By doing this, you're half way there! These experts have spent a great portion of their life overcoming and breaking through the same resistance you are facing. All you need to do is access the right book, video, course, etc., and they will show you the way, it is that easy.

Here is an example of an experience I just had and how I used this step to overcome the resistance. I was experiencing enormous financial pressure in my business. I had let go of my sales team because they had become complacent, I had unfinished projects and some of our AR's were getting stretched out longer than they should. I was training a new sales team and it was taking them time to get up to speed, I was feeling completely overwhelmed. This was some serious pressure, enormous psychological resistance to overcome. I knew I needed an answer and I knew where to find it. I started my search..."Seek and you shall find." I came across a new book by a sales training expert that I had taken a course from some years ago. I started reading, watching his YouTube videos and BOOM! I got the answer!

This has never failed for me and it won't for you. When you are struggling to find answers and to get a break through, get around the experts. These experts are individuals who want to help you crush your resistance!

STEP 4

In addition to getting access to these experts, there is another thing you need to do. This advice was given to me by an extraordinary, successful businessman named Lou. This man was 85 years old and was a business genius. When I told him about the type of business I was starting, he gave me the following advice. He said "John, find yourself someone who is very successful and working in the same type of industry you are, however, find them in a different city (so you are not in competition with them). Reach out to them by phone or personal visit, and ask them if you could call them from time to time to discuss business problems and issues as they arise." Lou told me he couldn't count the number of times this had helped him. I followed his advice and when resistance occurred, I reached out and asked for advice. This has benefitted me enormously. When you do this, you will have an experienced expert working with you, and guess what, you will probably find that you will end up benefitting them as well.

Look to the experts and they will show you the ways to blast through your resistance and soon you will become an experienced expert yourself! Only a fool tries to do it all alone! Remember that resistance is a signpost on your road to success indicating:

...BREAK THROUGH JUST AHEAD!

About John

John Patrick Muldoon (Calgary, Alberta, Canada) is a self-taught business enthusiast who has succeeded at many start-up companies, basing his achievements around sales and marketing. Presently, he owns and operates a company that does over $6 million in sales annually.

John has spent over 25 years practicing and mastering the principles of personal and business success. He is passionate about sharing his knowledge and experience with others to assist them in reaching their full potential in life and business. John has overcome numerous obstacles throughout his life and in business by studying and practicing the psychological, metaphysical and spiritual laws of success.

CHAPTER 27

THE GROWTHSTAR FORMULA:
5-STEP BLUEPRINT TO SKYROCKET YOUR NEW BUSINESS SALES™

BY JONATHAN GRAVES

*"Give me six hours to chop down a tree and
I will spend the first four sharpening the axe."*
~ Abraham Lincoln

If you want extreme results with your business sales growth, you have to be willing to take extreme measures.

This principle will continue to stand the test of time across all aspects of our lives. The highest performing business leaders, athletes, scientists, entrepreneurs, etc. all share this common characteristic.

They push the limits further than any of their competition, during both their preparation and as they execute their attack strategies.

**How to GROW Your NEW Business
Leads, Referrals and Sales by 350%**

Since graduating college in 1998, I have been in the business of helping businesses drive revenue and sales growth. After spending over $30+ million dollars of our own capital testing NEW breakthrough opportunities to help our clients work smarter, I created *The Growthstar Formula*™ to help you achieve fast results.

The Growthstar Formula™ is a 5-step blueprint that is specifically built to help you skyrocket your NEW business sales. When implemented correctly, your business can easily experience a 350%+ increase in your NEW Business Leads, Referrals and Sales.

Here is a quick snapshot diagram:

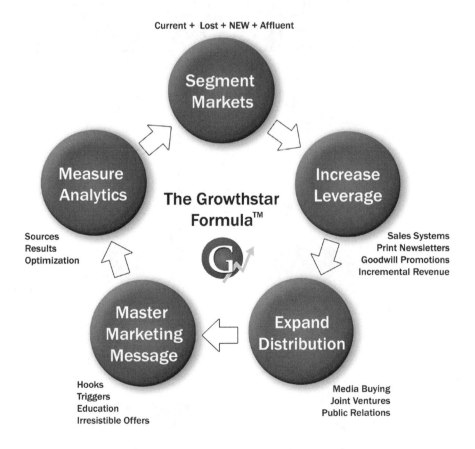

© Copyright Graves Organization, Inc.
All Rights Reserved

STEP #1: MASTER MARKETING MESSAGE

The first step is to create your *Master Marketing Message.* Your *Master Marketing Message* is what you are going to use in all of your advertising to capture your prospect's attention and entice them to want to learn more about your business.

Making tweaks to your *Master Marketing Message* will have an enormous impact on the pulling power of your front-end advertising. Front-end advertising is defined as ads that draw NEW customers into your sales funnel.

This step is so powerful that making a couple of small tweaks to your message can increase your NEW customer leads by 350% all by itself.

Here are the four ingredients you need to create a winning *Master Marketing Message.*

1. Hooks
Your "Hooks" are the biggest problems that your product or service helps your prospects solve within your marketplace. Don't worry about making these "Hooks" unique. They should shine a light on the biggest pain points that your target market is experiencing. You will use these "Hooks" as attention grabbers within your advertising headlines.

Focusing the headlines of your ads on the biggest problems your prospects are experiencing will supercharge the pulling power of your ads.

Here are a couple of quick examples:

Chiropractors: **Is Your Day Job CRUSHING Your BACK?**

Lawyers: **Need a Lawyer That Won't SQUASH Your Bank Account?**

Loan Officers: **Need a Fast Business Loan WITHOUT the Headache?**

2. Triggers
Triggers are used to further increase the pulling power of your marketing by further <u>engaging your prospects</u> into the body of your ads. There are a number of *Triggers* you can use, these are two of my absolute favorites…

> **(i). Prospect of Gain Triggers (Psychological) How the reader of your advertisement can increase this:** *his/her mental, physical,*

financial, social, emotional, or spiritual stimulation, satisfaction, well-being or security.

(ii). Fear of Loss Triggers (Psychological) How the reader of your advertisement can *decrease* **this:** *His/her fear of poverty, illness, accident, discomfort, boredom, and the loss of business or social prestige or advancement.*

3. Education

The body copy of your *Master Marketing Message* needs to focus on HELPING your prospects get the education they need to make a smart purchasing decision. You do this by helping to educate them for FREE.

Free education tools include: *Free reports, samples, trials, consultations, demonstrations, videos, teleseminars, webinars, face-to-face meetings, estimates, proposals, etc.*

4. Irresistible Offers

Creating your unique *"Irresistible Offer"* is absolutely critical to your long term success, as it gets you away from being a *"commodity"* and into offering a unique *"one of a kind"* opportunity.

The goal of this 4th and final piece of your *Master Marketing Message* is to provide a 100% unique solution that your prospects cannot get their hands on anywhere else. It needs to be a one-of-a-kind solution that will help your prospects fulfill their biggest desire and/or how to solve their biggest problem.

Here is how you do it…

Find Something about Your Product or Service that is 100% Unique.

If You Do Not Have Anything Unique… CREATE IT.

Give it a NAME.

This lead magnet will serve as your *"Irresistible Offer."*

Here is a quick example…

FREE Consultation!
XYZ Realty's Exclusive

"TD3 Home Sales System"
Will Reveal 3 Proven Strategies of How to Sell Your Home for TOP
Dollar EVEN in a Down Market!

Notice how the *"TD3 Home Sales System"* is an offer that the reader can ONLY RECEIVE by calling XYZ Realty. It is 100% unique. This 100% unique problem solving solution, plus the hooks, trigger ads and educational value of this ad make this an *Irresistible Offer.*

STEP #2: MEASURE ANALYTICS

The second step is to set up proper performance marketing analytic tracking systems so that you can MEASURE the results of your advertising.

You can't grow that of which you do not have the ability to measure. You need to have a clear understanding as to how each of your advertising channels are performing so you can make smart marketing decisions.

Here are the ten critical marketing analytic questions and answers you need to know:

1. **How many visitors does your website/offer page receive a month?**

2. **What is the current conversion rate of your website?**
   – meaning, what %age of visitors pick up the phone or email you to learn more or request an appointment.

3. **How much does it cost you to drive a NEW Lead?** *These can either be inbound phone calls or web forms.*

4. **How many sources of traffic do you have that are delivering NEW customer leads?**

5. **Can you provide detailed reports that show which of your leads are coming in from each free/paid marketing channel?**

6. **Can you track your lead cost broken out per marketing channel?**

7. **What % of your NEW leads are you converting to NEW customers?**

8. **What % of your NEW customers is coming from paid marketing vs. referrals?**

9. **What is the average "Lifetime Value" of each NEW customer worth to you?**

10. **How much are you looking to pay to acquire a new customer?**

To properly measure your marketing analytics, you must obtain a clear understanding of each of your advertising *sources* and the corresponding pulling power *results* of each source.

This will provide you with the tools and expertise needed for *optimization*, where you will cut advertising waste and GROW profitable channels.

STEP #3: SEGMENT MARKETS

Once you have your *Master Marketing Message* and your ability to *Measure Analytics* and track your results, now you are ready for the third step of the *The Growthstar Formula*™, which is, to *Segment Markets*.

Segmenting your markets provides you with the ability to create custom marketing messages tailored specifically to each of your four major market segments.

These segments include:

1. Current Customers
Your current customers should be your number one source of NEW sales growth. They are counting on you to deliver NEW products (everyone loves NEW) and to keep them educated on what is going on within your field of expertise.

What they really want is to feel appreciated, as they should be.

To stay top-of-mind with current customers, you want to reach out to them as often as you can to provide additional value-based information and NEW product/service offers as you bring them to market. You can do this via holiday promotions, NEW product launches, newsletters, VIP service offerings and special announcements.

Effectively marketing to your current customers will show them that you appreciate their loyalty. This will increase their frequency of purchases with you, effectively growing your overall lifetime value per customer.

2. Lost Customers

Lost customer activation campaigns work very well. You can leverage holiday promotions, sales, discounts, premiums and incentives to drive lost customers back into your sales funnel. You should look to deploy lost customer activation campaigns 2 to 4 times a year as part of your ongoing sales system.

3. NEW Customers

Targeting NEW customers is pretty self-explanatory. We all love to go after NEW customers. Unfortunately, this process can be very expensive and can get very expensive at times if you do not know what you are doing.

It is critically important that you have a strong handle on the first two steps of *The Growthstar Formula*™ before you start to aggressively purchase advertising to generate NEW Customers. When just starting out, first make sure you have the ability to *Measure Analytics* and track all paid ads. Then launch "Seed" marketing to test your *Master Marketing Message* (along with landing pages, sales closing rates, etc.) before you get aggressive with your media buying.

4. Affluent Prospects

Not all customers are created equal. It is a lot easier to target the higher echelon of your target market than it is to go after the bargain hunters and bottom feeders. Creating a separate marketing budget and attack strategy that specifically goes after the affluent prospects within your marketplace allows you to present special offers to markets that will provide the least buying resistance.

STEP #4: INCREASE LEVERAGE

The fourth step of *The Growthstar Formula*™ is to *Increase Leverage*. Leverage is your ability to use a quality or advantage to obtain a desired result.

There are four very important business assets that you want to leverage.

1. Sales Systems

Sales Systems utilize technology to automate pre-determined communication processes of your *Master Marketing Message* across all of your market segments (Current Customers, Lost Customers, NEW Customers, Affluent Prospects, etc.). When used properly, Sales Systems that have been built by trained marketing professionals are the most powerful business assets that you can leverage.

You want to utilize a cross-platform strategy with sales systems that deploy your *Master Marketing Message* across as many marketing channels (print newsletters, direct mail, email, telephone, events, etc.) as possible.

2. Print Newsletters

Print Newsletters are a fantastic tool to increase your brand equity and *"Top of Mind"* awareness across all four of your *Segment Markets*.

Think about it, how many emails do you get a day?

It is very difficult, if not borderline impossible these days, to establish a strong connection with your customers via email alone. Look to use email as a supporting media tool, not as your number one source of customer interaction.

Print Newsletters are among the strongest tools I have ever seen that will help you grow your brand equity and celebrity authority within your marketplace. You absolutely NEED to leverage this valuable asset.

The key is to keep them short, educational, fun and entertaining.

Let your personality shine through and look to help your subscribers get an inside look at what your company is all about and how you can help them.

3. Goodwill Promotions

We all love a good deal, it is human nature.

The key to successfully running long term deals and not diminishing the strength of your brand is to leverage what I call *Goodwill Promotions*.

Goodwill Promotions provide a **"reason why"** you are running the promotion and provide a limited time call-to-action to receive the deal. To accomplish this, deploy a cross media strategy (print newsletters, email, direct mail, outbound phone, etc.) that provides a healthy mix of holiday promotions, lost customer activation promotions and customer appreciation promotions.

Look to have one unique promotion go out to your entire list every one to two months with an expiration date. Provide a **"reason why"** you are running the promotion.

These my favorite holidays to run promotions that you should leverage:

New Year's Day (Let's kick some tail this year!)

Valentine's Day (Love is in the air, fun holiday)

Memorial Day (Everyone is pumped for summer)

Independence Day (FREEDOM!!!)

Thanksgiving (Thankful for all that we have)

Halloween (A fun promotion, everyone gets in fun mood)

Run each promotion only once a year. This will keep your promotions fresh.

This works best when you combine your *Print Newsletter* that provides educational value to your list with your *Goodwill Promotions* that increase frequency with deal-based call-to-action incentives.

4. Incremental Revenue
The fourth business asset you want to look to leverage are incremental revenue streams of income for your business. There are dozens of ways you can add incremental streams of revenue, no matter what industry you are in. When you leverage Sales Systems, you can incorporate these incremental offerings into your sales cycle for each of your *Segment Markets*.

STEP #5: EXPAND DISTRIBUTION

Once you have the leverage to support your growth efforts, it is time to hammer down on the fifth and final step of *The Growthstar Formula*™, which is to *Expand Distribution*. Your distribution methods are the media tools you will use to spread your *Master Marketing Message* out into the world and GROW your business.

Media Buying

Media Buying gets fun when you have a *Master Marketing Message* that out-pulls your competitors ads by three times. Now your ads will receive three times the number of calls, plus you will have the backend sales systems, print newsletters, goodwill promotions and incremental revenue streams in place to monetize your inbound leads, even those that do not turn into customers right away.

Joint Ventures

Joint Venture partnerships are perhaps the most overlooked and under-utilized sales channel I see when meeting with business owners. When used correctly, this channel can drive a very significant spike in NEW customers and business.

To do this effectively, you want to look to partner with similar businesses in your marketplace that are complementary but not competitive. I recommend that you identify the TOP joint venture industry verticals and narrow it down to just one to start (so you actually get started).

Then, purchase a targeted list of this target market from a list broker and deploy a three-pronged attack (direct mail, telephone and email) to set up introduction conference calls and follow up meetings to explore how you can partner together.

Public Relations

Public Relations (PR) is the practice of managing the spread of information between an individual or an organization and the public. In other words, it is when you look to utilize mass media to get spread your *Master Marketing Message* and grow your brand.

Here are three of the top mass media PR vehicles:

1. **Book Publishing:** Write a book on your particular field of expertise. You can then leverage that book in all of your marketing materials to grow your brand as a leading expert authority in your field.

2. **TV Appearances:** With the help of trained PR professionals, you can become a guest speaker on television programs that are looking for expert advice and discussion topics around your area of expertise.

3. Newspapers and Magazines: You can provide free expert advice as a guest editorial contributor across major newspaper and magazines publications. This will provide free third party expert educational value for the publication's readers in exchange for mass media exposure for your business.

CONCLUSION

This has been a brief overview of the high level strategies that power the *The Growthstar Formula*™.

This 5-step blueprint to attacking your sales growth is being brought to you as a culmination of all of our years in the field—testing and learning—while helping over 3,000 of our personal business clients drive smart revenue growth.

You can use this proven 5-Step blueprint to help you skyrocket your NEW Business Leads, Referrals and Sales growth by over 350%.

This truly is *"The Winning Way."*

About Jonathan

Jonathan Graves is the founder of multiple marketing and sales-oriented businesses and is widely considered by many to be one of the key industry leaders in the direct response advertising field.

Since starting his career in 1998, Jonathan has helped many Fortune 500 companies, over 3,000 local businesses and entrepreneurs from across the world leverage his industry-direct response marketing and sales knowledge to capitalize on new GROWTH opportunities.

Jonathan has worked with some of the largest, most prestigious brand-name clients in the world. This list includes: Priceline, Lawyers.com, Avis Rent-A-Car, Brookstone, Incorporate.com, Jetblue, Carnival, Orbitz, Match.com, ADT and dozens more.

Most importantly, Jonathan's direct marketing and sales strategies have helped his clients drive over $500 million in estimated gross sales since 2004.

Jonathan earned a Bachelor of Science (BS) degree in Marketing from Virginia Tech. In his free time he enjoys spending as much quality time as he can with his wife and two children.

You can learn more about Jonathan by visiting: www.jonathanhgraves.com

CHAPTER 28

MOTIVATION IS TEMPORARY; INSPIRATION IS PERMANENT

BY JOSEPH J. CULIN
– The Black Belt Mentor

Those who know the truth learn to love it.
Those who love the truth learn to live it.
~ Bob Proctor

The quality of our lives will be based on the decisions that we make. As a matter of fact, decisions are the *only* thing in this life that we have total control of. However, this also requires us to be great thinkers, and concentrated thought is one of the hardest things to do. That is why so few people do it.

Why is it then that some people achieve great goals? How are they motivated to pay the price in time, money, effort or risk? Is it Motivation or Inspiration that leads us to great heights? As human beings, we have amazing God-given abilities and virtually unlimited potential. The divine gifts of Reason, Imagination and Intuition are ours to use so that we may create any life that we desire. And it's all right here, right now. Available to anyone who is willing to Awaken, accept the gifts, and to put them to use.

Consider this old Fable: Once upon a time an old man was stopped on a dusty road by several townspeople. The people, knowing the old man to be very wise asked him "Are you a god?" "No," he replied. "Are you a Saint?" Again, he replied "No." "Then, please tell us; what are you?" The old man simply replied, "I am Awake."

The purpose of life, and one of our greatest responsibilities, is to Wake Up, and to see our oneness with God. To awaken to the possibilities, opportunities and promise that is in front of us all. And to reach out and make use of the resources that can make our lives, and countless others better, happier and more productive.

AMATEURS COMPETE; PROFESSIONALS CREATE

When I opened my Martial Arts Leadership Academy, I was programmed to compete. I was a competitor both in and out of the ring. Yet there was always a feeling of lack and limitation. I was locked in the philosophy of *competition*. Competition tells us that there is a limited amount. That whatever you have to fight to get, you have to fight to keep. What is yours today is someone else's tomorrow. In order for me to have more, someone else must have less. It has temporary meaning, fleeting satisfaction, and fluctuating fortune. All rewards from competition, and our ego, are both temporal and feverish. And all competitive thinking is rooted in our ego.

Motivation alone is not enough. If you have an idiot and you motivate him, now you have a motivated idiot. ~ Jim Rohn

The concepts of Motivation and Inspiration are similar to the elements of Ego and Truth. Any lasting happiness in our lives is *never* born from our Ego; but by living in divine Truth. Let's look at the concept of Motivation a little closer.

Haven't we been taught that we must use motivation in order to make more money, help our children to earn higher grades; or push our employees to increase productivity? Think of these words for a moment: ***Motivate Make, Push.*** When I hear words like this I can't help visualizing getting behind someone and pushing them across the floor, while they resist and drag their heals as they dig in. Yet, in most cases, this is exactly what we end up doing!

The fact is, virtually any motivation techniques that we may use on ourselves or others are temporary.

Let me say that I do believe that some motivation techniques do work; such as fear motivation to keep our children safer ("don't put anything in the light socket; or stay out of the street or a car can hit you."). Or by putting a lackluster employee on a measured program or they would be fired. I believe that these, if used properly, *can* have a degree of effectiveness.

However, I believe that the core concepts of what we consider motivation to be flawed. Pushing an employee never works in the long run. I have trained staff members in Martial Arts Academies to restaurants; Fortune 100 hi-tech companies to nail salons; from day care centers to high-dollar Law firms. And the result is *always* the same: Motivation, even at its highest level; is temporary.

I'll give you a great example of an attempt at motivation from one of my 8-year old Leadership students. She asked me, in one of the Leadership classes that I teach weekly: "Mr. Culin, how can I *make* (motivate) people like me??" My answer was direct and to the point: "Madison, I said, that's an easy question to answer: *YOU CAN'T!*"

Now, imagine the child's face, and the parent's gasps when I said that! "Then," I continued, "you can't *MAKE* anyone do anything. **If you want to be more liked, then become more likeable!**" Wow! What a concept! *Inspire* them to like you by the person you are and the actions that you exhibit.

PEOPLE DON'T RESIST CHANGE;
THEY RESIST *BEING* CHANGED

Imagine, for a moment, a rope lying on the floor. The rope is in a perfectly straight line. Motivation can be equated to "pushing" the rope from behind. What happens to the rope when we push it? It bunches up and gets all tangled. Now, not only is the rope not moving forward, but also we now have to expend energy to untangle it!

Now imagine the same rope, but this time we are standing at the front. And we gently *pull* the rope. What happens now? It moves in a perfectly straight line; in the direction that we want, devoid of any entanglements. Our lives work on exactly the same principle! Inspire people with a strong enough Vision, and they will *want* to change!

INSPIRATION = IN SPIRIT

To be inspired is to live in the world of Truth. It *pulls* us into the future. It instills in us a feeling of hope, belief and possibility. It gives us a powerful image to work with. There is no resistance when we are inspired. We are completing volumes of work almost effortlessly. We are in a zone called Activity in Repose. Completing multiple tasks seemingly at rest. Like a top spinning at full energy and speed; and looking like it is standing still – *calm* and *rested*. Feelings of fear, doubt, worry and anxiety are set aside, leaving us the ability to create and achieve.

It's never the wind that blows across us all,
but it is the setting of our sail.
~ Jim Rohn

I often watch the sailboats from my home overlooking Lake Travis in Austin, Texas. There could be a hundred boats trying to get from point A to point B, but only a few are moving. The wind is hitting all of the boats, but the ones who set their sails just a little differently are moving ahead. This is a great lesson! What small changes can we make to make our boat fly into the direction of success? Remember, virtually all reasonable people want more—more money, better health, stronger relationships, spiritual connection, a satisfying career. Obtaining higher results from inspiration seems effortless for those who understand Truth. And the seeking of, and obtaining these things is praiseworthy! Never feel ashamed for being inspired by someone who is rich. Put aside being envious of those who have developed strong and deep relationships. Never curse those who have good health and always seem to be in the right place at the right time. We are ALWAYS in the right place at exactly the right time! And, we can have anything others have, or it's equivalent! We just have to follow the law. And, the law always works!

Remember that we have infinite potential and have been granted great gifts from God. And, since we have been given these gifts, we now have the responsibility to use them.

You are fully responsible for everything you are,
everything you have and everything you become.
~ Brian Tracy

So, you may ask, how DO we help our children, our employees, and ourselves attain a higher level of our infinite potential? Responsibility is the key. Responsibility tells us that we are in charge. That we must take the steps to make things better in our lives. That we can pray for wisdom, strength and guidance, but we must take the steps ourselves. "Pray, but move your feet" is a wise Quaker saying. And, it is very fitting for those who are awakened and inspired to enter the world of Truth.

SUCCESS IS NEVER A BY-PRODUCT
OF LUCK, BUT OF STRICT LAW

Egocentric life consists mainly of living life from the outside in. We see, hear, smell, taste and touch. Heck, my dog can do all of these! Yet, look around you. How many of the people that we associate with on a daily basis *react* to what they see, are influence by what they hear, or are only convinced that something is real only if it can be touched?

Their level of awareness is barely higher than that of an animal, whose only motivation in life is strictly instinctive. Hunger motivates them to eat, a sound motivates them to come or sit. In order to truly go after the things that we desire and to obtain the awesome potential that we all possess, we must leave the temporal aspects of our lives that is governed by our ego.

Competition is governed by our ego. The ego lies to us, telling us that we are unlucky, unfit or just plain unworthy. Ego tells us that in order for us to win, someone has to lose. Companies must "capture" the market share, or it's all over. What a restricted way to live!

Don't believe me? Then complete this sentence: "Opportunity only comes but _____."

Of course, most people would say "Once in a lifetime." WHO lied to us when they told us this? People who adopt this limited view of the world most certainly lose *all* motivation to succeed if they truly believed that the one and only opportunity already slipped by them!

Or how about this one: "The early bird gets the worm." Who said that there is only ONE worm?? If the worm isn't in front of you, then create the opportunity to be in front of it!

INSPIRATION AND THE TRUTH DEFINED

Lets separate ourselves from the Motivational to the Inspired. Begin to understand the elements of Truth. Purity, Humility and Justice are the basis of this understanding. A person of ego is always defending his petty interests and opinions. A person of Truth, who is inspired and aspires, takes up arms only against himself.

It is demanded of man that he shall continue to strive after better things, after greater perfection, after higher and still higher achievements; and in accordance with the measure of his obedience to this demand, does the angel of joy wait upon his footsteps and minister unto him; for he who is anxious to learn, eager to know, and who puts forth efforts to accomplish, finds the joy which eternally sings at the heart of the universe. First in little things, then in greater, and then in greater still, must man strive; until at last he is prepared to make the supreme effort, and strive for the accomplishment of Truth, succeeding in which, he will realize the eternal joy. The price of life is effort; the acme of effort is accomplishment; the reward of accomplishment is joy. Blessed is the man who strives against his own selfishness; he will taste in its fullness the joy of accomplishment.
~ James Allen

About Joseph

Joseph J. Culin is the founder and CEO of Culin Karate Center Ltd., one of the most successful Martial Arts Personal Development Academies in America. This Academy helps students in the areas of physical development, discipline, confidence and courtesy as well as self-defense. He holds Black Belts in several Martial Arts styles, and is currently a 6th Degree Master Instructor in the Korean art of Tae Kwon Do.

Joseph began his Academy following a very successful 20-year career at IBM, where he was involved in the development of security software used in the banking industry as well as in hospitals.

In 1996, he tested for his Black Belt in the art of Jhoon Rhee Tae Kwon Do, by Grand Master Jhoon Rhee himself. Master Rhee was Bruce Lee's friend and Instructor; took Muhammad Ali to the Black Belt; as well as testing Tony Robbins and members of Congress to the Black Belt level. This relationship and mentorship by Grand Master Rhee has had a great and lasting effect on Mr. Culin.

In 2007, Joseph was inducted by his peers into the United States Martial Arts Hall of Fame, for Outstanding Instructor of the Year in all 50 states. He is a Certified Instructor by the (ACMA) American Council of Martial Arts and by the Cooper Institute of Dallas, TX.

In 2002, he was named to Team America, a United States International Martial Arts Competition Team, to compete for the Gold Medal at the World Cup event in Honolulu, Hawaii.

Joseph is a graduate of St. Edwards University, in Austin, TX., where he graduated in 1992 with two degrees under full Scholarship.

He is also an accomplished Speaker, Mentor, Author and Business consultant, as seen on Fox News.

He resides in Volente, TX with his wife Julie and their two children.

For Information or to book Joseph, please visit
www.BlackBeltMentor.com
www.JoinKarate.com.
www.facebook.com/BlackBeltMentor

CHAPTER 29

SUCCESS ON YOUR OWN TERMS: HOW TO BUILD A BUSINESS AND LIFE THAT YOU LOVE

BY KATE BEEDERS

This is a really important subject for every entrepreneur. Our business is one of the greatest gifts we can give ourselves when we have a passion we want to share with the world and want to make a difference. The problem is it is so easy for an entrepreneur to get blocked, struggle, and head down the wrong path while trying to grow their business. When that happens, entrepreneurs tend to go into the place of frustration, disappointment and overwhelm. I have seen this happen time and time again with newbies and seasoned entrepreneurs.

I'd like to share with you how you can make those changes to build a business and life that you love. One of my favorite expressions I have is, *"The point of success is to enjoy the journey."* That is my mission!

Before I left the corporate world as a successful Business Development Executive, I was faced with a very big dilemma. Although, I loved my customers, there was something missing. I was making a lot of money, taking great vacations but working a zillion hours. As soon as I returned home from one vacation, I was booking the next trip. Things seemed out of balance and I was very stressed out. I felt as if I was working to go on vacation and there was something really backwards about that.

I believed there had to be a way to have balance in my life. But, everywhere I looked, I wasn't seeing anyone have that. Either, people were working very hard for their money or else had a job they loved, but were poor. There were no role models who seemed to have it both ways. I wondered if it were even possible. That question was one of the primary reasons I started my own business – to search for that answer.

During one of the worst economies ever, I started my business. I was truly ignorant of all it took to have a successful business. I didn't know that the majority of all businesses fail in the first few years. I thought that if you were really good at something and got business cards, the money would follow.

With my background in business development, I quickly built a prominent business and became known as a leading Success Coach. I had amazing clients, I garnered several accolades, and I had the income to match. I thought other entrepreneurs were experiencing the same thing. I was sadly mistaken.

As I looked around, I saw so many of my peers having trouble in the following areas:

1. Attracting ideal clients who valued them.

2. Making the money they needed.

3. Charging what they were worth (aka: their Self Wealth Worth).

4. Not taking action or taking the wrong action.

5. Not getting their business (and themselves) out in a bigger way.

They kept asking me what I was doing as it seemed so much easier for me. They wanted my secrets to success. That's when I started truly understanding each and every one of us has our own personal gifts to share with the world. This was mine.

I created a formula called the *Success Activator System*™ *f*or building a successful business quickly.

The Success Activator System (SAS)™ is a combination of my years of experience and expertise in the areas of Marketing, *Tapping* and the Laws of Attraction.

While I can't bring you to your full potential in one chapter I am really excited that I can get you started on your road to HUGE success. Below are first steps and real life stories that you can implement into your business RIGHT NOW.

Let's begin!

1. <u>You must have clarity of what you want.</u> As the expression goes, *"You can't hit a moving target."* Interestingly, I've found many entrepreneurs don't really know what they want, or even more importantly, are afraid to proclaim their hidden desires.

This is especially common for women who are wives and mothers. One of my clients, *"Susan,"* had a very hard time with this first step. She was a wife and mother of two grown children. For over twenty years, she took care of everyone else by putting herself second (and even third). No one had ever asked her what she really wanted. At first, when I asked her that question, it made her very uncomfortable. Not until I was able to shift her mindset to know she was worthy of this, was she able to share her desires. Once she did, she was on her way to actualizing her dreams of filling workshops.

Let's get you started with the vision of your business one year from now. Even if you've done this exercise before, I highly recommend you do it again as entrepreneurs often lose sight of this.

Here are a few of the questions you want to answer:

(a). What's your big "why"?

(b). What do you want your business to look like?

(c). Who are your ideal clients/customers and how do you want to work with them?

(d). How much money do you want to make?

(e). How will your life improve once you have this success?

(f). How will you feel after you've achieved this success?

Write your answers down in the form of a short paragraph and post it where you will frequently see it.

2. <u>This second part of my formula is critical as many entrepreneurs get stuck in their beliefs.</u> *How much do you believe you can actually achieve your vision a year from now?* On a scale of 1-10, rate your believability.

The reason this step is important is because I want to uncover what's holding you back from actually making your vision a reality. Your mindset is at least 90% responsible for your success (or your failure). What you believe is what you will attract. If you don't believe you can have it, you won't. End of story.

Beliefs are held in our subconscious mind, which is one million times more powerful than our conscious mind. These beliefs tend to fall into two categories, either *"core"* or *"limiting."*

<u>Core beliefs</u> are what we believe about ourselves. Examples are:

-I'm not good enough

-I'm afraid of success

-I'm afraid of failure

-I'm not good with money

-It will be too hard for me

One of my clients, *"Lisa"* worked with me because she was procrastinating about getting her website published. She (like many entrepreneurs) was a perfectionist, and had been holding off for over a year, waiting until everything was *perfect.* Lisa looked around and compared herself to successful people in the industry and thought her site didn't compare. Through our work together, I was able to help her understand that everyone has to start somewhere and that our own results improve with experience. After that, she quickly got her website published.

<u>Limiting beliefs</u> have to do with our views of the world and how we fit in. Examples are:

-There aren't enough hours in the day

-There's too much competition

-No one in this town would pay for this

-Not in this economy

-No one's spending any money

"Nancy" lived in a resort area that was busy nine months out of the year. For the 15 years she had been in business; she experienced a complete slowdown during the winter three months. All of her friends, who owned businesses, shared the same experience. She believed things would never change. I was able to help her shift her beliefs to create the business she wanted and have healthy revenue in those other three months.

Go somewhere quiet and take 30 minutes to write a list of all of the beliefs you have that are in the way of your success. Don't judge your beliefs. Just write.

Now, look at your list. These blocks are in your way and will continue to be in your way. These blocks will cause you to *"subconsciously"* sabotage your own success. Think about the times this has happened to you (or someone you know) in the past.

You're all set to do something that you're really dreading, but...

  – An emergency pops up...

  – You (or a family member) get sick...

  – You have a technical glitch...

  – You procrastinate instead of doing what's really important...

"Betsy" came to work with me because the previous month she blew her golden opportunity. She had been offered her first ever speaking paid *"gig"*. When the organization that hired her offered her $10,000 (because that's what they paid the previous speakers) as excited as she was, there was an even bigger part of her that was totally freaked out about this opportunity. She felt undeserving and was afraid she would blow it. Guess what happened? She got sick, lost her voice a few days before and never spoke at the event. Betsy was smart enough to not want that to happen to her again, so she hired me to clear out the negative beliefs she had. Since then, she's fully engaged successfully in all of her speaking opportunities.

The technique that I am an expert in to clear out negative beliefs is a phenomenal tool called *tapping*. It's the most powerful mindset technique I have ever experienced.

I came from a very traditional background and never, in a million years, would have expected that I would not only regularly use a technique like this, but also have built a successful business around it. This technique, when used by an expert releases negative stories, thoughts/beliefs and replaces them with positive ones.

This technique has helped hundreds of thousands of people around the world with various issues...anything from cravings...anger... disappointment...fears...overwhelm/stress...health issues...to PTSD. I use tapping to help my clients get "unblocked" and quickly getting into action.

When you look at your list of blocks, most likely, they can be cleared through the use of tapping with an experienced, highly trained/certified expert, such as myself. Once I clear out the negative beliefs, I replace them with positive ones, leaving my clients feeling in control, empowered, calm, focused, able to get into action, and attract abundance while feeling safe. You'll be amazed at how quickly your mindset shifts with *tapping*. Once your mindset shifts, anything and everything is possible.

Several years ago, I realized I had a fear of public speaking, which happens to be one of the top three fears in the world. I was offered an opportunity to host a radio show. As excited as I was about this, I also felt like a *"deer in the headlights."* I had never hosted a radio show in my life, or even been a guest on one. All of these fears popped up....*"What would I say?"..."Would people be interested?"..."How would my show compare with others?"*

Through the help of a fantastic *tapping* practitioner, I was able to let go of all of those fears and instead felt very excited about the radio show. Releasing that fear has led to so many more opportunities for me, such as, speaking on telesummits with over 500,000 listeners, having leading experts on my radio show, interviewed by many top people, speaking on stage and hosting my own live events. If I had never *tapped*, I don't even know if I would still have a business, as my fear would have held me back from putting myself out in a bigger way.

3. <u>The last part of my system is getting you into action.</u> This seems to be a piece that many entrepreneurs have a hard time with. They procrastinate. Many think that just by being really good at what they do, they'll make the money. Others are taking action to take action, without any real thought, clarity or strategy. You have to take *"right"* action.

If you're a newbie, clients aren't just going to come knocking at your door. You have to do the marketing, create programs/products and be able to "sell."

"Tina" was successful in the corporate world but was finding running her own business a very different experience. Especially, when it came to talking about money. When a prospective client would ask her rates, she would quote an amount, but then quickly offer a discount. She did this over and over again because deep down she felt very uncomfortable about what she was charging. She didn't think she was worth it. I was quickly able to get her to start to value her own worth. Not only did she get a new client that day, but at a much higher rate.

If you're a seasoned entrepreneur, it's equally important to look at what you're doing and how that fits in to your vision.

"Sandy" was making well over six figures when we worked together, but she was working every weekend, not going on vacations, not spending time with her family and not having any fun. She was taking lots of the wrong action by saying "yes" to everything even though it didn't line up with her vision. Through our work together and use of the *Success Activator System*™, she was able to *"fire"* her demanding clients, set boundaries for her weekends, raise her rates and finally go on that much deserved vacation with her family.

The really interesting thing I want to share with you is that success is not linear. That's a secret that most people don't know. If you're like me, you probably thought that once someone is successful, that's it. I learned a very valuable lesson earlier this year. Several things happened to me on a personal level where I had to put my business off to the side and take care of more pressing priorities. I put all of my other marketing efforts on hold.

Before I knew it, my business that I was so proud of, had almost disappeared. With the help of my coaches and the *Success Activator System*™, I worked through my fears (and there were many) that were blocking me from building my business back. As a result I built my business even faster than I expected. In fact, I didn't just get back to where I was; I built an even stronger, more solid business.

Here are the most commons responses I got at a recent event when I asked people I met if they were entrepreneurs:

"I wish I could be an entrepreneur."

"Maybe someday I can be an entrepreneur."

"I'd like to be an entrepreneur."

You made the decision to be part of today's fastest growing and most desirable industry. Be proud and enjoy it! To have the business and life you desire, you must have clarity about what you want, release any negative beliefs/stories in the way, and get into *"right"* action.

Reading this chapter has shown that you have a passion you want to get out in a much bigger way. Remember to ask yourself, "Am I dreaming BIG enough?"

Here's to your brilliance!

Names were changed for the purpose of this chapter.

© 2013 | Success Coaching with Kate | www.KateBeeders.com | All Rights Reserved

About Kate

Kate Beeders has been known worldwide as a Mindset, Money & Marketing Expert since 2010, and is founder of Success Coaching with Kate. Having been an award-winning Business Development Executive for over 15 years in Corporate America and more recently, an expert in helping Heart-Centered Entrepreneurs quickly make huge, life-changing mindset shifts, it's not a surprise that other established Thought Leaders and Marketing Experts turn to Kate when they're stuck in their own businesses.

She is a highly sought after Thought Leader, speaking at top events like 2011 and 2012 Tapping World Summit with a worldwide listening audience of over 825,000! Kate was also honored as an "*Exceptional Woman.*"

However, her greatest accomplishment is having the courage to follow her own path (which means manifesting amazing opportunities for skyrocketing business growth that others did not believe possible) and reaching six-figures in year 2 of her business.

With well over 25 years of business experience, Kate is now dedicated to working with small business owners, many of whom have quickly added thousands of dollars in sales after exposure to Kate's groundbreaking *Success Activator System™*. As a result of Kate's expertise and teachings, these entrepreneurs learn to quickly get unstuck, get moving and get the cash flowing. Once Kate touches someone's life, their journey is never the same.

Kate lives in the Boston area with her exceptionally smart, fun and the best Cairn Terrier in the world. Her most important mission is to teach entrepreneurs how to have *success on their own terms*.

For more information about Kate's *Success Activator System™* and to learn how you can build a business and life that you love, visit: www.KateBeeders.com

CHAPTER 30

7 STEPS FOR SUCCESSFUL NEGOTIATION RESULTS

BY OKSANA MAZOURIK

Negotiations are a big part of our everyday lives. We negotiate for the price of our house, our salary, our car and much more. Knowing how to negotiate well will make your life much more comfortable by both generating and saving you a great deal of money. And, the best thing you can do to help determine a successful negotiation outcome is to prepare! You can have a great product or service but if you come unprepared to your meeting it will significantly reduce your chances of getting an order or signing a contract. So take the time to prepare to get the best possible results because good preparation will be a key determinant for a successful outcome of the negotiation. In this chapter, we will look at 7 steps you can take to achieve successful negotiations with an outstanding final result.

STEP 1: PREPARE A NEGOTIATION STRATEGY

In preparing your negotiation strategy be sure to cover the following aspects:

- **WHAT IS THE OBJECTIVE (DESIRED OUTCOME) OF THIS NEGOTIATION?** Write down a list of all the "goals" which you would like to achieve through this negotiation. Then prioritize them in a list starting with the most important objectives of this negotiation.

- **MAKE A LIST OF YOUR "KEY SELLING POINTS":** Why should someone collaborate with you (or your company)? What do you offer that others don't? … An excellent service? … Faster delivery? … More competitive prices?

- **IS IT A NEGOTIATION FOR A SHORT-TERM OR LONG-TERM COLLABORATION?** Do you want to get the most out of it through hard bargaining (if it's a one-time transaction) or build a strong relationship? Are you planning on working again with this company or person? Or, is it a one-time sale after which everyone goes their separate ways?

- **BE PREPARED TO ANSWER QUESTIONS:** Put yourself in the other person's shoes and think through the various potential questions you are most likely to get asked. If you prepare the answers to these questions ahead of time, your approach will be more professional and your negotiation will go much smoother.

- **TRY TO DETERMINE WHAT IS MOST IMPORTANT FOR THE OTHER PARTY:** Focus and put emphasis on what your audience is most interested in – what is of most interest to them? Talking in terms of the other person's interest is a great way to move the negotiation/project forwards. It generates enthusiasm and eagerness from the other party to work with you because you are offering them exactly what they are looking for.

- **ASK THE RIGHT QUESTIONS:** If it is already an area in which you have a great deal of expertise, you will know exactly what questions to ask (best to have your list of questions ready in the form of a checklist). However, if it is a transaction in which you have limited knowledge – such as buying a used car – then you would be much better off preparing all the questions with someone who has the knowledge and experience in this area before finalizing the transaction. If you do not ask the right questions it is likely you will not find out about possible hidden problems until it is too late.

- **KNOWLEDGE IS POWER:** Be as informed as possible about the company you are working with because the better informed you are, the better the outcome is likely to be (even if it does not conclude in a deal).

- **PUT EMPHASIS ON PROFESSIONALISM** (efficiency, flexibility, brand-image profitability etc.): People like working with someone reliable and who knows his/her area of expertise.

- **STRUCTURE YOUR POINTS OF NEGOTIATION INTO TWO CATEGORIES—"STRATEGIC" AND "TECHNICAL":** Strategic points determine the "make or break" points of the agreement. Whereas, technical points would be points that need to be "discussed for a correct common understanding," and would be considerably less likely to be a reason for the agreement not to go through. Therefore, in your negotiations, start off by discussing the strategic points. Once the strategic points have been agreed upon, both parties basically agree to work together and it is just that some technicalities need to be worked out. Then go through the technical points together.

Tip #1: Get started by writing down a list of all the points that come to mind that you would like to cover with the other party. Now review the agreement and divide the points into two categories, strategic and technical. Once that is done, prioritize each point (within each category) in the order in which you want to address them in the negotiation.

Tip #2: Open the dialog with a 'lighter' point (basically whichever is most likely to get a positive response from the other party).

STEP 2: PREPARE SOME MORE FOR THE NEGOTIATION

Once you have prepared your negotiation strategy, prepare some more physically and psychologically by doing the following:

- **GET SOME GOOD REST:** Getting a good night's sleep before the meeting will help you focus and be at your 100%.

- **BE POSITIVE AND CONFIDENT** (not arrogant, just confident): Go to the negotiation with a smile, a positive attitude and confidence that everything will go well. You should feel sorry for the person who does not have your product or service. Be sincerely convinced of this, let your positive energy flow and let your enthusiasm and confidence set the overall spirit of the negotiation.

- **BODY LANGUAGE:** Let it work for you and not against you.

- **PERCEPTION:** People judge (consciously or subconsciously) – therefore, try to look professional and presentable. Have a look in the mirror before you go into your meeting.

- **PRODUCT SAMPLES:** Make sure you have all the product samples and information with you for an outstanding presentation.

- **MAKE PREPARATION A PRIORITY:** Make preparation for your negotiation meeting an important task on your list.

- **LEARN PEOPLES (FIRST AND LAST) NAMES** before you meet them – especially if it is a difficult name to remember.

STEP 3: THE NEGOTIATION SETTING

- **CREATE A POSITIVE AMBIANCE:** Create a comfortable and friendly ambiance for your meeting. A positive setting is more likely to produce a positive result and a greater willingness to collaborate.

- **KNOW YOUR AUDIENCE:** Is it a large multinational company? A local company? In the case of a foreign company, take cultural differences into account. Keep in mind that aspects that could be important to a large corporation could be completely irrelevant to a smaller-sized company and vice versa.

- **NEGOTIATE WITH THE DECISION MAKER:**
  – **Always negotiate with the decision maker.** This does not mean make the others feel left out, but try to ensure that the decision maker is present at the meeting.

  – **Be cautious of the two-party negotiation approach.** This is basically a technique where you negotiate everything with one person (presuming they are the key decision maker) and then they take all the negotiated points and submit them for "final approval" (after which you are most likely to get another hefty push to renegotiate all your conditions even further).

STEP 4: ESSENTIAL THINGS TO REMEMBER DURING THE NEGOTIATION ITSELF

- **STAY ON SCHEDULE:** By staying on 'schedule' you thereby ensure you have sufficient time to cover all important points.

- **OBSERVE BODY LANGUAGE and REACTIONS:** Observe body language and reactions. Business people are quite accustomed to controlling what they say, but the same cannot be said about controlling their facial expressions, mimics and body language. Expressive body reactions such as raising your eyebrows, frowning or even gently rolling your eyes come naturally (and therefore subconsciously). So use it to your advantage for greater insight into the situation.

- **MESSAGE RECEIVED:** Make sure your messages are going through. Make sure that you received a confirmation response, such as a verbal yes, an okay or a nod.

- **POSITION YOURSELF ON THE SAME SIDE AS THE OTHER NEGOTIATING PARTY:** Talk in the spirit that this is a mutually-beneficial deal. In conversation, where possible, unite yourself with the other party as "we" rather than separating each other as "you" and "us".

- **K.I.S. "Keep It Simple":** Over-complication can make the whole deal fall apart.

- **BE ENTHUSIASTIC:** Show willingness and enthusiasm to collaborate and to resolve all questions together.

- **FOLLOW YOUR NEGOTIATION PLAN:** While keeping a friendly ambiance, remember your key meeting objectives and the discussion points of your negotiations plan (be flexible, if required, to move things along smoothly).

- **THINK OF NEGOTIATIONS AS A DANCE:** If you are waltzing in the ballroom and there is an obstacle (for example another dance couple) naturally you would not run them over, but adjust by taking a little extra turn. Apply the same principle in negotiations.

- **GIVE AND TAKE - POWER BALANCE:** If you make a concession that favours the other party, make a counter-proposal for a concession that favours you on one of the 'things' you want.

Keep a balance.

- **FOCUS:** Silence your mobile phone, don't type on any devices and don't scribble on notepaper. All these gestures show disinterest.

- **SUMMARIZE YOUR KEY POINTS OF DISCUSSION:** After having discussed a key point, make a quick recap to make a 1-2 sentence recap to ensure everyone is on the same page.

- **NEGOTIATING IS A DISCUSSION NOT AN ARGUMENT:** If you are negotiating, it means both parties are interested in reaching an agreement. Negotiations are meant to improve relationships not ruin them.

- **EXPRESS UNDERSTANDING:** Express understanding, not necessarily conceding, but showing understanding.

- **GOOD NEWS SHOULD BE DIRECT (LOUD AND EMPHASIZED):** Not-so-good news should be diplomatic (quieter, and de-emphasized).

- **EXPRESS YOURSELF CLEARLY:** Formulate your message or thought in your head before saying it out loud to help your recipient understand your message clearly.

- **THE MOST RELIABLE NOTES ARE YOUR OWN:** Take notes during your meeting about the key points to which you can refer to for verifying if they have been implemented in the agreement.

- **BE SOLUTION-ORIENTED:** If you reach an obstacle in your discussions, remember to be solutions-oriented and to try to move forward smoothly.

STEP 5: TIPS – IF YOU GET STUCK OR FEEL AN UNCOMFORTABLE TURN IN THE NEGOTIATION

If your negotiation is not going according to plan, here are a couple of useful tips to get back on track:

- **SEPARATE THE PEOPLE FROM THE PROBLEM:** By separating the person from the problem, it will help you stay on better terms and resolve the issue more easily.

- **ACKNOWLEDGE THE PROBLEM:** Acknowledge that you understand the problem and ask how "we" – you and the other party – can find a solution. This will decrease the chances of a confrontation and restart a dialog aimed at getting results.

- **KEEP YOUR EYES ON THE PRIZE:** Do not get caught up on a point in the agreement that is not a deal-breaker for your negotiation.

- **USE YOUR CREATIVITY:** If you are at a point where neither party is budging, use your creativity to find solutions, ... 'think outside the box' ...break the tension.

- **LAWYERS AND AGREEMENTS:** Remember agreements are prepared by lawyers. Your goal of the agreement is to generate more income for you and your business. A lawyer's job is to defend if sued. Hence, the two objectives are not necessarily always the same.

- **LAWYER LANGUAGE:** If you get stuck on a legal phrase that does not make sense to you, then just ask them to re-write it in more "simple language" for the purpose of avoiding any confusion or misunderstanding.

- **"TIME-OUT":** If you are in a position during the negotiations where you are beginning to feel uneasy, not in control or unbalanced, then take a short break. However, take a time-out only if you are on the 'losing' side. It will give you the chance to gather your thoughts and discuss matters with your partners (but it also gives the other party a chance to regroup, so think wisely whether you want to use this option, because it mostly benefits the party with the disadvantage).

STEP 6: CLOSE THE DEAL

- **MOMENTUM:** Keep the momentum by making a prompt follow-up.

- **CONTRACTS:** If you have the option to go for a simple 2 to 3page contract with to-the-point clauses using clear and direct language, and without getting all kinds of lawyers and legal teams involved, that would be your best option. All product details can be added as annexes.

- **VERBALLY AGREED-UPON POINTS:** Make sure that all the verbally agreed-upon points have been put into writing in the agreement.

- **COMPARE TO YOUR NOTES:** Verify whether all verbally agreed-upon points have been implemented, do this by referring to your own set of notes.

- **UNDERSTAND THE AGREEMENT:** If the contract was prepared by the other party, read through it carefully multiple times to make sure you fully understand it with all associated implications. Highlight anything that is not clear to you, or if you think it could have a double meaning.

STEP 7: IMPLEMENT THE AGREEMENT AND START GENERATING RESULTS

- **GET STARTED:** There is no PAUSE after the negotiation has been completed. On the contrary, it is ACTION that should be taken.

- **BUILD YOUR REPUTATION:** Always be someone trustworthy, it will help you keep your existing clients, bring in recommendations and generate more business in the long term.

- **EVALUATE:** Evaluate what went well and what could have gone better during your negotiation.

About Oksana

Oksana Mazourik is an international marketing and sales expert who has been connecting people and products together across the globe. Oksana is a great enthusiast for creating new ideas and concepts and bringing them to market. Her entrepreneurial family background taught her to always think outside the box for finding the best solution. Hence, the art of growing companies and creating new businesses comes naturally to Oksana.

Using her multicultural understanding and linguistic knowledge of French, English, German and Russian, Oksana started her career as relationship manager at InterMedService. Oksana organized media events, press conferences and coordinated medical service activities for International VIP clients in Switzerland, Europe, Russia and Japan.

Thereafter, Oksana continued her career building and managing accounts as Export Manager at SANKOM (www.sankom.com). She successfully helped bring new innovative health and beauty products to market in over 90 countries worldwide, generating multi-million dollar turnovers and winning a series of awards. The international scope of the business took Oksana across many countries in Asia, the Middle East, Europe and North America.

Having gained extensive sales and marketing experience, Oksana took the challenge to the next level as Vice-President at SANKOM. As Vice-President, Oksana's core focus was new business development and overseeing international sales activities. Oksana set-up a Homeshopping and Direct TV division within SANKOM, and established TV sales in 20+ countries internationally, for a wide variety of different products. Having successfully put this division on a profitable and independently operational level, Oksana's new focus was to launch a premium body shapewear brand for retail, Avevitta (www.avevitta.com).

Starting from ground level, Oksana and her team worked on negotiating supply and distribution agreements, developing a brand-positioning strategy, product packaging, product sales policies and a unique marketing approach as well as the overall business plan. As a result, they launched Avevitta within 3 months on the market, opened a show room and own-brand store with 300+ products.

Oksana holds a Bachelor in Finance and Media from Webster University in Geneva, Switzerland and an MBA in Management from the Swiss Business School in Zurich, Switzerland. She has also completed executive courses Harvard University, Boston,

USA. Oksana holds several utility patents, which are successfully sold and marketed worldwide.

Fashion and design has always been one of Oksana's passions. As a hobby, she had designed clothes for personal wear, but with her passion for new business development, this hobby soon transformed into an International Luxury Womenswear brand, Ana Azur (www.ana-azur.com).

Oksana currently serves on the Boards of multiple companies. Having worked with a wide range of companies, ranging from multi-billion dollar corporations to small-medium-sized businesses, Oksana is your go-to person to help you grow your business and bring new products to market.

You can contact Oksana at info@ana-azur.com.

CHAPTER 31

QUANTUM LOVE:
THE ENERGY OF SUCCESS

BY PATRICIA TELLO, PhD

The winning way to health, wellness, wealth and anything possible for human beings is by finding our real essence. When we become aware that we are at one with the universe and that it is our personal responsibility to be the best we can be on a personal level, we will have the key to open the universal collective happiness.

The greatest stories of success have the ingredients of perseverance, hard work, commitment and achievement. I am so grateful to have experienced all of these in my own life and enjoyed them with my loved ones. But you can be sure that I would not be a testimony of complete healing without having experienced love in a way that I would have never imagined.

I have been practicing with success for many years what I call Quantum Love, "The Therapy of Love." When I thought of writing a book about it, questions came to my mind, such as: How can everyone receive this message? How to explain that we are not discovering anything? In the research for that book, I must confess I went through doubt and fear many times. Many scientists, professors, and doctors with whom I studied and who are my mentors, teachers, and guides, have written many wonderful and excellent books with valuable information. They have vast knowledge and experience. I thought to myself, "How am I going to write a book using quantum physics and quantum medicine principles and make it simple and easy to understand?" But once again, my heart responded saying, "You are writing about love, and the more complex you write, the further it will be from its essence. Love is simple." There it was! I did not have to make it complicated! Love is simple, marvelous and easy to comprehend.

The Therapy of Love has brought me satisfaction, and now I have the opportunity to transmit it to people that are and that have been in my life. Everyone can give and receive love in every possible way. Love has always been there, and the interesting part is that it has always belonged to us, even before we were born. Love is within us as a symbol that demonstrates the connection with other people and with the universe.

Sometimes we think that following the rainbow will take us directly to the treasure. We also think that looking at the past and staying there will give us the security to hold onto what we know, without facing fears or deciding to experience something new. What will drive us to win in all aspects of our lives is not in the past or in the future; it is not even something new. The responsibility of evolution in this world is a hundred percent ours. The choice to change paradigms and decide to be the observers of our lives, changing preconditioned patterns, can only be transformed with Love. In order to enjoy a life full of love, we have to practice love consciousness.

Being completely aware of love as a principle, knowing that it exists and how it vibrates within us, experimenting with it, practicing it with consciousness until we make it really ours, is the vehicle that will drive us to enjoy infinite possibilities of happiness, healing, achievement and manifestation of all our desires and goals. Practicing love as a life principle is fundamental to reach success at any level. We will develop love consciousness with perseverance and everyday practice. Love awareness comes to us through people with whom we are connected: people who give us peace, by their joyful presence, and at the same time bring us support. Love will grow within us at the moment we are helping someone, when we are doing unselfish and altruistic deeds. Consciousness of love is fundamental to create balance and harmony in our lives. The openness of awareness is infinite when we achieve love a hundred percent.

Why love? Simply because there is no other word that embraces the same deep meaning in all languages and beliefs. How did I arrive at this conclusion? You would think that this was already written, said, and sung in millions of love ballads. I arrived to the conclusion of love by my own journey. I was able to defeat an incurable disease. I experienced a leap of healing when I realized that in order to see the light we also have to know darkness. It was a learning experience that turns into a complete healing when I felt unconditional love transmitted by my healer.

If we have a hundred percent negativity in our lives, the opposite of love is not hate as many of you would think. The opposite of love is indifference, no love, nothing. Without love, humans die. No sickness or disease can be overcome if there is no love to support us. There is proof of miraculous healings of the most dangerous and incurable diseases that exist, but still there is no scientific evidence proving that a fatality can be caused by a lack of love. Lack of love is the excessive influence of negativity, which destroys a human being. Why do we have to use creativity in negative ways that result in self-destruction? Why is it that many of the devices and procedures that have been created to simplify our lives in practical ways are being used against us, harming our physical, mental and spiritual health?

Love is today. Love is the connection with our present, with nature, with the universe. Love is being able to enjoy every moment. Love belongs to us just as the air we breathe. Love is vital energy. Searching for the meaning of love in our lives is very important. Making it grow from within and sharing it is fundamental in order to get the balance that we need. Religion, spirituality, and now science with quantum physics give us the basis with which to explain so much about the human being as observed from different angles. Love is a feeling, a thought, an expression, a path, an exercise, and a remedy for health. It is complete healing. Love consciousness makes us smile from the soul, from within our hearts, without limitations. With it, we are in tune with other human beings. Smiles are contagious; they are good energy we radiate outwards. If we are in the vibration of love, positive and in balance, our thoughts will be positive all the time, and we will attract to our lives progressive results, responses, and positive changes. In this quantum world, we are all connected, and positive vibration is shared with the people that surround us.

Love is here, always is, always has been and always will be. Unconditional love is timeless; it is the love that completes the meaning of wholeness. In the Therapy of Love, we find that love is not to believe in something; Love is to know that what we are and feel makes us big, because it is not the beginning or the end of a paragraph; Love is the content. Love is something that we do not perceive or see, but it is something that we can feel. Love is that subtle energy which is produced from our core, the heart, to create divine intelligence, and this brings us closer to awareness, to consciousness. Real knowledge is not to accumulate information. Real knowledge is to learn how to love. Love is the vehicle to achieve knowledge and not the goal. By making our intuition grow, we allow the expansion of our intellectual knowledge. If we observe nature and understand it as perfect love with perfect cycles, days, hours, and seasons, we can slowly accept that we belong to that perfection and forever-functioning universe.

At the moment of real love, we will make space for our evolution because we will enter a world in which we will do things that we now imagine impossible. We must prompt ourselves to understand that the universe and humanity are an intelligent wholeness that will take us to the consciousness of love. To grow in consciousness is to grow in spiritual love, and we have to work on this constantly to make it our own daily routine. Routine is a critical part of our inherited behaviors. We have to work daily, filling our interior universe with love. The difference between a person who achieves and one who struggles is his perception, intuition, intention, and creativity.

What science refers to as health is what religion calls God, and this is what spirituality calls consciousness or enlightenment. All of these terms are exactly the same thing! We have the universal language that science has proven, religion has taught us, and spirituality has enlightened. This universal language is Love.

How can we live in the present? We can by doing and being in the now, reorganizing past experiences and seeing the positive future. Thinking in the past should be to feel grateful that we are here for a bigger purpose, using everything that we have experienced as a lesson preparing us to become who we are. Remembering good experiences feeds our souls. Going over bad experiences, reorganizing them in our subconscious, we are able to store them away with a different reality, which will not allow them to make us uncomfortable, sad or traumatized. The moment we think of the future is to reprogram our destiny. We have infinite possibilities to create, invent, enjoy, learn and be the best we can be. Let's make the most out of ourselves, knowing that we have something wonderful that everybody collectively enjoys.

The good news is that we possess the tool to open the door to wellbeing, happiness and wealth. This tool is going to help us be and feel closer to our higher self, to lead us and enlighten our path so that we can change our preconditioned minds. We will not only reach overall health, but also our greatest potentials. This, the tool that will extract the best out of us, is love. Don't search for the truth. The truth will come on its own. Quantum love's reality is the decision to set out on our path to the universal truth, having that perseverance to achieve our goals, reaffirming that we are one with the universe, choosing the closest road to health and finally, helping us to cross the portal to positive health. All of the "extras" will come soon of their own accord when we vibrate in love. These bonus gifts are inner peace, happiness, motivation, determination, openness, energy, health, and wealth. The past exists for us to be thankful, to create. By being in the present, though, the truth does not need to be searched for. It will come by natural law.

The mind does not recognize positive or negative. It only recognizes the commands we give it to anticipate our coming events, even way before we can even perceive them. This is why there are so many people that say, "Why does everything always go wrong for me?" Well, there's the answer: it's because they have brought it into their reality by constantly believing it to be true. Isn't it true that when we are in love and happy, everything turns out the way we want it to? Everything just falls into place perfectly? This happens because our body aligns itself to how we feel and how we want to be. The only thing we want to experience is pleasure, the feeling of absolute happiness, believing that we can achieve anything we want which we believe will give us that feeling of completeness. In this case I'm referring to physical love, which we feel when we're physically attracted to our significant other. You see, the love that takes us deeper and much farther than physical love, the love that makes us overcome the impossible, is universal love, quantum love. This is the love that religions refer to, the one attributed by spirituality. It is the one that science speaks of as the best physical state of the body, health. We will discover that in the end, everything is the same. In the end, we will all talk about and relate to the universal language of LOVE.

About Patricia

Patricia Tello was born in Lima, Peru, her father a Pediatrician, and her mother a businesswoman. Her childhood was very family-oriented; she was also raised with a very strong approach to natural and alternative medicine, which is strong in the ancient Incas culture.

At age 18 she married and moved to Venezuela where she lived for the next 6 years, in Venezuela she finished her English studies at the University of Carabobo. She was dedicated to her family, but always with the idea of maintaining balance by starting with the family. She returned to Lima for three more years and began her search in creativity, she joined an Art institute, but realized that creativity is important in life and that it could be done from a different approach.

Due to her husband's job, they were relocated to the United States, settling in the Washington, D.C. Metro Area. She continued to dedicate herself to her family while she reached a very important position within the Hispanic community by writing motivational articles for the Washington Hispanic newspaper since 1999. She started working with the Hispanic community in the Washington, DC area giving tips of empowerment for the community to "Do it Yourself" and encouraging them on how to be healthy, live more organized and giving different ways to grow as an individual and as a community.

In 2005, she began a Radio show called *Revista Latina* with all types of tips about good nutrition, organization, and health improvement. She then became a producer of the project that soon was a TV show through a very prestigious Hispanic Network (Univision) with one-minute videos of practical tips for everyday living. During this time she was also invited to be the Latina presenter for many American cultural events.

While working on TV she became aware of the importance and the influence that TV personalities have on the community, and she realized that she wanted to gain more knowledge and accreditations in order to further motivate and help the people in a more profound way. Patricia's main goal was to help her community grow in so many aspects; she wanted to be an example of perseverance by proving that if she could, then everybody could do so too.

This is when she began her studies of Natural Medicine in Mexico and immediately enrolled in the university to get her degree of Bachelor in Health Science. Patricia continued her studies and received her Quantum Medicine, PhD Diploma in 2012, turning herself into a strong personality in her new path. She is a very active participant of Quantum Medicine, as a Quantum Activist. During this time she has developed therapy called *Quantum Love* and is in the process of writing her book *Quantum Love, The New Medicine* which will soon be published and shared with love for everyone.

CHAPTER 32

HOW TO BECOME A SUCCESSFUL ENTREPRENEUR IN FIVE SIMPLE STEPS

SHAWN CHHABRA

The Law Of Attraction is the name given to the belief that "like attracts like" and that by focusing on positive or negative thoughts, one can bring about positive or negative results.

I strongly believe in the *Law of Attraction* as it has always worked for me without fail. It works, but you need to learn how to use it properly! I am always focused on "what I need and what I want," and so it's a matter of focusing on your desired outcome. You must be strongly focused to achieve your desired outcome, and then it will work for you.

Here is the latest proof of the *Law of Attraction* at work: I wrote this book with Mr. Brian Tracy. I focused intently on writing with one of my favorite coaches, and Brian Tracy was one of them. This book is living proof that if you want something and focus on it you will get it!

How can an immigrant from a poor town get all this and more? I love to work hard because I love what I do. I have always been disciplined and focused.

I was born in an immigrant family in India where my parents did not have much support or opportunities. They started with nothing and I still have memories from my childhood of going for gleaning with my siblings for the wheat and rice from other farms -- all of our crop was gone. That kind of scarcity of food and resources made me stronger, as it developed a good work ethic, discipline, and the value of time.

My parents taught me the value of discipline, hard work and especially risk taking. They showed me what it meant to be inspired and to give all I could and leave the rest up to God. They also taught me the Law of Karma from the Holy Book *Gita* that we can only control our work and action, but not the outcome.

> *Takeaway: You cannot control what happens to you, but you can control your attitude toward what happens to you, and in that, you will be mastering change rather than allowing it to master you.*
> ~ Brian Tracy

During my initial years at West Virginia University, I faced some tough financial times. This taught me important life skills to cope, and I emerged stronger. The Law of Attraction worked and I got the opportunity to work with Dr. Charles Wales who developed "*Guided Discovery*" at the Center for Guided Design, WVA University.

I contributed to this by testing several concepts during the development of his new text book he was compiling for the classes being taught at university level. I learned a lot during that period and whatever I am able to write today, I owe mostly to Dr. Wales.

The learning from Dr. Wales helped me to develop the process being introduced here. I have been using the following 5 steps for all my activities and decision-making. It has kept me on the track to success, and will help you to become a successful entrepreneur.

THE 5-STEP PROCESS

I call it *Defining-Refining* because it is being defined - redefined and reevaluated, tweaked continuously. This process will help you make the continuous appraisal of your efforts, and will shorten the time you spend on a bad idea. You will quickly move towards the right direction.

<u>Step ZERO: (Pre-qualifier)</u>: This is about you! You must qualify for this initial phase in order to even try to become a successful entrepreneur.

If your answers are "YES" to most of the following questions, then this is for you. If not, then try helping someone else to reach their dreams.

> *If you don't design your own life plan, chances are you'll fall into someone else's plan. And guess what they have planned for you? Not much.*
> ~ Jim Rohn

- Do you ever dream?
- Are you passionate about your dream and motivated enough to act upon it?
- Do you really have the *"GUTS"* to risk anything for your dreams?
- Do you have courage to face the fear of failure?
- Do you have the basic qualities of successful people – like being personable and able to deal with various personality types? Are you trustworthy, sincere, and a good listener? Do you value and manage your time?
- Are you willing to work at least a *HALF-DAY* — EVERYDAY? Before answering this question, make sure you refer to WIKI: A day is a unit of time. In common usage, it is an interval equal to 24 hours. I love this definition of a day!

Are…You…Still…With…Me? (Good, then keep reading…)

> *Takeaway:* It doesn't matter where you are coming from. It's very important to keep your eyes focused where you are headed.

STEP 1: SITUATION ANALYSIS

You should define the situation by writing down every single thing that comes to mind. Whatever you are thinking to do, whatever you have around you, whatever you think you want to be doing.

Write down every single thought. Are you looking for a job or are you interested in starting a business? Keep thinking and keep writing as every single detail will be helpful in your next steps to make better decisions.

What are your major skills that might help you in business? Who are the people who may be willing to help you or guide you to be successful? Who are the people available to devote some of their time to your business success?

What type of business would you like to start and why? How are you going to get there?

EXAMPLE: *This is just a fictitious case study, and we have limited time and space to write the full details in this article. (I can show you the expanded version of these strategies in my book- (coming soon)- Title: The Winning Way - Shawn Chhabra's Way! Introducing the Defining-Refining Process!*

By the time you finish reading the chapter (or book) you will see how we can create a business out of thin air with bare minimum resources, and we will be able to plan the expansion of business for going from Garage to Global! This study will lead you to create something out of nothing, and ultimately everything!

SITUATION ANALYSIS:

- I am interested in the food business, maybe the grocery business
- I like to serve people as I used to work in an ice cream shop earlier in my career
- I can run a restaurant, and I will be happy if it's Italian

  I don't want to deal with chefs and maintenance or other liabilities with a brick and mortar business. I prefer to run the business like Tim Ferriss taught in his Best Seller 4-Hour Work Week! Therefore, it's running a food business without dealing with chefs, waiters, or any liabilities.

> *Takeaway*: Details are gold nuggets as this information will help you fine tune to a better situation to start the next phase of your life.

STEP 2: GOAL SETTING

In this step we are looking for all the possible goal options -- nothing good, bad, small, or big because at this time we just need the options list to evaluate later. Write down all the possible goal options. I would just keep writing every single goal that comes to mind, based upon the situation you just defined in the previous step.

Then you will list pros and cons to evaluate and pick the best goal option in the current situation. Later during the redefining cycle, you will try your second best goal option, if the first one does not prove to be the successful goal option that you had anticipated.

For example (possible Goal Options):

- I can do an Italian restaurant.
- I can start a food delivery business.
- I should start an online order-taking business to distribute food from multiple cuisines from local restaurants and outsource most of the operation.
- I can have a banquet business.

Your gut feeling will always help you define the moment and make decisions. You should know your goals and what success means to you, and sometimes it will not be the same as how other people measure success. You must have guts to pursue your own goals and ultimately succeed.

Success is not a matter of chance, you have to work assembling all the forces in one direction. It's almost like creating a magnet by aligning all the electrons (forces) in one direction. Find your dream goals, focus, and act on them.

You must know what you want otherwise you are just living a life like any member of the animal kingdom. That's just living to survive and nothing more!

We must finalize our best goal option for our case study as that info is needed in Step #3. Let's say we evaluated the situation and goal options in detail and our first choice of goal option is: **"All-In-One *Restaurant Food Delivery Business.*"**

> *Takeaway*: The moment you know what you want, what you want to achieve, what you want to become and what you want to be remembered for, you are already ahead of the game.

STEP 3: PLANNING PHASE

Now you are looking for planning and blueprint options to get to your goal you selected in Step 2. This is based upon the situation defined in Step 1, and our selected goal option to pursue is "All-In-One *Restaurant Food Delivery Business.*"

You need to write down all the planning options and evaluate and pick the best plan for the moment. In later stages you will be reevaluating the whole process, and have to pick the second or third best plan. This helps in case the first option fails to deliver the desired results.

EXAMPLE--Planning Options List:
- Buy an existing business
- Lease a van and hire a driver
- Talk to several taxi companies about their taxi drivers doing the deliveries

Let us say in this example we evaluated all the pros and cons and decided to pick, "***Food Pickup and Delivery Through Taxi Company***" as the best option to implement so far.

We can also source online and take phone orders through an outsourced company. If we outsource some functions, then we can probably run this business from our kitchen table or out of our garage.

Takeaway: Every experience, especially a failure will make you stronger, and prepare you for the next challenge. Don't start feeling negative when something goes wrong or someone mistreats you, as dwelling on these circumstances is simply a waste of time and energy.

STEP 4: FUN PHASE

Now is the time for action. Act upon whatever blueprint/plan you picked as the best option. You need to implement the plan to establish the business by contacting the restaurants so that they are part of your food supplier network.

You also need to partner with taxi companies for food pickup and delivery. You will need to plan on finding the customers who will order the food from you from menus in network restaurants..... Order taking and marketing can be outsourced.

STEP 5: EVALUATION

In this step, we will be evaluating and adjusting the strategies and actions for all the four steps. We will be doing this continuously. We don't have enough time and space to repeat these steps multiple times. The continuous evaluation helps correct things early and gives less chance of failure.

Planning and preparation have a crucial role in creating success. Planning provides us the opportunity to see if something we planned is not working, make tweaks, and reframe your strategies to move forward appropriately.

You must stay focused! You have to be evaluating if you are moving in the right direction or not. The moment you realize that you are not progressing as desired, just stop and go over these five steps again to tweak them. You need to find out in which step of the process you were not right in making the selection, and simply redo each step.

THE SOONER YOU REDO IT, THE LESS EXPENSIVE IT WILL BE

You want to take risks, but only educated ones. You must weigh risks and benefits thoroughly and always consider worst-case scenarios.

You have to make sure that you are not just taking the same action again and again hoping for a better outcome. Most failures and difficulties are opportunities in disguise.

Treat the failures as opportunities to improve. You are not the only one facing failures, as many of the greatest entrepreneurs have openly admitted that their initial efforts brought them many failures.

If you are facing failures and having tough times making decisions, then you need to take a timeout. Take a break! You probably need some down time to reflect and to be more efficient and productive.

If you are not getting the desired results, you need to revisit all the steps again in order to define the new situation. Then, look for the best option, and plan for it. You need to be prepared and ready for anything at any moment to be successful.

Embrace the change!

> *When I was young I observed that nine out of ten things
> I did were failures, so I did ten times more work.*
> ~ George Bernard Shaw

Takeaway: Give it your personal best, stay laser-focused. Focus on the things you can control and don't waste time and energy on uncontrollable situations. Learn that you can only control your own response and attitude and not every situation.

CONCLUSION

As you can see, we just created a business that offers all cuisines to be delivered to customers. We get the food from the best restaurants available at a discount, and then use local taxis for pickup and delivery.

In other words, it's a business in Tim Ferriss' 4-hour workweek style! It's a scalable business that can be franchised and can be expanded to other cities and countries. We can grow from garage to global business in no time and we created this business out of thin air!

Here are two thought-provoking quotations to think on:

> 1. *After you become a millionaire, you can give all of your money away because what's important is not the million dollars; what's important is the person you have become in the process of becoming a millionaire.*
> ~ Jim Rohn

2. Here is part of a poem copyrighted by Jake Steinfeld:

> *Success is failure turned inside out -*
>
> *The silver tint in the clouds of doubt,*
>
> *And you never can tell how close you are,*
>
> *It might be near when it seems afar;*
>
> *So stick to the fight when you're hardest hit -*
>
> *It's when things seem worst that you must not quit.*

Takeaway: Have confidence to set your goals and pursue them. Fear nothing, be accountable and take responsibility, take action, make decisions, and above all – be human. Celebrate your successes, big or small, and seek happiness!

About Shawn

Shawn Chhabra is a successful entrepreneur, educator, business coach and marketing executive who resides in Saint Louis, MO. He holds both his Bachelor's and Master's degree, and places great emphasis on a solid education. Shawn has leveraged his educational background to become an author, coach, mentor, and curriculum creator for several online institutions.

He has worked within several industries including food, clothing, retail, IT, and holistic health. He is a big believer in healthy living, and has put this concept into play with his work directly. He is very in tune with practicing what he preaches, and often writes about his life experiences to enrich the lives of others.

A Man Who Wants To Reach Others Through His Passions

Shawn has always wanted to reach people through education. He brings his vast expertise of business and holistic practices to his coaching and publishing business. Shawn believes in treating his clients like they are his brothers and sisters—this is modeled after his favorite Sanskrit saying: "the world is one family."

Shawn is featured as one of the America's PremierExperts® at: www.americaspremierexperts.com/directory/shawn-chhabra.php

Shawn has also been quoted on national media networks, including ABC, CBS, NBC and Fox affiliates.

In the process of expanding educationally and professionally, Shawn mastered the process of Defining-Refining™. This is a process utilizing the continuous evaluation and tweaking of strategies in order to lower the risk of losses.

He Has Put What He Has Learned Into Words For Others

Shawn Chhabra has authored several books, including the #1 Best Seller:

Weight Loss by Quitting Sugar and Carb (ISBN-10: 1494449285, B00GUXOCNM), and *Dash Diet: Heart Health* (ISBN-10: 1494966212, B00HAVX3UQ) and also the best seller – *Time Management, Life Management, Stress Management* (ISBN-13: 978-1495469022). The *Time Management, Life Management, Stress Management* is a book that shows you what it really means to stay in control of your life. Though you may feel bogged down by commitments and a lack of time to complete them all, sometimes it's simply a matter of staying organized. Shawn Chhabra's Time Management book can be an excellent tool in helping you to do just that.

It's Time To Take Control of Your Time and Your Life and Learn How To Do That!

Shawn is happily married to the beautiful Indu, and they have four wonderful children. He understands the value of family and this is his first priority in life. Shawn and Indu are proud parents of three daughters, Anshul, Taniya, Tarika and their son Anuj (Sunny) and son-in-law Matt Schwartzkopf.

Shawn and Indu have co-managed their wholesale computer business for the last 14 years. The computer business website can be visited at: www.laptopuniverse.com. Shawn has a website where he puts all of his work and practice into play and it is: www.shawnchhabra.com where you can learn even more about him and his work.

<u>Shawn's favorite quote:</u>
Give a man a fish and you feed him for a day.
Teach a man to fish and you feed him for a lifetime.
~ Traditional Proverb

CHAPTER 33

MY STORY

BY KELLEE SPILLMAN

Some could say I'm just a small town girl who just made a lot of good choices along the way to her success, however I would say they are wrong. I've been blessed along the way by SO many people! I will say the key to winning in life is to GIVE. You can never go wrong giving to people as long as it is for the right reasons. You never know who you will touch or the major influence you could have over someone's life. You never know what you will add!

My story is about not just about me but the great people I met along the way who gave to me in different ways to mold and shape who I am today. This has everything to do with my successes!!! Whether it was skills, advice, time invested into my life, words of encouragement **or most importantly**, belief in me! These have all been gifts to my life in one way or another.

GROWING UP

I grew up in Hemet, California "home of the newlywed and nearly dead" or at least it used to be. Forty years ago it was a simple town like "Mayberry." I was raised by a single mom from the time I was nine years old. My mom had been out of the workplace for a long time, and when herself and my dad divorced, she had to start all over. Her first job back was working for a retail Window Shade Company. She actually glued the trim on the scallops of window shades as her first job back to the workforce after nine years. Prior to that she had worked in the nursing field. I watched my mom work at that job day-in, day-out never complaining, and always grateful to have a job while being promoted over and over. The little shade shop known as Sun Control Shade Company, in Hemet, California eventually became a large wholesale window covering company called NS Industries. This company sold all types of hard window coverings throughout the entire state of California. The three-man little shade shop became a 125-man show as the company grew. My mom, **Lupe Overton**, grew with it – eventually becoming the overseer/ office manager for this successful growing operation.

BIG INFLUENCE OF MY LIFE

As I started junior high school, I was ready to start working. I made blinds every day after school to save for my first car. When I was in high school, I learned computers and was able to work doing data entry at the blind company. My mom made sure I kept busy with work and many outside activities, and sacrificed a lot to keep up with all of the expenses associated with the activities I enjoyed. Eventually I graduated high school and moved to Upland to live with my dad while attending school at Cal State, Fullerton. Soon after, I went back to work for NS Industries, only, at this point, as an outside Sales Representative in Orange County. The owners of NS Industries**, Dawn and Pat Ennes** would eventually become amongst the group of the most influential people in my life to this day. They had high very expectations and yet always showed me they believed in me! It was the BEST feeling ever! I watched them take a small shade shop and grow it with hard work, determination, perseverance, integrity, and "yes"- power and innovation! They were the best bosses I ever had and I am grateful to this day for their example!

MY SALES CAREER

Each day I convinced designers, decorators, homebuilders, and Home Building Centers as to why they needed to order their custom hard window coverings through NS Industries. I called on about 8-10 clients per day per city. My very first sales manager was **Bill Havens**. I still consider him the best sales manager I have ever had… rest his soul. I shall never in my life forget him as he taught me simple but extremely valuable sales skills. Bill had many little sayings that were solid sales truths that still play in my head to this day! He took the art of selling very seriously. He would go out on sales calls with me and analyze my every move from body language to eye contact to the inflection in my voice! This was all over and above my "spiel" as he called it. He would grade me on how well I did, and provide me with constructive criticism after each call. This man invested a ton of time and energy making sure I took selling seriously. When I would solidify a new account, I couldn't wait to share with him. At the age of eighteen, I was earning a great salary, had a company car and had an excellent commission package, so I stopped going to college and focused on my sales career.

TRANSITION TO REAL ESTATE

At nineteen, I was married and by twenty one I had my first born, Tyler. By twenty five, I had my daughter Khylee. At the age of twenty-six, I was still selling blinds as a wholesale blind rep but now I worked for a National Company. The recession had hit and the smaller operations like NS Industries didn't survive. There came a point where I decided – since my children were getting older – I didn't want to be so far away from them during the day. My territory kept growing and my drive was getting longer and longer. At the beginning of my sales career, I covered one county, then I covered three counties, and eventually was responsible for the entire state of California. The blind business was competitive and the sales people were stretched thin. I realized this was not good for my family, so I decided to apply at a local title company for a job as a sales representative at the excellent advice of my friend **Heather Jensen,** so I could work in a smaller territory closer to home. This transition began my career in Real Estate.

TRIAL BY FIRE!

I worked for Orange Coast Title as an outside Sales Rep for five years and loved it. My territory was Riverside then Moreno Valley, CA. I called on twenty to twenty-five Real Estate offices daily. My focus was to gain market share by getting new clients (agents) to use OCT as their title company! The market was tough at this point in 1993, and eventually Moreno Valley saw a 70% foreclosure rate. The recession was in full force and the housing market was suffering terribly. Nevertheless, I still had to make a living and was commission-motivated. By year 5 at Orange Coast Title, I was awarded Sales Person of the Year. Once I received my plaque, pen and check for $250.00 I decided to move on. 80% of the agents I was calling on had zero sales skills and were making good income.

At this point I stepped out of my comfort zone, obtained my Real Estate license and worked as a Manager at Home Life Real Estate in Moreno Valley, CA. A gentleman by the name of **Mando Hernandez** believed I had the ability to manage a Real Estate office. I don't know what I was thinking, accepting a job as a manager when I had never even had my Real Estate license before. Talk about trial by fire!! After all, I was managing Real Estate agents who had been in Real Estate a long time. Who was I to think I could offer them anything?? They were not too excited, let alone cooperative. Well, I tell you... my sales skills really came in handy here. You see, when I took over managing this office, the office had been performing poorly. In fact it was deep in the red. I took over and turned it around in a little over a year - teaching 'Sales Skills 101' to agents who desperately needed self-discipline! And although I had no Real Estate experience, I had excellent tried and true sales experience, and was able to give the agents the tools I learned along the way!! It was one of the most painful experiences of my life, but ONE of the best as I look back. I am grateful to Mando for seeing in me what I could not see in myself at the time, and taking a risk and providing me that opportunity! Eventually my family moved to Canyon Lake and I went to work for a Real Estate office in Temecula and added loans to my repertoire while practicing Real Estate.

GREAT CAREER MOVE

In 2000, I was offered a job managing an office in Temecula called Reliable Realty Inc. The company had no agents and sat dormant for a year, so the Loan Company, owned by two men, were on the lookout for someone to run it and handle the leads they provided. Eventually, I became very busy and had to hire agents to help with leads. We went from one to five agents in about a year's time. We moved from a cubicle in a professional office building to an actual office in Murrieta within a year. Our office continued to thrive, and in 2004 we closed 99 deals. I recruited agents and worked on my own Real Estate business at the same time. I was a working broker, which is often frowned upon. However, I was always was taught it is better to lead by example! On a side note, I decided to go back to college and finish my bachelor's degree in Business Management at the strong suggestion of my dad, **Hal Overton**. My dad is a STRONG advocate of learning and higher education and beyond. After all, he attained his Real Estate license at the age of seventy three!

A BEAUTIFUL PARTNERSHIP!

In 2005, I was afforded an opportunity to buy out one of the partners – which I took. I now owned 49% interest in Reliable Realty. In 2005, our little office sold 160 homes! In 2006 the market slowed and I started Reliable Realty Property Management. I had done research regarding Property Management as part of my school project and learned it was a necessary evil for Real Estate. By the way, I finally graduated from University of Redlands in 2007 just before turning 40! My Bachelor degree in business was a bit painstaking while running a business and having a family, but worth it!

THE NAME OF THE GAME – REO

In 2006 as the housing market crashed I learned everything I could learn about bank-owned properties and began listing and selling REO's (bank owned listings). I attended REOMAC – a conference in Palm Desert. At this point, I learned you had to spend money to make money. The conference set me back $1,200.00, which was a lot at that time when sales were slow. However, I was fortunate enough to meet a wonderful lady who became one of my very good friends. Her name was **Leanne Walker**. She had been listing and selling bank-owned properties in Denver for sometime and agreed to train me and introduce me to her contacts. **What a God Send**!! At one point with the help of my now best friend and agent **Naomi Putney**, I personally had 176 active REO listings at one time. I went to every Bank-Owned conference I could attend - one year I attended 12 conferences! I made every contact I could, and joined every organization I could while prospecting banks and asset management companies. I was building my personal team of people and building my office business at the same time. In 2008 and 2009, our office closed nearly 400 escrows!

MY BOUTIQUE REAL ESTATE OFFICE

In 2009, I bought my partner out of Reliable Realty and became sole owner. Our extraordinary little boutique firm made up of about twenty five agents moved to an amazing office in Old Town Temecula. We have not only continued to survive but have thrived in every market!

OPPORTUNITIES

In 2008, I was invited to be the VP of Corporate Affairs for NAHREP Inland Empire. Over time, I have been asked to be on the Advisory Board at MSJC. I have sat on numerous committees, and served as moderator and speaker on numerous occasions at Real Estate Conferences abroad.

LESSONS LEARNED

I have learned a lot of life lessons along the way. **Valuable life lessons.** Hard work and determination are all good, but it is the heart to give and help others which is the most important. All the people who helped me along the way get to where I am, I owe! My mom taught me to always look for how to be a blessing to others. My dad has taught me to stretch myself to the point of pain and never stop learning or growing as person! My kids have taught me humility! My friends have taught me that the richness of life has to do with what is free! I aspire to be successful, not for me, but for all whom I can touch and bless. I have learned if I follow my passion, the money will follow. Work hard, take chances, achieve goals, extend happiness to others. The ultimate key to my success has been giving back! It is my intention to give to others any way I can – including supporting our local charities.

THINGS I WISH I KNEW WHEN I WAS A FIRST TIME HOMEBUYER

I have sold over 600 homes as an agent working for buyers in my Real Estate Career and I have some important advice to give to buyers. It's simple and practical, and yet most buyers don't understand the concept until they are on their third or fourth home. My advice is this – don't be an emotional buyer! A home purchase needs to be thought of as in investment, and investments are to be thought of as something that will increase in value. However, I have buyers who still wish to buy without thinking about what the value will be when they decide to sell their home! Location is very important as we all know, but tax rates and HOA fees are extremely important, as it will affect the desirability of the house when the buyer sells. There are some areas in California that have a base tax rate of 1.25, but by the time you add the Mello Roos and

Special Assessments to the tax rate, you are looking at a rate over 3%. On a $300,000 home the monthly taxes alone would be nearly $800.00.

As a buyer you must buy something everyone else will want. You must look at a purchase as an investment and remember the key factors that will make it a good investment. Location, accessibility, style, amenities and yes, tax rate!

My words of advice for sellers:

Listen to your Real Estate agent. Do your homework and put your house in the best marketable position possible, and whatever you do ... DON'T overprice your home!!

About Kellee

Kellee Beth Spillman, CEO/ REO Director/Broker of Reliable Realty Inc., is a leader in the ever- changing Real Estate Industry. She is a licensed Real Estate Broker with extensive knowledge in foreclosures, REO dispositions and short sale negotiations. Since joining Reliable Realty Inc, Kellee Spillman has been instrumental in expanding the company and establishing its reputation as one of the top Bank-Owned Foreclosure Brokerages in California. In 2005, Kellee was made partner/ President at Reliable Realty. She bought out her partner in 2010 and is now sole owner of Reliable Realty.

Kellee's outside sales career began in 1984, but was introduced to the Real Estate Industry in 1992 when she took a position with Orange Coast Title as District Sales Manager. In 1997, Kellee received the Prestigious Sales Person of the Year Award and was then recruited by Home Life Real Estate in Moreno Valley as Sales Manager and Marketing Director for five Home Life Offices. Kellee was responsible for leading Home Life out of the red and making it the most profitable branch within the Home Life Franchise network. In 1999, Kellee was recruited by Reliable Realty Inc. located in Murrieta, CA where she practiced Real Estate and became proficient at loans. In 2005, Kellee earned her Broker's license. In 2006, Kellee started Reliable Property Management. Kellee continues to rapidly expand her successful Real Estate Brokerage and develop cutting-edge techniques in the field.

Kellee attended MSJC where she received her AS degree in Business then was accepted to University of Redlands School of Business where she received her Bachelor Degree in Business & Management.

In addition to the many organizations in which Kellee is involved, she regularly speaks at public forums and workshops. Such experiences include MT. SAJ, NAHREP-LA, NAHREP-IE. Kellee has recently been asked to speak regarding leadership at the University of Redlands. She most recently served as Master of Ceremonies for the NAHREP- LA Installation dinner and recently served as moderator at a REO commercial roundtable event. She has also taught numerous Real Estate classes at Mt. San Jacinto College and has been asked to apply as an instructor. She currently serves on the Real Estate Instruction advisory committee at MSJC. Kellee has sat on numerous committees including the REOMAC Sponsorship Committee. Kellee has sat on the board for the MBA and currently sits on the Board of Directors for NAHREP-IE as VP of Corporate Affairs. Kellee has developed very strong professional relationships – which have propelled her to become a leader in the Real Estate world.

On a personal level, Kellee is committed to community service such as feeding the homeless through Project Touch in Temecula, CA, an organization benefiting local homeless families. In 2010 Kellee was the recipient of the Presidents Volunteer Service Award.

CHAPTER 34

EMBRACE YOUR CAPE: FINDING THE SUPERHERO WITHIN AND OWNING IT!

BY KIMLEIGH SMITH

I always wanted to be a superhero. *Pow!*

Villains tried to stop me. *Wham!*

I still became one! *Bam!*

I was lucky, I had great role models. My parents *were* superheroes. My father was in the Air Force. He flew through the air protecting the world. My mother was an unstoppable force. A real-life superwoman who could do it all and taught me that I could too. There was no obstacle my parents couldn't overcome. I wanted to be just like them. I wanted to be a part of a family of caped crusaders, soaring into the stratosphere.

My first ten years of superhero training took place in Japan. In Kindergarten, all I wanted to do was act, and dance, and sing. Reading and writing? No time! I had to assemble my league of pint-sized superheroes and cheer them on to conquer the planet, or at least Kindergarten. *Vroom*!

Now, every superhero has their strength tested. My first test came when my family moved back to the States — Leavenworth, Kansas to be exact. I instantly felt the culture shock. In Japan, I was taught that all people were the same. In Kansas, I was told that people were different

311

and that being different was a bad thing, a reason to not connect, to not be friends. I chose not to believe that, though. You see, one of my superpowers was the ability to love all kinds of people. Judge someone else? Again, no time! With my cape tied firmly on I was busy soaking up life. I was unstoppable.

I acted, and danced, and sang my way through High School; and on top of that, I cheered. By the time I graduated I was ready to make the leap to college and cheer my way to a degree in Psychology. I received a small scholarship to study at Emporia State University, so I packed up my bedroom and zoomed off to college. I was so excited. In Leavenworth, I'd been surrounded by family, fed three squares, and lovingly guided through my days. That's how it should be and I was blessed to have had that experience. College was going to be my safe transition to adulthood. I would be in charge of my days but would still have the structure of my class schedule; I was going to live away from my parents for the first time, but the roof over my head would also be over the other students in my dorm; I'd have to feed myself but someone else would be doing the cooking.

I was also coming into my sexuality. *Late*. I was a late bloomer with no clue about the birds and the bees. I mean, I'd been told about them but I hadn't come anywhere near being pecked or stung! My friends had been exploring their sexuality for a long time. They'd held hands and kissed, and some had done much more. My attraction for boys hadn't started yet. How could it? Boys still had COOTIES! So, I graduated high school a v-i-r-g-i-n, utterly awkward when it came to boys. Emporia State University had enrolled a sexual rookie who was ready to make the leap to the big leagues... or so I thought.

"Everywhere we go! People want to know!

Who we are!

So we tell them!

We are the Hornets! The mighty, mighty, Hornets!"

My Freshman year was going great! My cape flowed out behind me as I swooped across campus from Psych classes to football games where I cheered on our team to victory! It was time to leap over campus in a single bound and celebrate with the football team at the victory party. *KaPow*!

All I remember was waking up in the hallway outside of my dorm room with blood streaming down my legs.

"Wow," I thought, "I'm having my period." That's what I thought had happened for the next eight years and I kept going on with my life.

I won the Miss Emporia Pageant and competed in the Miss Kansas Pageant. The scholarship money I won paid for the rest of my college. I graduated with a BS in Psychology and went to work in a group home until my undying love of the arts steered me and my cape to Chicago to pursue a career as a dancer. It was in Chicago that the acting bug hit, and I never looked back.

I loved my life in Chicago and got very comfortable there. As an actress I worked a ton. I knew instinctively how to take other people's words and speak their truths. My own truth, however, was hidden deep inside of me. My personal voice had no strength. Even more frightening, my legs had no strength. Seriously.

I kept falling down. *SPLAT*!

It had been happening on-and-off for a few years. My legs would freeze up and I would fall down. No worries though, I always got back on my feet. My life was great! My career was great! I was a performer, a dancer. Maybe I had a pinched nerve? A hazard of my job. Nothing a visit to chiropractor couldn't fix.

The chiropractor referred me to a therapist.

"Are you sexually active?"

"NO!"

"Have you ever been sexually active?"

"NO!"

"Would you ever like to be sexually active?"

"NO!!!"

Diagnosis? Hysterical paralysis. Emotionally I was so hysterical that I was unable to deal with my trauma, my legs were literally locking up and making me fall down!

I agreed with the diagnosis. I thought it was *hysterical.*

I never saw the therapist again. Even with my BS in Psychology, I couldn't see the truth. I was full of my own BS. I wasn't ready to face my trauma, so I ignored it and kept pushing through my days. My nights however, were getting out of control. I was seeing violent, sexual things in my dreams. Nightmares where I'd try to run but my legs wouldn't move, scream but there was no sound. My darkest truth was struggling to come out, but I'd keep it buried for a few more years. I'd lose my cape. I'd lose my superhero.

I did however, fall madly in love.

And when the man I fell in love with tried to become sexual with me, I punched him. And then I ran. I ran away from love. I realized that I couldn't accept love in my life. Something inside of me wouldn't let me. That was my turning point. I grabbed the *Yellow Pages* and found a hypnotherapist. Hey, it doesn't matter how you get there, *just get there.*

"I just want you to know, I'm not a victim."

I had to make that clear to the hypnotherapist. I was successful. My life had purpose. My art let me explore the depths of the human condition even though someone else had worked through the emotions and written the words. I was *not* a victim and I would show the hypnotherapist that in 5...4...3...2...1...

I was a cheerleader and they were football players. *Wow*!

There were three of them. *Wham*!

They gang raped me. *CRASH*!

"That's okay! That's alright!

Get back up!

... and FIGHT! FIGHT! FIGHT!!!"

My truth had been released. I could see it. Hear it. Feel it. *Finally, I could deal with it.* I was ready to fight for my life. I searched for my superhero and found out where she'd been hiding. She'd been behind the pompoms of that sweet, innocent cheerleader, pushing everything down, trying to protect me. She'd been jumping and shouting, turning cartwheels for years trying to get my attention; and she'd been taking care of my cape! Guarding it until I grew into a super*woman* and realized that shame and self-blame had no place in my life.

Soon, my superhero's strength would be tested again.

"Yes, I will donate my kidney to you, Stuart." To be honest, I'm not sure where those words to my cousin came from. I was scared but I knew I had to do it. Fear was standing in front of me and I made a conscious decision to face it. I say conscious because overcoming your fear doesn't happen passively. You have to be *active* about it. You have to look your fear in the eye so you can (as I like to say), start "Killin' Your Villain!"

Stuart looked at me and said, "Thank you, you're my hero." I felt my cape drape back over my shoulders and I wrapped it around me and embraced it. *Boom*!

As I recovered in the hospital I entertained the doctors, the nurses, *everybody*. I made them laugh. I laughed with them. Laughing *heals*! And that's when it hit me. I had a story that needed telling and I had a way to tell it. I had been brutalized back in college but I'd never lost my *funny*. I decided I was going to tell my story, on stage. I was going to share my story with an audience, and tell my truth, and laugh with them, and heal.

I grabbed my cape and soared to Los Angeles where I first performed my show.

My training as an actor came in very handy. As an actor you're taught that you can't use your emotional experiences until you own them. Until then, they own you. The process I went through to create my show became the foundation of my workshops. I started by writing down my strengths. It's a courageous step to acknowledge your strengths. Writing them down gives you something concrete to reference. You can look at your strengths right there on the printed page. You create your own personal power tool. I also wrote down my weaknesses. I'm a firm believer that you have to know your enemy to defeat your enemy. And then I wrote down the thing I was most afraid to tell anyone: I'd been gang-raped and I was going to say it … out loud.

I was going to own my good, my bad, and my ugly. I had to. I was made up of those three things. We're all made of those things. That comes with being human.

As I created my show I thought about my early life in Japan, of my beginnings, of the freedom and fearlessness of childhood. I remembered pretending to be (in my mind, really being) a superhero. If my mother called for "Kimleigh!" … I wouldn't answer. If she called for "Wonder Woman!" … I would. I realized that as children we fully own our stories, they're *ours to tell*. As we get older we learn to let other people tell us our stories. When that happens we give away our freedom and fearlessness.

My story was taken from me one violent night, but the first time I walked on stage I took it back. *SHAZAM*!

I named my show *"T-O-T-A-L-L-Y!"* because that's how I wanted to live, totally present and engaged – in full possession of my life and my sexuality. *"T-O-T-A-L-L-Y!"* is how I chose to tell my story but it doesn't matter how you choose to tell yours, you just have to tell it, whatever it is! Our superheroes show up because we show up! Telling your truth makes you powerful and free.

I'm honored to have my show tour the country and allow me to cheer on people who are bravely facing and owning their truths. Here's what I've learned and what I teach:

I am not a victim. I am never a victim. I am not a survivor. Survival begins the moment we experience trauma. We stand up and keep going. We're already that strong.

What I do is *thrive*, and I want you to thrive too! I fought the obstacles that were in my way and I won. I brought fearlessness back into my life. I saved myself and became my own superhero.

You're ready to be your own superhero. I know it.

Come soar with me!

About Kimleigh

Kimleigh Smith is a Best-Selling Author, an accomplished actress, and the founder of the "Embrace Your Cape!" philosophy. She is dedicated to helping people discover their personal superhero, own their power, and find emotional freedom.

She holds a BS in Psychology from Emporia State University in Kansas and has had a long and successful career as an actor and storyteller. Some of her many television credits include *The Mentalist, Parenthood, Lincoln Heights,* and *Heroes.* Garry Marshall cast her in her first major motion picture, *The Princess Diaries.* Make sure to watch Kimleigh strut her stuff as *Marzipan* in the new Jason Bateman film, *Bad Words.*

Kimleigh wrote and continues to tour her solo show *"T-O-T-A-L-L-Y!"*, a remarkably honest and open performance about her rape, the obstacles she overcame on her journey to heal, and the lessons she's learned. *"T-O-T-A-L-L-Y!"* has garnered her universal praise and multiple awards, including the *Washington Post's* "Editor's Pick" (Capital Fringe), one of *Wall Street Journal's* "Top Shows To Watch" (Fringe New York), and the "Best In Theatre Award" and "Top Of Fringe Award" (Hollywood Fringe).

Steven Leigh Morris of the *LA Weekly* says of Kimleigh, "She is without shame and she's earned that right. There's not a trace of self-pity; rather, super-hero determination."

The Director of General Education at Shenandoah University, Amy Sarch, writes that Kimleigh, "has become a legend and thanks to this legend, sexual assault awareness and prevention has become a part of Shenandoah University's public discourse."

Kimleigh is a highly sought-after performer, keynote speaker and life coach and teaches transformative workshops on topics such as *Living Authentically and Powerfully, Healing Through Forgiveness,* and *Owning Your Story.*

Begin your superhero journey and learn to embrace your cape by contacting Kimleigh at: embraceyourcape.com
kimleigh@embraceyourcape.com
www.facebook.com/EYCbyTotallyKimleigh
www.twitter.com/totallykimleigh

CHAPTER 35

LOSE FEAR TO BUILD A SALES TEAM THE WINNING WAY...

BY KIP L. CARPENTER

Fear is a big inhibitor and motivator, losing Fear can lead to Success.

Fear and growing up; imaginary or real... happens... At a young age, I realized you need to accept your fearful situation or overcome it...

We had dogs as I was growing up. Raising a large dog or two requires walks and the use of a collar for restraint. We used the old style metal choke collars, one end slipped inside the other to tighten up on the throat of the dog as he/she otherwise took off; compliance was mandatory.

You learn that sound of the choke collar; metal sliding against metal as it unfolds. I remember hearing that very familiar sound, in the 7th grade (12 years old), coming from the back of my classroom, only a couple rows back from my desk; it caught my attention.

Upon hearing that familiar sound, I looked back, and on more than one occasion; what I saw was the very same choke collar I used for my dogs, unfolding with 2 or 3 triangle cut fishing weights attached to it. The gang member with the dog chain swung it in a small circle as he looked at me. "Uh, oh", I thought; "There's a gang fight going on down the railroad tracks tonight and I have to walk that way home..." I caught my breath in fear.

Let me first tell you about me and my Winning Ways and how I can affect your business in a positive manner, before we go any further. January 2014, I became a Best-Selling Author as I co-authored a book with Dan Kennedy titled *STAND APART – The World's Leading Experts Reveal Their Top Secrets To Help Your Business Stand Out From the Crowd To Achieve Ultimate Success*. Being a very current 'Best-Selling Author' on business today; I have current techniques; information and ideas to help you achieve success now.

Since 2006, I have been building and rebuilding once highly effective sales teams, turning Gross Profit margins from mid-30s to 50s, with sales volumes jumping immediately 20-40% and sustaining on average a steady increase of 10+% annually.

It's not that the sales teams that I fixed were totally ineffective; after all, they were producing tens of millions of dollars in retail sales annually, but rather, they needed that little something extra I provided to give them an extra edge.

I was born on Kodiak Island, Alaska – before it was part of the United States; an island known for having the most ferocious bears in the world, the *Kodiak Brown Bears*. My family left Kodiak just before the Great Alaskan Earthquake and settled in San Jose, California.

I have a successful 30+ year career in business, which has resulted in:

- A Top Sales Producer and Sales Manager; conquering tangibles and intangibles.
- In a key executive position, I helped build a direct sales company to $1 billion in annual sales; I've served on the Presidents Clubs and Key Clubs of the Top Insurance Companies and Mutual Fund Companies in the world as an annual multi-million dollar producer and I've achieved huge success in the retail marketplace.

Personal development seminars were a big part of my training, along with advancing the corporate image. Learning how and why to choose high-producing sales people to join different companies, educated me on the interview and selection process. This training has helped me focus in on how I can identify good sales people and reignite whole sales teams.

Every business I joined, I became the Leader; achieving #1 – whether there were 100 or 350 people there ahead of me. Why is that?

Highly effective sales people exhibit characteristic traits and mannerisms that I look for – eye movement, hand and head movement, pronunciation, accentuation on certain words in their speech. I look at the whole thing and ask myself: Is this the complete package and would I buy something from this person? If these traits and mannerisms are present, I know I can fit this person in any place and they'll probably outperform a good number of the existing sales people.

To conclude: The gang member; as he looked at me and swung the dog chain in a small circle...

In this situation; What would you do? What did I do?

I looked him directly in the eyes; he had a cold stare back at me; and as he swung the dog chain in a circle ....

I turned around to do my homework. I flinched in the stare down!

It was human nature; that spinning dog chain thing gave him the upper hand... I think.

Regardless of any schoolroom situation, I did walk home down the railroad tracks that night.

In Junior High School at 12-13 years old, I had to walk down the railroad tracks to get home – maybe a mile or more with orchards on either side – anybody and anything can be hiding down those tracks ... especially when it's dark. More than once, I had to walk through active gang fights down the railroad tracks, I was confronted. I was young; I was worried and yes, ... I had fear. Thankfully, I was cleared by a gang member or two that happen to play school sports with me. "He's cool, let him through," they said.

I was packing a switchblade to school daily in the 7th grade (as a 12 year old); and as an 8th grader, in possible need of self-protection. I always worked to excel in school and sports – resulting in excellent grades and being a 2-time Presidential Physical Fitness Award winner. I may not have been able to fight them then, but I bet I could outrun them for a couple miles.

Look at your 7th or 8th grader; imagine them, unknown to you, to be packing a switchblade to school so they can get home safe. I have a daughter and three boys, and I looked at them at that age. I was amazed at how young and innocent they were. I chose to keep it that way for them; being young and innocent is a virtue.

It wasn't until I reached high school as a freshman that I stopped packing a switchblade, and I learned martial arts and didn't have to walk home down the railroad tracks anymore. – *One Fear Set Aside*.

In elementary school, my parents were getting a divorce and my mother's anger boiled over onto me, creating a rough home life. In an attempt to gain approval from my Mom at home, I turned my punishments into accomplishments; these included: Straight "A's"; playing three instruments; speaking five languages; Tournament fighter and Black Belt in Karate; lettering in sports in High School and College.

Struggles are a part of life. How a person deals with them shapes how they grow.

It was just as I entered high school that I ran away from my Mom's house taking my youngest brother with me; for our protection. – *One More Fear Set Aside*.

Fighting and Martial Arts Tournaments calmed my internal fears. The more times I fought, the better I became; the more confident I was in all things. You keep setting aside fears - You gain a lot of confidence and strength.

My Final Exam in college for my calligraphy class required us to write – in calligraphy – an original statement of our life. Here is what I wrote:

Fear is like a Flame.

Unless extinguished,

It will feed upon the minds of the weak,

Who will Fear the strong,

That Fear nothing at all.

~ Kip L Carpenter

In College, I got a degree as a Technical Illustrator. There was a problem however. The problem was... I loved to talk to people. You know what I was told Technical Illustrators do, ... "They draw, they don't talk."

"What?"

I can't be quiet 8 hours a day! I had fear of losing my creativity and my lively spirit if I was now unable to talk, laugh and carry-on! I set my Technical Illustrator Degree aside... and went into Sales!

I've learned that building a highly effective sales team is not a mechanical thing; building a highly effective sales team is a psychological thing, ... the psychology of sales; ... the psychology of people; ...the psychology of human nature. The key to building a highly effective sales team is Interaction, Understanding, Empathy and Strength.

How does it relate to your sales team today? Let me tell you...

- Sales people hunger for acknowledgement from the Boss; or the highest person that reports to the Owner. As a Top Manager, think of the number of times you may have direct interaction with a sales person – some more than others, right?

- So if at the end of the day, when the sales person goes home and they report to their loved ones that, "Today the Boss came by or called, and we talked and he/she said I was doing an awesome job and he needs more sales persons just like me." Does that make a day?

- Sales people are adrenaline driven... the *sale* is the score; then the lull and lots of talk of the sale... then quiet... Too much quiet with a high profile sales person and you lose them. They are action warriors of sales. They'll sell anything for a commission.

- When sales people are happy, they produce more sales and make more money - go out of your way (within reason) to make them happy; contests are good; there's inexpensive ways to have catalog contests, getaway trip contests, surprise gifts. Sales people are creative types, they'll sell almost anything for a bonus or prizes that benefits the ME; as in ME, I'm-the-most-important-person-in-the-World syndrome in all of us. (Feed that ME syndrome, it'll benefit you greatly.)

- Don't have the Fear mentality that a lot of business owners have; business is slow, I can't do a contest and give away stuff, because it'll cost me too much money. The reality is, it'll cost you too much money not doing it, your sales people will be stoked just looking at a sales catalog of what they could possibly win by accumulating points by selling certain products. You'll be stoked by picking those items you want sold that could possibly have somewhat higher profit margins to you. They sell a bunch, they WIN; they sell a bunch, you WIN. Perfect!

Management Leaders need the same type of Incentives; that will lead them to want to advance in your company.

- Whenever I was hired to serve in a management position for a company, I felt it a direct responsibility of mine to protect that portion of the business owner's empire. I'm not afraid to fire people, I don't necessarily like it, but I know if I don't do it in a proactive fashion, the business owner will find someone else to do it in my place.

Do you know that your managers hesitate or refuse to fire some of your sales personnel out of fear – the fear of confrontation. If it's necessary to fire a sales person, DO IT! It's a contamination to the rest of your sales staff, if you let that sales person remain. Improve your manager's mindset; have them realize that times change, people change and the sooner they learn to recognize the signs of change in your sales people, the quicker your sales teams will improve.

- Telltale signs include: complacency; tardiness; laziness; low personal sales; all of these require a managers non-threatening investigation and conversation with the sales person; to determine the need of change within the company or separation from the company.

Does one of your sales managers want a promotion to the next level? You as the business owner know this manager is great at what they do otherwise you wouldn't consider them for advancement; but you also realize you'll create a void if you advance them too soon.

Recruiting is the answer to fill the void. Do you realize that even your management staff have a fear of losing their jobs? There have been many instances of management staff not hiring an exceptional candidate because that person could take their job. You know who really loses in this situation? YOU! ... the business owner.

Here's an idea: Before you promote that Manager to a higher position, have them find their replacement, someone as good or better than them

- it'll change their prospective on recruiting.

Will recruiting someone better than them be difficult? Perhaps... I know it was for me.

The reality is that the sooner the manager wraps their head around this reality, the quicker they get that promotion. Win - Win. You get to promote a great employee without having a void in sales, management or production.

At one point, my wife and I lived in Lake Arrowhead, CA (a beautiful mountain retreat); and home-schooled our four children; for a period of a year or two. Our kids ranged in age from 4 to 11. We explained to them that if they could learn in this new environment, with home schooling, we could live and learn anywhere we wanted to. They all had a level of fear of losing; close friends, classmates, regular visits to the beach; since we lived in San Clemente, CA.

Lake Arrowhead provided a 2-story home with an under unit for storage, and heading into the winter, the kids and I daily went about collecting kindling and firewood from our immediate area. Once the first 15" snowfall hit, there wasn't any more kindling to be found, and we realized that our collecting of kindling and firewood proved to be a very warming experience. Our fires nightly kept us close. No TV and lots of books helped to center the conversation to us and what we are doing as a family.

I drove to Newport Beach to work each day, fighting massive traffic in both directions;

it was 2.5+ hours one way, each and every day. However, once home, at approx. 5000' up in the mountains, I stood in the front yard, raised my hands, and looked up in amazement at the sky and the clouds and how quickly the clouds moved past me at that altitude.

I was truly amazed each and every day.

Looking back, our kids now think that living up in Lake Arrowhead was one of the best times of their lives. We had to move back down to the flat land, because our kids were needing science labs and learning experiences we were not able to provide.

The end product: Outstanding! X4!

Our kids are currently applying themselves in the area of higher education and business; and we are very proud of them.

Daughter: Graduate, Vanderbilt University;

Son: Graduate, USC Business School;

Son: Junior, Notre Dame University;

Son: Freshman, Stanford University.

You know why our kids have done so well? For the same reason your sales teams will do well... consistency - perseverance - accountability - follow-up - teaching/training. That, as well as the elimination of any and all fears through Interaction, Understanding, Empathy and Strength. I've had opportunity to implement this many times and it works.

www.KipLCarpenter.com

About Kip

Kip L. Carpenter was born on Kodiak Island, Alaska – before it was part of the United States – an island known for having the most ferocious bears in the world, the *Kodiak Brown Bears.* Kip's family left Kodiak just before the Great Alaskan Earthquake, and settled in San Jose, CA. Much later he moved to Southern California.

In elementary school, his parents were getting a divorce and his mother's anger boiled over onto him, creating a rough home life. In an attempt to gain approval from his Mom at home he turned his punishments into accomplishments; practicing three instruments 45 minutes daily; reading 50 pages a night; practicing sports at school for years. Kip ran away from home entering High School and moved into his Dad's house, while continuing to excel on his own; the pattern of over-excel (prove your worth) was set in his mind.

Accomplishments included:

- Straight "A's"
- Playing three instruments
- Speaking five languages
- Tournament fighter and Black Belt in Karate
- Lettering in sports in High School and College.

Every business he joined, he became the leader, achieving #1 whether there were 100 or 350 people there ahead of him. Why is that?

A successful 30+ year career in business has produced: A Top Sales Producer and Sales Manager; conquering tangibles and intangibles. In a key executive position, he helped build a direct sales company to $1 billion in annual sales; he's served on the Presidents Clubs and Key Clubs of the Top Insurance Companies and Mutual Fund Companies in the world as an annual multi-million dollar producer; and he's achieved huge success in the retail marketplace.

What can he share with you? Since 2006, he has been building and rebuilding highly effective sales teams, turning GP margins from mid-30s to 50s, with sales volumes jumping immediately 20-40% and sustaining on average 10+% annually. It's not that the sales teams that he fixed were totally ineffective; after all, they were producing tens of millions of dollars in retail sales annually, but rather they needed a little something extra, that he provided to give them that extra edge.

Kip is also a best-selling author with the best-selling book *Stand Apart,* which he co-authored with Dan Kennedy.

If all Kip could do for you was methodically improve your sales, your GP's and your sales teams overall effectiveness, would you be interested?

During his spare time, Kip and his wife Chris, of 29 years, spend time with their four children. Daughter: Graduate, Vanderbilt University; Son: Graduate, USC Business School; Son, Junior, University of Notre Dame; Son: Freshman, Stanford University.

To learn more about Kip L. Carpenter and how he can effect positive change for your company —

Visit: www.KipLCarpenter.com.
Call: 949-226-8026 or
email: Kip@KipLCarpenter.com.

CHAPTER 36

THE PLATINUM PRESCRIPTION BUSINESS OWNER: TAKE CARE OF THYSELF

BY LINDA DRAKE

Twenty-five years. Yes, I founded and owned a business for 25 years. I was like every other business owner: frustrated, fearful, anxious, and yet committed, rewarded, and fulfilled. The stresses of starting, growing, and managing an enterprise are often overwhelming. In retrospect, I learned a great deal from the ebbs and flows of owning a national, and then global, business. I am writing this chapter as a reflection and prescription of entrepreneurial principles I now know to be true.

The very first is **Business Owner: Take Care of Thyself.**

This is not going to be a feel-good chapter or an expose about taking yoga classes or walking or going to the gym. This is an analysis of the core of our being and how we achieve congruity in our personal and business lives, which in entrepreneurial terms are usually synonymous.

Why is congruity critical? I believe that small business and entrepreneurism are the heart and promise of America. At twenty-seven million strong, we have contributed more to the economic survival of the U.S. than big businesses. We pay our taxes (many times a much larger proportion of our profit than large multinationals); we fund our businesses (often with our own cash); we support our families (doing our level-best to shield them from our own anxiety); we meet payrolls (often by a hair); we support our communities (there are endless needs); we train and counsel our employees (everyone's problem is the most important to them), and we give with every last drop of blood, sweat and tears that we have – in order to breathe life into and often resuscitate the business.

And WHO – may I ask WHO – takes care of us? For this question, I only have one answer…*the buck stops here*. The important responsibility we have is to ourselves!

I am sure you know, consciously and unconsciously, that you are the engine that ignites and drives your business. As a business owner, no matter where you are and what you do, you walk no beaten path. Every single solopreneur or partnership, franchise or corporation, is unique and all of it, every bit of your business, in whatever form, hinges on you.

As we do battle on the playing field every day, we forget as business owners that we are the *platinum* core of our business – the most precious element. You see pure platinum is rare, desirable, and yes, harder than iron. Yes, this describes you! You are the commodity that must be valued as you create the American dream for yourself (and so many others). You, the business owner, need to recognize consciously your contribution to your critical importance in the midst of the mayhem, the stretch goals, and the conflicts as you reach for the brass ring. The truth is that with so many balls juggling in the air, so many decisions to conclude, and so many variables, we can easily lose ourselves, our core, and often…our health.

So let's **STOP.** For a moment, **STOP** and think about it. If you are the core element in your business, the most precious cog, where would the business be without you? In most cases, the answer is that your business would be another failure statistic instead of the success you envisioned. While platinum is a metal that is resistant to tarnish and wear, you are not! What are the keys that will keep you, the entrepreneur, healthy, happy, and on the road to your ultimate goals?

One of my stories…

(My husband will not be happy that I wrote this…)

Twelve years after I founded the company, the American dream was alive and well. We were pumping…we were expanding our offices and our client portfolios. We were winners in a highly competitive game and our employees −2000 at the time −were amply rewarded. It had been a good financial year. I was living the dream…but my marriage was failing.

My husband and I owned the business together, though I was the majority shareholder at 55%. What occurred were some very basic business conflicts that were eroding our relationship. So, as marriage and business partners, we entered traditional counseling. A year later, we decided to stand the test of time, though I had acquiesced to more than I believed that I should. We celebrated that year-end in style as we watched fireworks from a hotel room in Las Vegas. We had a terrific time, yet I knew I was incongruent with my fundamental beliefs. That was January. I would learn more when the phone rang on the last Friday afternoon in March.

"Mrs. Drake?" "Yes," I responded. "This is Dr. M. Your breast biopsy has tested positively for cancer. Make an appointment with my office next week." Silence. The earth moved, but in the wrong direction.

Please note: none, and I mean none, of my family members had ever developed breast cancer, and I later had all the genealogic tests. I did not then or even later, see myself as precious to the business.

This was a serious error. I let myself get out of alignment with my personal direction, my instinct, and my intention. I believe that this acquiescence to my partner's beliefs and to market conditions played havoc with my mind and, consequently, with my body.

Here I was…the lynch pin…the conduit…and now, the wounded business warrior. After a two-year cancer battle (that was funded ironically because I had the financial resources derived from the business), I reached wellness physically. What I can now tell you is what I should have done psychically. If I had only known then what I know now….

The Platinum Principle: Congruity – The best gift you can give yourself is you.

A lot of the conflict you have in your life exists simply because you're not living in alignment; you're not being true to yourself.
~ Dr. Steve Maraboli, Behavioral Psychologist

What is congruity? Congruity or congruence is the state in which one's internal and external stories match. Further, it's really the story that we tell ourselves about ourselves, or the internal story that we want to be seen externally. The basis of congruity is derived from psychology and can sometimes be characterized as "story matching" which is authenticity – conducting your life in such a way that your words, behaviors, and actions all align with your values. And, interestingly enough, it is congruency that enables us to examine the world with a broader lens, i.e., see possibilities.

Contrarily, incongruence is defined as what is incompatible with what is suitable, acting out or thinking with disparate or discordant elements. Psychological literature and studies demonstrate that in those parts of our lives where we evidence inconsistency between our core beliefs and our behaviors, we get derailed (an accident waiting to happen). In those areas of our lives where we live our values, we have greater levels of contentment and enjoy much more success. This is the power of congruency!

The truth is that more often than not, many of us don't see the incongruence in ourselves. What we are left with is the "dis-ease" of this conflict and its resultant tension. It is incongruence that culturally suppresses our gut reaction, or intuition radar, that signals threats to our own authenticity and the authenticity of others. Suppression of our own beliefs is not any different than suppressing a group or a nation; the result is often chaos, hostility, anger and a tsunami of negative energy. Incongruity can be a nightmare of misdirection on the playing field or as simple as a "little white lie" we tell ourselves. And, incongruity breeds myopia yielding a state of limited views and narrows our focus.

How does incongruity manifest in our daily lives?

Incongruity lurks in the mental dissonance of:

- Scott, the solopreneur graphic designer who struggles with a proclivity for perfection by investing too much time on small jobs and not enough time on marketing.

- Doug, the business owner that has deep-seated self-doubts that interfere with his role as CSO (Chief Sales Officer...prospects read the tea leaves!).

- Carrie, the entrepreneur, who agonizes about firing a long-term, underperforming personal friend.

- Kent, the seriously overworked small business owner, who puts up with tantrums from employees in conflict or crises, which only compound his sleepless nights.

- Melanie, the successful entrepreneur, who somehow can't uncouple from the business for family or personal time.

These are the kinds of incongruities eating at the heart of America.

So how do we become more congruent, more authentic? Concurrently, how can we enable ourselves to become more self-aware, mindful, and successful in our personal and professional lives? There are several ways.

Literature abounds with endless books that can walk us through a re-examination of our purpose and ourselves. Sometimes this is just the ticket, but more often than not, these exercises can become out-dated quickly, or we entrepreneurs become bored and move to the next big thing. In a like manner, we can attend seminars that for the moment shed light on our circumstances, but unfortunately, once back in the trenches, we lose touch with those insights.

We can turn to meditative downloads and centering exercises. Useful? Absolutely, although meditation is often not compatible with the typical businessperson's type-A personality! We can hire periodic consultants whose job it is to get in, make course corrections and exit on time and on budget. A cautionary axiom: *Quick fixes seldom create lasting solutions!*

Or, we can hire seasoned thinking-partners and/or join mastermind groups that enable us to learn from trained, capable peers, many of who have gone through this identical process repeatedly. This is the road preferred by many.

The business coach option creates personal accountability for you and your business and can facilitate quantum leaps in your own thinking. A business coach involves you in a committed conversation. What does that mean? Simply this – through coaching conversations you form a bond with the coach. This is more than an agreement; it's a pledge to take action on what is most important for you.

Why does this choice produce the greatest likelihood of consistent, decisive results? There are many reasons: coaching is personal, it's private, it's specific, and it's all about you. (This is one time you do not have to share!) Accredited coaches bring impersonal, objective views that enable you to maintain your focus and accelerate your strategic direction. One last point, the top 20% of successful businesses use coaches. Now, there's a goal worth attaining!

The above methods are only a few suggested pathways. The more critical issue is not how we get there, but that we get there.

> *Nobody goes into business for business reasons;*
> *everybody goes into business for personal reasons.*
> ~ Brian Tracy

The quote says it all. As business owners, we have personal reasons that literally drive us into our offices every day. Beyond the desires to make money, influence people or leave a legacy, you had a dream in the beginning. That dream was the big, bodacious goal that you could see, taste and touch. You and the dream were inexplicably intertwined. At whatever stage you are in your business, you need to continue to realign yourself with the dream and, just as certain as the seasons, those dreams will change.

Self-alignment is the unequivocal centering of you and your business. It is a repetitive and evolving act. It is the critical adhesive that cements, yet reconstitutes the foundation for your business. This is neither a stoic nor static exercise: the realignment of your psyche and your business requires a deep unearthing of all the emotions, all the devotion, and all of the excitement and engagement with which you began the business. I strongly urge you to realign yourself with your dream at least annually to maintain integrity with yourself. Subsequent, periodic check-ups with this prescription are also highly recommended!

Lillian Vernon, one of America's most accomplished leaders in the catalog industry, was once asked what were her greatest challenges? Her response: "Staying alive as a business, staying ahead of the game, and melding my business with my personal life." The issue of creating and maintaining alignment and congruity in business transcends time.

I brought an immense amount of passion to my quarter-century business. Zero to fifty million takes a lot of burning desire. I only wish that I knew much earlier how much of a difference clear, congruent paths would have made for me. My counsel to other business owners is that finding the key to congruency will unlock fulfillment in your life. Congruity, however you find it – through meditation, at seminars, in books or with the help of a seasoned coaching professional – is the best gift you can give yourself.

On a personal note…

Some of us were born to work. I fall into that category. But, today, my business mission, passion and interests are totally aligned, i.e., I am applying my large and small business lessons with a coaching practice that supports the heart of America. Interested in a complimentary session? Contact me, but hold onto your seat! Alignment will make you soar! And by the way, I am still cancer-free and still married. Alignment also heals.

One last impression…I want to share the immortal and brilliant words of playwright William Shakespeare:

To thine own self be true, and it must follow, as the night the day, thou canst not then be false to any man.

…Including YOU!

About Linda

Linda Drake is a seasoned entrepreneur, corporate executive and certified transformational business coach. As the Chief Pathfinder and Founder of Trailblazer Advisors, Ms. Drake brings insight to opportunities in the business environment by coaching for entrepreneurial and team success. Her process, Leadership Success Journeys, uses the most incisive tools for client self-awareness guiding the client in any stage of the business lifecycle. Linda's scope and experience is broad, but concentration on the client is narrow…her laser-focused coaching achieves maximum results!

Linda was the founder of a global information services company headquartered on the east coast. For 25 years, the company provided international business process outsourcing for customer service, database management and quality assurance to Fortune 100 corporations. The company, winner of the State Quality Award, achieved ISO 9001 registration, the first company of its kind to do so worldwide. A certified woman-owned business, the company also received the Better Business Bureau Torch Award for Marketplace Ethics.

Ms. Drake is the recipient of numerous state and national awards, including Entrepreneurial Woman of the Year, the *Philadelphia Business Journal* Women of Distinction Award, Ernst & Young's Delaware Valley Entrepreneur of the Year, and the coveted Pioneer Award from PACE, the Professional Association for Customer Engagement. Ms. Drake also won the Women Impacting Public Policy (WIPP) Member of the Year Award for leadership as Membership Chair. As a networking early adopter, Linda founded a women's professional organization still in existence after 30 years. For her efforts, she was awarded the Alliance of Professional Women's Trailblazer Award for leadership in the state.

Ms. Drake served for 12 years on the Board of Directors for a publicly-traded financial institution. Ms. Drake served for 15 years on the Board of the State Chamber and 6 years on the Board of the Breast Cancer Coalition where she chaired the Strategic Planning Committee. Ms. Drake was the Founding Co-Chairman of "Advocates of Hope" Conferences, which in concert with the State Chamber of Commerce, raised awareness in the workplace about the prevention, diagnosis, treatment and post-treatment counseling for issues involving cancer. Ms. Drake also chaired the Top Corporations Selection Panel for the Women's Business Enterprise National Council (WBENC). Ms. Drake actively supports professional organizations including the

International Coaching Federation, Chambers of Commerce, the National Association of Women Business Owners and the EWomen Network.

Linda graduated *magna cum laude* from Kent State University with a B.S. in Education, and continued graduate studies in Communications at the University of Massachusetts. She is a breast cancer survivor and the proud mother of two fine sons.

Linda.Drake@TrailblazerAdvisors.com
Website: www.TrailblazerAdvisors.com
Facebook.com: facebook.com/Linda Drake
Linkedin: http://www.linkedin.com/in/lindadrake
Twitter: @linda_drake

CHAPTER 37

AIM HIGHER
THAN INCOME

BY LOUIS BRINDISI

Poll a group of high school graduates or fledgling college students why they've selected their specific major and many will respond, "Money" or "Income." Although, I compliment these ambitious individuals for understanding the need to become self-supporting, those of us who have lived a little, or, in my case a lot, realize that our goals must become much larger. Don't get me wrong, the desire to make money and not to struggle financially was certainly a goal of mine when I started out. However, as I contemplate my life's work and the challenges and successes I have encountered along the way, I am compelled to share what has become apparent to me during the 53 years that I have practiced law. I have come to appreciate that it was not solely the monetary gains but truly the challenges that made my life fulfilling, and the achievement of overcoming them that has made my life meaningful. What I learned from the challenges applies to all businesses. When, at any stage in life, you reach an impasse or commence something new, I would suggest that you apply these basic principles to excel:

What are your core values? What is important to you is always your guiding light.

- Make your business or career choices based on fulfilling a need.

- It is not always important to have the "right" people like you.

- Be your own barometer. Sometimes the winds of change blow

you in a different direction.

- Do not be afraid to change the course of your business. Get to know your community and care about the people with whom you work.

- Aim larger than the income you want. Set your goals to have impact.

I was born just after the Great Depression in Utica, New York to Italian and Armenian immigrant parents. Utica, located on the Erie Canal approximately halfway between New York City and Buffalo, and called the gateway to the Adirondacks, drew many immigrants intrigued by the area's industrial development.

My father, Angelo Brindisi, emigrated as a baby with my grandparents from the Calabrian region of Italy. My mother, Mary Murad, was also an infant when she arrived here with her Armenian family from Syria. Both families knew the hardships of war and poverty. My father had to quit school at a very young age to help support his family and consequently never received a high school education. My mother, on the other hand, had the privileged opportunity to attend high school.

My parents eloped very young, having met when my father's taxi stand was fortuitously located near my maternal grandparent's grocery store, where my mother worked as a cashier. After their marriage, his lack of education resulted in subsequent fluctuations with regards to his capacity to earn a consistent wage. This monetary instability, coupled with the unlikely blending of Italian and Armenian culture, created a dysfunctional family environment complete with parents who argued constantly.

In addition to my father's unpredictable employment history, he also had a gambling addiction that resulted in multiple occasions when he would come home and throw money on the bed and say, "We're rich" – only to return the next night to say, "We have to move," because he lost our home in an unlucky bet. Losing my childhood home on numerous occasions caused me to attend five different grammar schools during an eight-year period.

Because both of my parents were working, I was primarily unsupervised and out on the streets when I was approximately 6 years old. I grew up in East Utica, which was a predominantly Italian neighborhood. At that time, there were many "tough guys" living in this part of the city.

The neighborhood influence to be a lackluster student and barely scrape by was strong, but I was very close to my mother's youngest brother, John, who was only two years my senior. I respected him greatly, especially for his strong educational convictions. He became my mentor and helped me navigate through some very difficult times. When my Uncle John attended LeMoyne College in Syracuse, New York, I followed him there shortly thereafter.

What are your core values? During college, I gained a considerable amount of weight. After completing college, I went on a very strict diet and with great determination lost what I had gained. It was at this time that I began to develop the necessary skills to overcome what I considered the challenges in my life. I decided I no longer wanted to be heavy and began to value my health, knowing that it was a vital component of my future successes. It was also a strong desire of mine not to experience the financial struggles that I witnessed as a child. It was with this mindset, fostered by my mother, that I chose to attend Albany Law School. I actually did quite well in law school because I focused on my studies and my goal of obtaining a law degree.

After clerking for a year following my law school graduation, I went into practice with my Uncle John, fittingly also a lawyer, into the newly created firm of Murad & Brindisi. Somewhere between college and the opening of our law firm, I learned that determination often arises out of core values and what is important to you. It became apparent to me that my core values needed to become the foundation of my successes and I began to measure each future decision against the standard core values that I had set for myself. I focused on the skills that my father seemed to have lacked in his ability to support himself monetarily. I used the lessons learned from this situation as my guiding light to chart a course of success for my own business by determining and fulfilling a need providing a particularly specialized type of legal counsel in the Utica area.

The desire to fill a need and to make money propels most businesses. Perhaps because of my neighborhood of origin, when I got out of law school it became evident to me that many of my childhood acquaintances required legal counsel. In recognizing this need, I decided to become a criminal trial lawyer.

When I started practicing criminal law, the case of <u>United States vs. Miranda</u> had not yet been decided and it was common practice for the police to interrogate defendants using violently aggressive tactics to coerce confessions out of them. They would also routinely hide clients so their lawyers could not speak to them. In those days, most of the attorneys in Utica entered into plea deals. The majority of them did not want to try these cases; therefore they would plead their clients down to a lesser offense or enter a guilty plea. Contrarily, I took on the police and law enforcement. If police beat a client, I brought police brutality charges and civil rights actions against them. When they hid clients so that you could not talk to them, I would bring a *habeas corpus* proceeding. My core values guided me to see the possibilities in representing the underdog. My acquittals range from alleged murder to manslaughter, assault, robbery, burglary, grand larceny, gambling, rape, counterfeiting, money laundering, RICO and conspiracy cases, as well as cases and crimes involving criminal violations of the interstate commerce laws. The commonality among these cases was the core belief that each defendant was presumed innocent and had the right to a fair trial guaranteed to them by the Constitution of the United States. *When you find a need and fulfill it, you strengthen your business.*

It is not important to have the "right" people like you if your core values and opportunities take you on a different course. During that time period, I represented numerous high profile organized crime figures — including the "King of the Gypsies." I soon became an expert in First Amendment Law, arguing these constitutional law cases in a three-state territory of New Jersey, Pennsylvania and New York. My clients owned private planes and would pick me up and fly me to the various cities where I would handle their cases.

In Utica, my uncle and I became known as the "Young Lions" for taking on the establishment when trying these cases. We had no fear, but the results were that many law enforcement officials disliked us immensely due to the acquittals that we attained on behalf of our clients. When my Uncle John decided to run for a judgeship and won, we dissolved Murad & Brindisi and I became a sole practitioner. I continued to be unpopular with various members of law enforcement but it was important for me to become a champion of the "common" people. In upholding this belief, I lost the respect of the "right" people but my personal self-respect was worth more than my popularity with the opposition. I became my own barometer.

Be your own barometer. Sometimes the winds of change will blow you in a different direction and alter your belief structure. I soon built a very successful criminal law practice that eventually generated the financial security that I had hoped to achieve. However, my world changed on January 4, 1983 when my wife, Jackie, of almost twenty five years of marriage, died of cancer, leaving me with five children to raise. The youngest was only 4 years old. On the same day, a young associate in my office was murdered, making it the most devastating day of my entire life. From it came another life lesson and rebirth that transformed my priorities as well as the future of my law practice.

Do not be afraid to change the course of your business. You must believe in your business practices for it to succeed. You strengthen your business through fundamental adjustments to keep it in line with your beliefs. When I realized that a criminal had tragically taken my associate's life, I vowed never to try another criminal case. My core value was still to help the underdog, but I was compelled to find another way to accomplish that goal. I decided that my life had to change and therefore became dedicated to assisting the community in other ways. I rechanneled my energy and found my niche handling serious personal injury and wrongful death cases.

Gerry Spence, a great, nationally-known trial lawyer, was asked, "What does it take to become a great trial lawyer?" His answer was simple. He said, "You have to care."

Knowing your community and caring about people changes the scope of your business. I have cared for my clients throughout my career and have done everything in my power to obtain successful outcomes in their cases. My practice is now limited to the trial of serious personal injury and wrongful death cases arising as a result of a motor vehicle accident; defective products; medical malpractice; with a strong emphasis on construction accidents involving violations of the Labor Law of the State of New York. We protect the rights of the workers whose employers provided inadequate safety devices that resulted in their injury. My law firm has handled and tried numerous cases and has won million dollar settlements on behalf of these injured individuals.

My serious injury cases have included everything from brain injuries, birth defects, amputations, quadriplegics, paraplegics, and those who suffered from severe brain injuries and burns. I have handled defective product cases involving SUV rollovers and tire defects, seatbelt failures, airbag injuries, seat-back collapse and roof-crush injuries. I have also handled cases involving the failure to warn, and other design and manufacturing defects. I have tried cases involving the Federal Employer's Liability Act; elevator crashes, medical malpractice, legal malpractice, discrimination, slip and falls, construction accidents and nursing home negligence. The pattern here is that I have a passion for justice and a strong desire to help others find hope and security throughout their struggles. Knowing the needs of and caring about the people living within my community has built my business into a legacy beyond the financial success for which I had originally aimed.

Set the bar higher than the income you want to achieve in your business. When I was young and building my business for financial gain alone, I did not consider the legacy I would leave behind.

I married and had five children while fresh out of law school. Later in life, I had one more child from a subsequent marriage . Although I built a financially successful practice, I was not the most attentive husband or parent. Frankly, I worked all the time. Even though the long hours that I devoted to my practice, over the years, meant extended absences from their daily lives it was important for me to provide the economic stability that I had lacked as a child from my own father. This was my way of showing my love for my family.

Although we did have our occasional vacations, most of my time was spent practicing law in the courtroom. I did, however, as a father, instill in my children a great deal of love and respect and taught them that the most important thing in life is family. These core values are still a part of each of them today and they continually bring me great pride by demonstrating, on an ongoing basis, their love for one another. With regards to career advice, I have taught them to resist focusing solely on their future income-earning potential. They have learned, through my example, that you will not be remembered by how much money you acquire but instead on how positively you impact the lives of others. Additionally, the successes you are blessed with achieving should always be shared in philanthropic ways with the community that fostered those successes.

Fifty-three years later, the knowledge that I choose to impart to the next generation hinges on a few solid beliefs. Build your business on a set of core values garnered from the strongest influences in your life including family, school and mentors. Know that the greatest businesses do not offer products; they fulfill needs. When your career or business no longer aligns with your core values, do not be afraid to change the course of your business to better reflect the evolution of your principles. Changing course requires you to rely on your own barometer. It also means in my situation, that the "right" people may not share your commitment to doing what is legally ethical for others. Believe in yourself and stay true to your core values. Acknowledge that no matter where your business is located you will reach the most people when you know and support local needs. I have demonstrated this, during my lifetime, with the legal counsel that I provide and the charitable ways that I consistently give back. Target your business objectives, not solely to gain wealth but to change your profession and ultimately people's lives. Monetarily supporting yourself and your family are wonderful goals, but in the end the real measure of your wealth is how much you would be worth if you lost it entirely.

About Louis

Louis T. Brindisi was born in Utica, New York on October 20, 1934 and has lived there all his life, having attended local grammar schools and high school. He attended LeMoyne College in Syracuse, New York and graduated with a Bachelor of Science Degree in Economics in 1956.

In 1959, he graduated from Albany Law School with a Juris Doctor Degree and was admitted to the New York State Bar in 1960.

After law school, he was married to Jacqueline Brindisi, now deceased, and has six children, two of which, Eva Brindisi Pearlman and Anthony Brindisi, have become lawyers, and are now partners in the law firm that bears their names. With 54 years of trial experience, he has handled thousands of cases, both civil and criminal.

Lou is a member of the American Bar Association; Oneida County Bar Association (where he has lectured attorneys for CLE credits); New York State Bar Association; Florida Bar Association; American Association for Justice (Past ATLA District Governor updating national decisions of Courts from the field of medical malpractice, products liability and personal injury); New York State Trial Lawyers; New York State Academy of Trial Lawyers; National Board of Trial Advocates, where he holds the rank of Advocate; Multi-Million Dollar Advocates Forum; the Association of Trial Lawyers of America; American Society of Legal Advocates; the Motor Vehicle Trial Lawyers Association; Mass Tort Trial Lawyers Association; Medical Malpractice Trial Lawyers Association; the Association of Plaintiff Interstate Trucking Lawyers of America; American Society of Legal Advocates and the Association of Motor Vehicle Trial Lawyers.

He has been named by Lawdragon as one of the top 3000 Plaintiff's Attorneys in America. He is also been named as a New York State Super Lawyer.

He has also been named as one of the top 100 Trial Lawyers in New York State by the National Trial Lawyers Association. The Association is a national organization composed of the top 100 trial lawyers from each state. Membership is obtained through special invitation and is extended only to those attorneys who exemplify superior practice in the field of law.

Lou has been selected by his peers to be included in The Best Lawyers in America, and the law firm which he has founded has a ranking in the *U.S. News* - Best Lawyers "Best Law Firms" Rankings.

Lou is a featured attorney/author in the *Consumer's Advocate* book published by Celebrity Press. Lou has been named a member of the National Academy of Best Selling Authors in recognition of his best-selling book *Consumer's Advocate.*

CHAPTER 38

UNLOCKING THE SECRETS TO LONGEVITY — A SCIENTIFICALLY PROVEN APPROACH TO HELP YOU DISCOVER HOW TO PREVENT AND REVERSE DISEASE NATURALLY

BY DR. LUC LEMIRE

MY PERSONAL JOURNEY

I was quite young when I first developed rashes all over my body that were so dry that my skin often cracked and bled. The burning sensation, the itchiness and the pain kept me awake at night, not only plaguing me physically, but also poisoning my self-esteem. I felt ugly when I looked in the mirror and convinced myself that I didn't fit in with the 'normal' kids. I hated going to the beach, because taking my shirt off exposed my secret to the world and made me feel vulnerable. At night I would lie awake in bed, in agony, thinking to myself: "What have I done to deserve this? How did I end up with a skin condition that could guarantee me a spot in a horror movie?" The saddest part of it all is that

I struggled with this for years because nobody had answers.

I consulted with countless Doctors over the years. None of them could give me concrete evidence that they knew what we were dealing with. Each Dermatologist had a different diagnosis. They did all have one thing in common however: Every one of them diagnosed me as having some sort of rare condition that had a minimum of 20 letters in its name--so difficult that even an Ivy League graduate with a PhD in Latin would have a hard time pronouncing it. The treatment protocols were essentially the same too: "*Try* this lotion, potion or pill and we'll *see how it works*." They were willing to prescribe the latest, and most powerful drugs on the market, but none of them knew, with certainty, what was wrong with me, so they couldn't know the effects of these drugs on my unknown condition, or how detrimental they might be to my overall health—they were just shooting in the dark and hoping.

Nothing ever worked and I suffered for years, simply because I wasn't asking the right questions. The simplicity of the solution was elegant, and hidden in plain sight of my Doctors and myself from the beginning: *The Questions That We Pose*. The reason they could not solve my medical mystery? My team of Doctors was not asking the right questions!

ASKING THE RIGHT QUESTIONS

This journey that I had been on for years gave me an appetite to learn everything that I possibly could about health and vitality. I wanted to understand why some people were healthy while others were sick. To this day, my continuing quest is to discover the cause of disease and how to reverse it naturally. I continue to study scientific literature and have conducted years of research to uncover the common threads and secrets that the healthiest people on this planet understand inherently.

Imagine if you woke up every morning and your vehicle had a flat tire. You head over to the local tire shop to get a *diagnosis* and the technician *prescribes* the following: "Go buy a pump and use as needed and come back to see me in 2 weeks." During your follow-up consultation, you explain that your tire continues to be flat every morning. Your specialist asks you a few questions to assess how well this treatment plan is working: Do you find the pump easy to use? Are you able to fill up your tire with it? Do your arms or wrists hurt when you use it? Has the flat tire prevented you from driving the car? Because your answers indicate that the pump is sufficient for your needs, he concludes that he has indeed solved your problems and that you just need to keep filling the tire as needed for the rest of your life.

This solution would be ridiculous, right? You would not accept that answer from the tire shop, and yet, this is exactly what many of us do with our Doctors—blind trust and "take your medicine." Because of this blind trust, we use drugs to mask symptoms, which seem to allow us to carry on with a normal life, without ever addressing the root cause of the problem.

One simple question from a different perspective would have totally changed the outcome of the tire scenario. That one magical question is: Is there a slow leak in this tire that needs to be repaired? The obvious answer is yes, and what a difference this one question makes in the approach to solving the problem. From this illustration, you can see how the quality of the questions you ask, determines the direction of the treatment path?

Modern medicine often takes a similar approach with health problems. When a patient presents to their Doctor's office with chronic headaches, asthma exacerbation, Crohn's disease, or any other condition, they are prescribed drugs, surgery or a combination of the two. Do you really think you get headaches because you don't have enough aspirin in your bloodstream? Do you honestly believe that you cannot breathe well because you are lacking bronchodilators in your lungs? Do you believe that you have Crohn's disease because you have an extra foot of intestine that needs to be removed? Of course not.

The reality is that drugs don't make you healthier. Pharmaceutical toxins simply mask the symptoms of sickness and move your health either sideways or downward, but never upward towards balance. Furthermore, according to Dr. Lucien Leape of the Harvard School of Public Health, "180,000 deaths per year occur from medical mistakes, the equivalent of three jumbo jet crashes every two days!"

The right question to ask in these situations is: *"Why are we sick?"* as opposed to *"What can we do to cover the symptoms?"*

In fact, masking symptoms typically aggravates the underlying cause of an injury or illness, and often accentuates the problem. In addition to worsening the disease, the side effects can be as devastating as the illness itself. To find true solutions to your problems, your focus needs to shift toward understanding the cause of sickness.

WE DEVELOP SICKNESS...WE DON'T CATCH IT

In my 20 years of research, I have discovered that sickness and disease is nothing more than the result of something we lack in our body (*Deficiency*) or something we have present that shouldn't be there (*Toxicity*). These are the *only* two routes to sickness. I've also come to the conclusion, that disease can only be eliminated once we introduce the polar opposite of its cause into the body – that is *Sufficiency* and *Purity*!

Another discovery that I made, is that taking toxic drugs or removing body parts will never restore health because these actions never deal with the cause of your illness. Removing a sick organ doesn't make you healthier, just as adding air to a tire with a slow leak doesn't fix that problem either. It may help in the short term, but the problem will inevitably re-manifest because the underlying *deficiency* or *toxicity* is still present.

There's a time and a place for modern medicine and these procedures. In an acute crisis, it may be necessary to save a life. I'm completely supportive of measures used to save someone's life in an emergency situation. But as quickly as possible, treatment should focus on satisfying any *deficiency* or eliminating any *toxicity*. The patient who undergoes heart surgery, for example, but returns to their toxic eating habits afterwards, will inevitably end up back on that operating table in the future because the cause of their problem was never addressed.

Unfortunately, the vast majority of people feel that they catch disease from bad germs, bad genes and bad luck. The reality is we get sick from making bad choices. We don't *catch* disease, we *develop* it.

DON'T BLAME YOUR PARENTS, BLAME YOUR BAD CHOICES!

Back when I was studying genetics during my Biochemistry degree, I learned that genes control our traits and our health. I was taught that you receive your genes from your parents at conception, and that that they are the blueprint that will determine all physical, behavioral and health characteristics for the rest of your life. This is what we've been taught as a society through conventional health education from an early age--that we are slaves to our genes and that *they* will control our destiny.

In recent years, a new science, called Epigenetics, has emerged. This science demonstrates that *we* control our genome rather than being controlled by it. It has proven that genes are not self-actualizing, meaning that they cannot turn themselves on and off. Genes are simply blueprints and therefore cannot accomplish anything on their own. Genes function based on the environment to which they are exposed. This is significant because conventional medicine is based on the notion that we are victims of our genetic blueprint--that we are simply the result of how healthy our ancestors were and that we will fall prey to the same diseases that our biological ancestors suffered.

Epigenetics shows us that our preconceived ideas of genetics are not accurate. Coming back to our automobile analogy, genetics is the frame of the car and without you driving the car, it goes nowhere. *You* decide the direction in which *you* will travel. It's the choices that *you* make on a daily basis that influence *your* health: *You* decide how to fuel your car and how to maintain it in optimal running condition. Your levels of health are nothing more than the cumulative effects of all the choices you've made in the past.

If you are sick, your body is talking to you and telling you that you are out-of-balance. Therefore, you need to restore homeostasis in the body in order to recapture your health. While drug companies are busy studying sickness and looking for answers in the medicines they prescribe, holistic practitioners are studying health and finding that true healing comes from within. Western medicine believes that curing occurs with an outside-in approach: Give the patient a drug (from outside the body) and hope they get better. Holistic practitioners on the other hand, understand that healing only occurs from the inside-out—once you re-establish function within the body.

You may be asking yourself the following question: What requirements do I have in order to re-establish a state of balance and express my full health potential?

(1) Proper nutrients,

(2) Positive thoughts and

(3) Adequate movement.

These are not only the three pillars of health, but also the only three parameters that affect genetic expression and therefore your complete health. This is the foundation of the *3GX Longevity Blueprint ™* that my wife and I formulated and have been teaching people in our Wellness Centre and around the world for the past 12 years.

The 3GX Longevity Blueprint ™

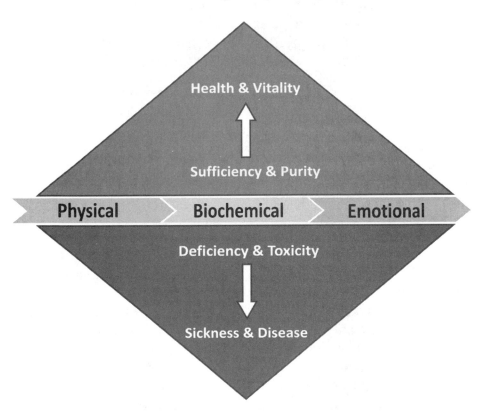

Only **3** parameters affect **G**enetic e**X**pression:
Physical, Biochemical and Emotional Stress.

If you're ready to reclaim your life, I encourage you to spend some time exploring *your* 3 pillars of health. Be honest with yourself about whether or not you are providing your body with the *sufficiency* and *purity* needed in the physical, biochemical and emotional pillars. Once you provide for your body's true needs, you will drive health and vitality upward, all the while avoiding sickness and disease which are simply a result of *deficiency* and *toxicity*.

Just as you can't drive a car forward and in reverse at the same time, you can't be moving toward health and sickness simultaneously either. Your health will only move in the one direction that you push it toward. So make an effort to swing the pendulum toward the life of your dreams and I guarantee you that you will move in that direction. But you must stay focused and keep your eye on the goal—optimum health and vitality. Yes, you will fall down, you will deviate and you will get discouraged at times, but when the breakdown is big enough, the breakthroughs are even bigger! So make sure you clearly understand why you are on this new journey and if your *why* is big enough and loud enough in your mind, you will push forward and you will always have a phenomenal breakthrough.

Always remember that you were born to be well, you were designed for greatness and you have an unlimited health potential, but your choices will often get in the way. And this is why I've written an eBook to help you make better choices along your journey to better health and vitality. It's entitled: ***The 7 Dangerous Habits That Are Threatening Your Health and Leading To Premature Death***. In this book, you will discover what you may doing on a daily basis that is increasing your odds of developing life-threatening diseases and what you must do to reverse those odds.

Emerson once said: "That which we persist in doing becomes easier - not that the nature of the task has changed, but our ability to do has increased." By developing persistent patterns that are congruent with your genetic blueprint, and creating *sufficiency* and *purity* in all three pillars of health, you will increase your body's ability to cope with the daily demands of the environment we live in, and become successful at creating a world-class life that will ensure vibrant years ahead!

Yours In Health,

Dr. Luc

About Luc

Dr. Luc Lemire is a wellness expert who specializes in preventing and reversing diseases naturally with his highly-acclaimed, *3GX Longevity Blueprint ™* that leads to shifts in health that most Doctors would say is impossible.

He is the president, founder and research director of the *Whole Body Wellness Centre & InnerMiracles.com.* He has also served on the National Chiropractic Examining Board, a Nutritional Scientific Advisory Board, and as the chapter President of the Heart and Stroke Foundation. Dr. Lemire has also been named as one of America's PremierExperts® in recognition of his success and knowledge as a Best-Selling Author and International Speaker in the Health and Wellness industry.

He is a board-certified specialist whose seminars have become famous for two reasons: first is his world-class content – which is easy to implement; and second, the fact that these proven strategies will literally reverse premature death. This has led him to be called *"one of the greatest wellness experts of our time."* This is the primary reason that many of the world's leading companies hire him as their keynote speaker. Some of his clients include: Wal-Mart, Union Gas, Hydro One, Government Agencies, The Art Institute of Dallas, London Life, Freedom 55 Financial, large insurance companies, banks, as well as a number of School Boards, Colleges and Universities. At these fun, entertaining and life-changing events, you will emerge from your experience with the latest advances in scientific research and the knowledge and skills to create long-lasting change in your life and your expression of health!

Dr. Lemire is that rare health authority capable of guiding you down the path of lifestyle change, including the recalibration of the subconscious mind, optimal nutritional protocols and principles of physiology and exercise. For contact information for Dr. Luc, visit:
www.InnerMiracles.com
www.WholeBody.ca

CHAPTER 39

WINNING FROM WITHIN: ON BEING PRESENT AND RESILIENT

BY LUPE-REBEKA SAMANIEGO, Ph.D.

THE WINNING PATH

Lately, it seems to me that in many settings, no matter where I look - school environments, work and corporate settings, homes, airports, and institutions, individuals everywhere are struggling with loss. But this is a book on 'the winning way,' you may say, what does this have to do with loss? There exists a vital bond between losing and winning. In feeling powerless, one gains new strength.

I think of Nelson Mandela and the world mourning his loss while celebrating his legacy. He lived a life exemplified by the winning belief that "the greatest glory in living lies not in never falling, but in rising every time we fall."[1] Mandela brought dignity and freedom to South Africa by engaging in a winning path that symbolizes "not merely {casting} off one's chains, but {living} in a way that respects and enhances the freedom of others."[2] Nelson Mandela, indeed a hero, emerged with exemplary resiliency by moving beyond 'casting off his chains' to become a respected and loved inspirational leader.

---

1 *Life Commemorative Special: Nelson Mandela 1918-2013.*
  Life Books, Managing Editor: Robert Sullivan. 2013.
2 *Life Commemorative Special: Nelson Mandela 1918-2013.*
  Life Books, Managing Editor: Robert Sullivan. 2013.

And I also think of Tommy* whose mother died suddenly when he was three years old. In his marriage he held on to the relational needs of a helpless three year old who missed his mom. He feared losing his spouse and clung emotionally to her. With desperate attempts to keep her close, Tommy desired primarily for his spouse to 'physically hold him' especially when he felt distressed. As a 35 year old, he needed to move experientially from the past and feel in the present the deeply buried anguish and hurt of the loss of his mother. As he faced his anguish and mourned his mother, he began to relate to his spouse, not as a substitute mother, but as a loving partner. He developed an empathic awareness of his spouse's needs and began to ask, "I wonder how she experienced me all of these years?" He engaged her directly in the here-and-now of the present. He learned to resonate with her feelings and respond accordingly. In engaging empathically and winning the present love of his spouse, he also won the ability to express genuine emotions and developed resiliency in dealing with ruptures and disruptions.

And I remember Kevin* who frequently would engage in impulsive and emotional encounters with partners outside of his current relationship. He began to integrate the past with the present and processed his past from a new perspective. He saw the emotional connections between his past traumatic history and his present way of sustaining his self-esteem through brief sexual encounters. As he faced his emotions and sense of himself, he let go of a fantasy of perfection and power that got in the way of winning in life. Kevin began to access his own feelings of feeling flawed and came to accept that there are flaws in every human bond and connection. He began to find newer and healthier ways of sustaining his energy and his self-esteem. It is at this time that he truly began to experience 'being in love' as well as holding on to a passionate connection. He found the 'winning' path by developing more resilient ways of relating and increased his self-confidence in relating to others.

Our 'winning way' thus includes separations and departures from those whom we love and also the ideas we cling to. It also embraces the inescapable fact of the coming of age and the coming of our last phase of life. And yet, throughout all phases of living, we gain so much. We

---

* Confidentiality Note: Tommy and Kevin are hypothetical individuals based on the author's 30 years of clinical experience. Any reference or resemblance to any one person or organization, whether living or dead, existing or defunct, is purely coincidental.

really win by losing. In feeling and leaving and letting go, we become more resilient and embark upon our winning path.

OUR INNER AND OUTER LENS

Many books have been written about how to win in life. Among the paths include routes to obtain status, money, power, celebrity, and leadership skills needed to get ahead. They frequently focus on an outer lens.

By looking within, we take a deeper dive using an inner lens. This path embraces an inner guide emphasizing the role of our inner minds. Our inner lens focuses on our emotions, our sensations, and our intuitions. By focusing within, we also begin to know our passions, our perceptions, and notice our desire for connection with others. We begin to notice, for example, that we experience grief when we lose. And we feel passion when we love; vitality when we are affirmed. We also feel righteous anger when treated unfairly, coupled with physiological sensations, judgments, and desires.

It is important to stress, however, that it is within our conscious awareness where we attach meaning to our experiences. Our conscious mind thus creates the meaning we make out of our experiences in the world.

Going even deeper, decisions are frequently made below our level of awareness in what we refer to as our unconscious minds. Our initial impressions of someone come from experiences that are thus out of our self-awareness; this is also true of our inner biases created throughout our lives. Yet these submerged experiences are at the core of what makes us feel alive, shape our judgment, and help us with skills needed to win. On the other hand, our inner biases may also interfere with our winning path. Our conscious mind may fool us by creating narratives in order to make sense of what is out of our conscious level of awareness.

For example, individuals may engage in many altruistic activities that may mask a craving for external recognition. They may tell themselves that they are engaged in an activity because they desire nothing else than 'to help others.' Nonetheless, a deeper dive into their inner mind reveals that they are also striving for a connection with others, and yearn to be noticed and outwardly praised by those they help.

The 'winning way' therefore acknowledges our inner lens by tuning into what emotions and experiences move us forward and what holds us back.

WHAT HOLDS US BACK

In order to win, however, we need to face what holds us back. More importantly, by deepening our self-concept, our self-esteem, and our self-confidence, we begin to face our losses and get onto the path of winning. We let go of blame. We forego putting on others feelings that belong to ourselves, and looking outside of ourselves to find what we are lacking inside ourselves. "If only" phrases become a thing of the past, such as, "If only my boyfriend would love me more, I would feel more beautiful; if only my boss paid me more, I would be more successful; if only my parents had noticed me more, I would respect myself more."

It is in accessing, feeling, and accepting our deepest emotions that we begin to experience joy and a genuine freedom to live a life of vitality. The buried fear, anguish, sadness, anger, shame, and/or hurt begins to emerge. It is in being present that we can succeed. By noticing our range of emotions, experiencing them, and embracing them, we are more able to manage them. In feeling fully, we live fully as we become 'unstuck' and embark upon the winning path.

What are common emotional reactions that hold us back? It is not the emotion that holds us back. What holds us back lies in the manner in which we respond and how we regulate our emotions when triggered by the following examples:

- Feeling/being threatened or disrespected
- Feeling/being treated unfairly
- Feeling/being unappreciated
- Feeling/being not heard or listened to
- Feeling/being overwhelmed with emotions or deadlines

Psychologists, neuroscientists, anthropologists, and researchers now tell us that our thoughts, as well as our emotions and biases that occur below our level of awareness are what interfere with the winning path. Within a matter of seconds, we quickly form a negative impression of someone walking into the conference room in a business meeting. We become uncomfortable around this individual and may not be fully aware of where the discomfort is coming from. Perhaps it is in the unfamiliarity of their physical appearance or the accent in their voice. We thus may consciously choose to stay away from him/her and thus miss an opportunity to get to know and engage and learn. By becoming aware of our inner lens we become open to new experiences. Being open to experiences and engaging openly with others is on par with 'the winning way.'

So how do we access the 'winning path' into our emotional inner life, you may ask? A beginning path involves the concept of presence.

ON PRESENCE

A teacher instructs her student 'to stay present.' She is desiring that her student remain focused and pay attention to a task. Presence, however, is a journey that we take into ourselves. Presence is a winning path that we plunge into by engaging in a focused awareness of 'who we are' and 'how we are' in the moment. When we are present, we are being ourselves in the moment. We notice the external environment as well as our internal world. We are embracing what we are feeling, sensing, and viewing with full awareness of the moment that we are in. We are not in the past nor in the future. By being in the moment we also notice others, as well as ourselves, and the mind-state that we are in. We accept others and ourselves as we are being in the moment. A significant benefit of 'presence' is that by becoming aware and being attuned to the present moment, we can simply focus our thoughts. And we move away from anxiety and worry toward the winning path of feeling calm and centered.

Simple yet powerful awareness statements bring about an intention to focus on the external environment as well as our internal sensations in the present moment. It is important to remain in the here-and-now. We put aside, for the moment, tomorrow or what occurred yesterday. We temporarily leave out the future. Simple awareness statements bring about powerful internal changes. One shifts quickly from an internal anxious mind-state to a calming experience.

The following include examples beginning with the wording "I am aware..." and illustrate how one can focus on staying present:

- "I am aware of.....my breathing."

- "I am aware of….my sensations in my body, my muscles, my gut feelings."
- "I am aware of… my hands touching the doorknob."
- "I am aware of …the sun shining brightly and the air blowing on my face."
- "I am aware of ….getting out of my car and into a relaxed mind-state."
- "I am aware of…the beauty of the landscape as I look out my window."

According to psychologists and researchers, presence is a 'state of being' where we 'take in' an experience in the moment by entering into a brief and temporary space of noticing our external environment, while simultaneously noticing our internal world of sensations and emotions, and experiencing them without criticizing ourselves or others. For example, we become fully aware of our external environment and may notice that others are shouting, or crying, or laughing while we ourselves may notice that our bodies are yearning to escape the situation. We do not criticize the experience. We observe and accept it 'as is.' We may decide to regulate our internal sensations simply by consciously focusing internally on how we are breathing.

The role of conscious awareness is therefore significant for 'presence' to occur. We are not fully present when we engage in auto-pilot responding or are waiting anxiously to 'get our turn' to speak. When we are not fully aware of the beauty of life and others in it, it is an indicator that we are living too rushed, too frantic, too preoccupied, and need to move into a winning state of being fully alive and fully present in the moment.

I am reminded of a conversation that I overheard on an airplane as I flew from Santa Clara to Denver one Sunday morning. Two young men who were returning from a 'Brain Conference' were exchanging notes as they enthusiastically discussed the newly discovered brain research. They had a background in engineering and computer science. I learned of their ages when the 40-year-old announced that his 20-year-old son had an infant daughter. He was remarking to the 39-year-old that his spouse was very concerned that their 20-year-old daughter-in-law was feeding the baby while multi-tasking. "She holds the baby with one hand, props the bottle up on a pillow to feed her, while she is texting on her cell and 'surfing the net.' What ever happened to cooing to your baby?" he remarked.

I was reminded of the importance of being present and being responded to with presence from the first moments of life. Babies, similar to adults, need to be held and be seen, heard, felt and touched. Babies need to be affirmed in order to grow up and feel alive just like adults need to have a boss who cares about them in order to experience vitality at work. We all need to 'feel felt' so that we can 'feel within.' As we mature, we will then be better able to observe our emotions and sensations, reflect upon them, as well as regulate them at the same time. We will then be more able to engage in the winning path of life by moving toward choice, action, and change.

BENEFITS OF BEING PRESENT

Research studies tell us that the more we are fully present, the more we win. Our engagement with others becomes more positive and we feel more centered as we experience inner calm. Other benefits include the following:

- We move away from a state of worry and anxiety toward calmness and contentment and become more resilient with disruptions in life.
- We perform better all around because we become more focused.
- We can improve our overall health while we receive benefits at the cellular level, and may even strengthen our DNA.
- We increase our energy and decrease our stress as we lower our blood pressure.
- We improve our ability to resolve conflict because we do not get triggered so easily as we engage with others in a more calm and centered manner.
- We have better relationships and an increased ability for intimate and meaningful connections, especially as feelings of despair, anger, and hurt move into a space of less importance.
- We can engage in laughter and play more.
- Learning becomes easier because we are more centered and can think more clearly.

- Presence improves our ability to lead others with empathy and compassion without being overwhelmed because we can sense, hold, and titrate within us powerful emotions and internal sensations.
- We thus make better overall decisions.

For the past three decades I have been engaged in the inner world of individuals. It has been a gift to be part of a journey toward self-understanding and self-integration. Together we learned where they have been, who they are now, and understood how they have coped in hurtful and traumatic ways. Many come fearing self-discovery. And while I continue to gain a profound appreciation for the uniqueness and complexity of human life, these individuals have taught me a deep respect for 'the winning way.' In taking a deeper dive into their inner minds, they faced and shared their emotional life stories with me and did not allow their life-disrupting experiences to overtake them. Instead, they learned to develop the strong resiliency skill of 'presence' and set out on a transformational journey that defined their lives. It is here where they embarked upon the winning path.

About Lupe

Lupe-Rebeka Samaniego, Ph.D., licensed Clinical Psychologist, inspires individuals daily to transform their lives. She is an expert in human development, human behavior, and traumatic stress. She is also a collaborating author of the recently-launched International Bestseller book, *The Expert Success Solution.* For over three decades, Lupe has influenced individuals to create meaningful connections, live with inner calm and vitality, and make a difference in their lives. Lupe is also a Certified High Performance Coach. Her passion led to the creation of Colorado Center for High Performance Living where she guides professionals, through her workshops on Life-Auditing for High Performance Living,™ with skills leading to a life of vitality, inner calm, and meaning.

A sought after psychotherapist, speaker, and mentor, Lupe integrates brain science within a developmental framework and influences individuals daily to deepen compassion and empathy. In addition, Lupe has extensive teaching experience, authored articles on topics related to loss and trauma, and received awards for her contributions in teaching and service. To honor her and continue her legacy, the Graduate School of Professional Psychology at the University of Denver, Denver, Colorado, created the Lupe-Rebeka Samaniego, Ph.D. endowed scholarship fund that benefits future generations of psychologists.

Lupe obtained her pre-doctoral clinical internship at the University of Colorado Health Sciences Center and later a post-doctoral NIHM fellowship in Child and Adolescent Psychology from the same location. She received training in adult psychoanalysis from the Denver Institute for Psychoanalysis, Denver, Colorado.

Contact information:

Visit: www.drsamaniego.com

CHAPTER 40

TRADE THE MARKETS WITH UNCONVENTIONAL WISDOM — THREE PSYCHOLOGICAL MINDSETS YOU MUST HAVE TO BEAT WALL STREET

BY MATT CHOI, CMT

INTRODUCTION

It's eight o'clock in the evening – the time of day when I am at my best. My kid is sound asleep and my wife and I just finished dinner and a glass of *pinot noir*. With the U.S. markets closed and Asia yet to open for trading, it gives me a window of serenity where I can think about the markets without all the noise. Crude Oil is trending up and I found a price to go long. I put in my buy limit order, target, and stop loss and let the market come to me. Looking at my open positions I find my bonds trade up two handles, and with FOMC minutes tomorrow I decide to take profits. I am done for the night. It's time to catch the newest episode of Criminal Minds.

It's easy to understand why so many people are attracted to trading. Unlike the typical job with many rules and guidelines, trading has no boundaries. You have the freedom to set your own rules, you choose where and when you work, and you decide how much money you want to wager on each trade. What else gives you such flexibility to make money with a click of the mouse? What else is so simple where you can make money by just guessing correctly whether a stock, a commodity, or a currency will go up or down in price? But if trading is so simple, then why do most traders lose money and fail to achieve consistent and profitable results?

When I first started trading, I believed that beating the markets requires perfect analysis. I spent hours and hours studying the markets trying to understand why it moves the way it does, hoping to predict the next big move. Over time, I felt like I knew more and more about the markets, but my trading results were not improving at all. It wasn't until a few years after I started trading when I had an epiphany. I realized that the way we typically think makes it very difficult to achieve success trading the markets. In fact, the mindset that we learned in school and from our work experience is opposite to what is required to become a consistent and profitable trader. The bottom line is that although trading is simple, it is difficult to master because it is counterintuitive and paradoxical. For the rest of the chapter, I will show you the three psychological mindsets I acquired to become a consistent and profitable trader, all of which you can adapt for your own trading if you have an open mind.

(1) ACCEPT MARKET UNCERTAINTY

The first psychological mindset to acquire is to accept market uncertainty. This means that you believe each trade you take is a random event, and the outcome is out of your control and has nothing to do with any of your analysis. Think about it, there are millions and millions of investors, traders, and institutions betting on the markets each day, creating infinite combinations of buying and selling dynamics. It is the cumulative action of all these participants that moves the markets up or down. So unless you know why and how much each and every market participant is buying or selling, it is impossible to predict what the markets will do. And because you can't make such a prediction, you must accept the fact that markets are random and uncertain.

Before I go any further, let's circle back to examine why most people fail at trading. As human beings, we are brought up to believe that there is a correct answer to most things in life – there is an answer to why a car wouldn't start, why one has a heart attack, or even why gravity exists. So when novices start trading, they also seek an answer to why markets move. They listen to tips from TV anchors who make bold market predictions to increase viewer ratings. They listen to advice from brokers who make a living off of transactional commissions. And when all those fail, they spend thousands and thousands buying systems only to find they don't work either. Finally they start doing their own analysis, spending hours and hours ciphering through company balance sheets and reading charts, but still fail to achieve consistent profitable results.

The truth is, no matter how much time you spend studying the markets, you will never know what all other market participants are doing. There is no trading textbook that will tell you whether the markets are going up or down next week. Novice traders often believe that trading success is directly related to how much you know about the markets, and such belief is reinforced when they get lucky and their analysis correctly predicts market direction coupled with a few winning trades. This gives them a false sense of security that markets can be conquered strictly via analysis and knowledge. However, trouble arises when they encounter a losing streak. They begin to doubt their analysis techniques, and naturally they resort to doing even more studies on the markets but to no avail, and the more frustrated they become.

Don't get me wrong – market analysis is important. You need to have an arsenal of tools to analyze the markets, and you need to be confident that these tools give you an edge. My trading turned profitable when I stopped searching for new analysis techniques and started to believe in the tools I already had. I started to accept that markets are uncertain, and as such in the short run, I will have randomly distributed winners and losers. However, in the long run, I trust that my edge gives me a higher probability of winning than losing. Believing in market uncertainty is critical in acquiring a trader's mindset and lays the foundation for the next phase.

(2) FOCUS ON "NOW"

"The only source of knowledge is experience." – Albert Einstein

A child learns not to touch the stove again after being burned by the hot element, and a chef makes changes to his recipe after negative customer feedback. We've all been conditioned to learn from our past experience, and for the most part it works, because if we change our behavior there will likely be a different outcome. The child won't get burned if she doesn't touch the stove, and the food will taste less salty if the chef uses less salt.

But in trading, it is detrimental to associate your trading decision with past results. Recently a friend who just started trading asked me for help. He had a setup trading gold futures that was generating winning results. He had a six-trade winning streak, and he became so confident that he doubled his next bets. Then all of a sudden he had four losers in a row, wiping out all of his previous profits. He then modified his setup thinking that his original strategy no longer works. He took the next four trades with his new setup but only one was a winner. He got very frustrated and is now taking a hiatus from trading. Our minds are conditioned to associate with the most recent events. After losing consecutive trades, novice traders develop fear that hinders their decision-making ability, which in turn causes them to change their strategy, deviate from their trading plan, or even worse, creating a perception that the market is out to get them. On the other hand, when novice traders experience a few winning trades they become euphoric and overconfident, which in turn leads to overtrading (i.e., not waiting for their edge) and risking too much money on each trade, which is how most traders lose their entire account.

Professional traders understand that each trade is uncertain and random, and as such they look at each opportunity independently of previous trades. This is a very difficult mindset to acquire because it is unnatural for us to wipe the slate clean each time we are making a trading decision without thinking about recent results. After all, isn't it natural to feel fearful and rejected when you lose five trades in a row? Or isn't it natural to feel happy and confident when the strategy that you created gave you six straight winners? Great traders only focus on opportunities that are happening NOW. They have no emotions when trading because they see the markets as neutral and are simply giving out unbiased information. When their edge appears they take the trade without hesitation. There is no hesitation because there is no association with previous winning or losing trades. Once you can fully accept market uncertainty and can focus only on opportunities that are happening now, you are ready to acquire the third and final psychological mindset to become a successful trader.

(3) THINK PROBABILITY

By now you must be wondering that if markets are uncertain then how can I achieve consistent and profitable results? Although markets are uncertain in the short run, long-term predictable results are achievable. To illustrate this point, I will use blackjack as an analogy. Based on the game rules, it is mathematically deduced that the casino has a 55% probability or edge for winning each hand. That said, in the short run, any player can get lucky and have a five, ten, or even fifteen game winning streak and in doing so beating the house. However, the casino understands that in the long run after millions of blackjack hands are played, the odds will play out and it will win very close to 55% of all hands. And because they understand their edge and have the deep pockets to stay in the business, the casino does not panic when some lucky player walks away with large winnings.

Similar to the blackjack game rules, your analysis, setup, indicators, and entry/exit rules give you an edge trading the markets. You will have both winning and losing trades in the short run, and in the long run your edge will give you a higher probability of winning than losing. When you encounter a losing streak you do not panic and continue to trade without hesitation when your edge appears, and when you are winning and making money you continue to risk the same amount on every trade because you know that a losing trade can be just around the corner. Being able to think in probability also helps you become a more disciplined trader. When you finally see trading as just a numbers game, you will no longer need to rationalize why markets move the way they do. You won't need to tune into CNBC and listen to all the so-called experts tell you why the markets went up or down, because you know they don't have the answer either. You will be able to trade with less emotion and less stress, and this allows you to think more clearly and as a result – make better trading decisions.

FINAL THOUGHTS

At the beginning of the chapter I said that trading is simple but difficult to master. I hope you now realize that trading is difficult to master *because* it is simple. Most traders fail because they think the markets are solvable problems when in fact they are uncertain and random. They fail to see that traditional education not only hinders, but also acts as an opposing force to acquiring a successful trader's mindset. As a result, they overanalyze the markets and wipe out their accounts looking for answers that don't exist. The good news is you will be able to see the markets in their simplest forms when you acquire the three psychological mindsets described in this chapter. Not only that, you will also be able to compartmentalize your thinking to leverage these winning mindsets only when trading the markets. I wish I discovered all this earlier in my trading career, it would have saved me tons of money and I would have become a consistent and profitable trader much earlier.

I will leave you with a few recommendations on how to acquire the three psychological mindsets so you too can become a successful trader:

I. First, you need to develop a few edges or strategies and apply them to no more than five markets. My trading took a leap forward when my mentor suggested that rather than trading every market and being jack-of-all-trades, I should become an expert and trade only a few of them.

II. Second, after you discover what you want to trade and how to trade them, develop and stick to your trading plan with proper risk management. The key here is to risk as little as possible on each trade. I suggest no more than 0.5% of your account so you can preserve your capital while you master the trade. The less money you lose on each trade the less pain you will feel and the more you can maintain the winning mindsets necessary to make proper decisions.

III. Third, you should get a mentor to help you develop your trading business. While having a mentor is no guarantee for success, he or she can make sure you have the right mindset and help you focus on your goals. For me, I attribute my success to my own hard work, but at the same time I can honestly say that with my mentor's help I was able to achieve success years faster than I originally expected.

IV. Finally, you must apply the three psychological mindsets at all times to keep trading simple. If you can do all that, I assure you that you will see a breakthrough in your trading, and very soon you will become a consistent and profitable trader well on your way to achieve great success in life.

About Matt

Matt Choi is a successful, self-taught, professional trader with over 13 years of experience trading the markets. He is a CMT (Chartered Market Technician) who specializes in trading stocks, commodities, Forex, and bonds. He is also the founder of CertusTrading.com, an online trading education and consulting firm. An entrepreneur at heart, Matt owned and managed a successful car dealership after obtaining his MBA from McMaster University while he traded the markets on the side. He always knew that his passion lies in the financial markets because the opportunities there are limitless, and it can give him the mobile lifestyle that he wants. So he sold his business to focus full time on his trading.

Matt's first exposure to the financial markets came at the tender age of 10 when he would wait outside the Hong Kong Stock Exchange while his grandfather finished making his trades. The constantly changing stock prices on the green screens, along with his grandfather's investing philosophy, fascinated Matt. During the early 80s, Hong Kong was going through an economic boom and Matt's grandfather was convinced that HSBC, being the largest financial institution, would be a good long-term investment; so he invested his hard-earned money and multiplied his investment more than 500 fold. With unwavering belief in his analysis and consistent strategy, Matt's grandfather went on to pick a few more big winners, such as Bell and Nortel.

His grandfather's rags to riches journey ignited Matt's passion in the markets. Although Matt's trading strategy differs from his grandfather's buy-and-hold approach, they share the same attitude toward trading – which is one of conviction, diligence, and consistent strategy.

Unlike many professional traders whose experience come from working on the exchange floor or for large hedge funds trading other people's accounts, Matt's experience and knowledge was accumulated after years of trading his own money. Having been through the school of hard knocks, Matt knows firsthand all the common mistakes of the typical trader and has developed profitable trading strategies and a winning mindset that beat the markets. While he enjoyed the freedom that his trading success brought him, he wanted to help other traders achieve the same. So he founded CertusTrading.com to share his hard-learned knowledge and unique experience with other traders so that they can also enjoy the freedom that trading success could bring.

Matt lives in Toronto, Canada with his wife, son, and Wheaton Terrier. In his downtime, you can catch Matt enjoying soccer – but only on TV now, after a knee injury made him hang up his cleats. As an avid foodie, he enjoys travelling the world with his family, savoring gourmet cuisine and local delicacies.

You can reach Matt at: matt@certustrading.com or on Twitter @mattchoitrader

CHAPTER 41

WINNING WITHOUT WORRY

BY PAUL EMERY

PART ONE

When working towards being successful there are many tools available: studying with mentors, attending seminars, reading personal development books and of course, hard work. Why is it that with all this at their disposal, some people are still not reaching the potential they strive for? Is it because the right guidance or tools are lacking? Or isn't there the ability to take action and implement all they have learned? If so, then why?

It's because of what I call your 'Success Stoppers'. These are the psychological barriers that include stress, worry, anxiety, anger and above all, fear. These stop people, perhaps like you, from being the very best they can be. Winners!

'Success Stoppers' impact all areas of your life, relationships, health, work performance and therefore bottom-line. Here are some cases from recent clients: One had such a strong fear of failure that his business lagged behind his competition because he lacked the confidence to do what was necessary to grow his business. Another was always tired and often got sick, so lost productive workdays because he never took holidays due to his fear of delegation. A third was frequently irritable, frustrated and angry, and worked below her potential due to sleepless nights stressing, worrying and over-thinking about her business.

Fortunately, they all overcame their challenges in a short while, and without medication or months of therapy. They did so by using a few simple, proven strategies alongside the latest cutting-edge mind/body methods. I provide these in Part Two of this chapter to help you let go of any current challenges you may have.

If only these innovations were available from my mid-teens onwards, there wouldn't have been 35 years of suffering high levels of stress and worry. In fact, my biggest obstacle was a fear of public speaking, maybe you too have experienced it from time to time! The uncontrollable anxiety, the racing heart, sweaty palms, blank mind and the unbearable and uncontrollable 'fight or flight' feelings. There was frequently a feeling of insecurity and nervousness and not just in front of strangers or groups, but also around people who I knew.

Tired of suffering, by my late teens I confided in my doctor who diagnosed a 'Social Phobia.' He said I would grow out of it, which wasn't much help at that time! In order to become calmer and more confident, I studied every self-development book around, from the *Power of Positive Thinking* to *Self-hypnosis*. They helped a little, but I never made any real improvement.

Over the coming years the symptoms continued – maintaining pressure on my social activities and stretching to increasingly affect my career, work success, performance and ultimately promotion prospects.

Therefore, business meetings were traumatic. I'd do almost anything to avoid them or not contribute to a discussion, even with something of value to say. When being called upon to speak, my insecurity would quickly reappear. The speech that came out was a nervous, incoherent, jumbled mess, even though I knew my work well and excelled at it. At those times it was obvious the management would never consider a promotion.

Further anxious years passed. Unable to solve the problem by my thirties, it was time to seek assistance. I turned to friends and work colleagues who were surprisingly sympathetic and understanding and offered some advice. Though helpful and comforting, and even with sharing this, the anxiety remained.

As the years passed, seeking professional help through attending sessions held by therapists became necessary. They were all useful, but, frustratingly, no one could cure me. Eventually I gave up hope after being told I was a complex case. That it was a hard-wired issue. Subsequently anti-anxiety medication was later prescribed, which was quickly stopped due to its terrible side-effects. Medication as you know, is never a real long-term solution – as it often just suppresses the symptoms without addressing the root cause.

This led to gaining a growing fascination with psychology and the decision to train as a counsellor. By studying the subject and working amongst teachers and other students perhaps it would somehow help alleviate the problem. Not so, as once again nothing was gained leading to an increased hopelessness.

My career progressed onto an executive level and was going quite well. Then the company's 10th anniversary arrived and the role I played for them required a speech in front of 500 industry people as well as the media. Imagine the horror!

Luckily though there was a month to prepare. Fear aside, to be a successful speaker, I know you've got to concentrate on the basics; be familiar with the subject, plan, rehearse, etc. I also introduced Mnemonic techniques to the script to make it easy and importantly unforgettable.

Come the night, nerves did set in but confidence was high as I had practiced and memorized the script from back to front. The time drew close and the anxiety increased as the crowd swelled. Once being introduced and called onto the stage straight into the spotlight, the feelings returned. The heart started to race and my mind went blank, wiping out all that had been learnt. Frantically, the speech was rushed through with anything that could be recalled. It was nowhere as good or as comprehensive as planned.

The reception was lukewarm which was embarrassing and disheartening. I knew the subject and was capable of doing better. It was yet another blow, not only for confidence but also for career prospects.

Anxious years passed. I then discovered the groundbreaking solution orientated psychological techniques of NLP (Neuro-Linguistic

Programming), which you may be familiar with. NLP is based not on 'the why' you have a problem but rather how you create it – what you see, hear or feel for example. Once discovered, it can be changed to create relief from your problem. I was good at helping others using its tools, so I opened up a small part-time coaching and therapy practice.

Another magical find was the powerful techniques of the now widely popular EFT (Emotional Freedom Techniques). EFT is proven to remove any negative emotional response by means of simple 'tapping' on specific nervous system (acupressure) points to calm and neutralize stressful thoughts.

Incorporating NLP and EFT into my practice, results with clients were nothing short of amazing, and with a very high success rate! It was often possible to quickly alleviate any emotional stress, everything from fear of flying, sadness and relationship problems to war veterans suffering from PTSD. But with everything the tools and techniques could accomplish, and all the successes other practitioners had, neither I nor they could still alleviate my fears! There still was a piece missing as to why it didn't work for me and a handful of others

Nonetheless, whilst continuing to help others I also worked in full-time employment to earn a decent living. Unfortunately, the job involved giving occasional presentations, which, as they were stressful, led to avoidance in many cases. In the ones that were unavoidable I'd distract the focus away from me, either by using power-point or through group discussion. Unfortunately, at one point during work the anxiety became so bad the only option was to quit the job. Career, income and life had really started to be impacted now.

By my early forties, the biggest and most profound changes finally happened upon discovering the original calming and relaxing (tapping) method of TFT (Thought Field Therapy), alongside other revolutionary and powerful curative methods. Also by identifying food sensitivities and intolerances which also affected my emotional and physical well-being. These were the final piece in the puzzle that enabled me to increase my success rate and help those clients previously un-helpable.

Through a simplified yet comprehensive approach, the new discoveries did, in a very short while, what all other therapies and techniques couldn't. They cured my Social Phobia and fear of public speaking!

Encouraged by my increased results, soon after I opened up a full-time coaching and therapy practice to pass on my knowledge to help others.

The biggest realization and milestone about how successful the strategies and techniques helped came during my first appearance on live TV. Not only was the interview intensive featuring my life, work and success, but I was also asked to coach an audience member live during the show to help with a smoking problem they were currently dealing with - which I effectively accomplished.

Never in the past would that have ever been possible, or plausible. Even the mention of going on TV, let alone live TV would have made me tremble. In fact, it wouldn't have even been up for discussion. No fear or anxiety showed whilst performing the coaching techniques, which was a complete success. I was confident, calm and relaxed throughout – making the show a great triumph.

It was a challenge to have remained persistent for many decades to discover the help that eventually enabled me to become the relaxed and confident person I am today. It's easy now to talk calmly and confidently in front of anyone – even large groups or celebrity clients – and not through fear or anxiety any longer, but with passion and excitement.

It's a revelation to know that despite the odds, any psychological challenge holding people back can be overcome, no matter how long it's been around. All you need is the how. Fortunately, it's no longer a 35-year quest for you as it was for me, the tools are here now with me to share and help you with any limitation you may want to let go of.

PART TWO

Two Amazingly Effective Stress Busters!

My QEPR (Quantum Emotional and Physical Release) coaching and therapy consultations incorporate all the latest groundbreaking techniques and tools. One such recent huge advance in psychology and a powerful addition to QEPR is Havening. Some people aren't aware of these advances, yet all have been researched, developed and scientifically proven effective throughout the years.

With nothing to lose but the problem, give both my Stress Busters a go! Don't let the disappointment of past failures, or the fear of trying something new and different stop you from experimenting and succeeding in life. *Video of the techniques below can be viewed at http://www.quantumepr.com/blog/winningway

(Disclaimer: Do not use these techniques without a qualified practitioner if you suffer from a psychological disorder or severe trauma. Always consult your doctor before attempting any self-therapy.)

I. Havening

Havening (www.havening.org) is a 'Psycho-Sensory' therapy that is a massive break-through in modern psychology. Developed by Dr. Ronald Ruden, who, upon studying the brain discovered that sequences of repeated soothing touches to specific parts of the body, alongside eye movements and distracting visualizations, have predictable and calming effects on our feelings. In fact, Havening reduces stress chemicals, increases the feel-good chemical Serotonin and quickly de-links negative and bothersome feelings from thoughts. It is usually performed by a qualified therapist but is also highly beneficial when self-applied.

There are three aspects to 'Self-Havening':

1. Retrieval of an emotion by recall.

2. Havening touch. This entails softly stroking down the arms, face then hands in a comforting fashion. These areas on the body are shown to produce strong electrical delta waves to the brain's emotional center, the *amygdala*. These waves in turn release an enzyme which permanently unhooks then strips away the specific stress-causing receptors from your *amygdala*.

3. Distraction techniques. This prevents continuous re-activation of the stress producing receptors.

How to reduce a stressful thought:

1. Eyes closed – take 30 seconds to bring to mind a distressing thought.

2. Rate feeling zero to ten – zero being no emotion ten the highest possible.

3. Eyes closed looking at the back of the eyelids 'clear your mind completely' of the problem as you begin self-havening: Cross your arms over and gently but firmly continuously stroke down from your shoulders to your elbows.

4. At the same time, visualize walking up a staircase of twenty steps. As you climb, 'each step causes the distress to diminish and for

you to feel safe, peaceful and calm.' Count aloud as you climb the steps in your imagination. Continue the arm self-havening.

5. After reaching twenty, continue the self-havening and hum a tune that makes you feel good, or is neutral in nature, e.g., Row, Row, Row Your Boat, Happy Birthday, Twinkle, Twinkle Little Star etc., for two verses.

6. When finished humming, open your eyes and look straight ahead, keeping head still. Look hard to the right and hard to the left, hard to the right, hard to the left. Close eyes and take a relaxing breath in and out.

7. Close your eyes again and continue gently arm-havening as you rate your level of distress again.

8. Repeat the entire sequence 1 - 6. But now instead of self-havening your arms, smooth across your forehead and cheeks at the same time from the center out, as if smoothly and comfortingly washing your face.

9. Repeat the entire sequence again 1 - 6. But this time, self-haven your hands by smoothly performing circular hand-washing type movements.

10. Repeat all above 1 – 9 until you feel the problem has diminished or gone.

II. Stress Reduction Breathing

A simple, but extremely effective breathing technique that's proven to lower stress and Cortisol levels, is quickly calming, makes you less reactive, emotionally stronger, helps you sleep better, improves your heart and raises your anti-aging DHEA hormone:

- If comfortable to do so, inhale slowly and smoothly through your nose, tongue resting on your gums just behind your top teeth, for a count of five seconds.

- Then exhale slowly through your mouth, tongue resting on the bottom of your mouth, also for a count of five seconds.

- Repeat for 5 to 20 minutes at a time, several times daily or as often as possible.

About Paul

Paul Emery helps his clients successfully overcome any psychological barrier to success and lead better, more fulfilling and confident lives by utilizing innovative, ground-breaking techniques.

Paul is great…it helped me!
~ Kate Moss, Supermodel and Icon

Born in Bristol, England, Paul grew up with an interest in personal development and subsequently studied at the 'University West of England' qualifying as a counselor/coach.

Identifying the needs of others to improve their lives, especially dealing with stress and worry more effectively, he also studied the innovative works of people like Anthony Robbins, Jack Canfield and Brian Tracy.

He really mastered his skills whilst employed in the corporate and business world of retail, telecommunications, education and finance.

Encouraged by the tremendous coaching results he got, he decided to train formally and be mentored by other recognized leaders in the personal development and psychological field, notably Dr. Richard Bandler, Paul Mckenna, Gary Craig, Dr. Roger Callahan and Dr. Ronald Ruden.

Paul is certified as an NLP (Neuro-Linguistic Programming) Master Practitioner, EFT (Emotional Freedom Techniques) Trainer, TFT (Thought Field Therapy) Advanced (Optimal Health) Practitioner, and more recently, a Havening Techniques Practitioner.

In 2002, he successfully launched his coaching and therapy practice that thrived by offering a rapid, no nonsense "Guaranteed Life-Changing Results" service.

Paul's service is centered on his philosophy that any psychological or emotional challenge can be easily and effectively overcome by the right guidance and tools.

His goal is to enable his clients to become more relaxed, confident and successful, to help them effectively conquer any limitation that holds them back, bringing out the optimal person they can be—the very best in all areas of their lives, in any situation, at any time either at work or at home.

He also believes in empowering his clients by teaching simple, yet effective tools and techniques for them to manage any challenge that may occur in their daily lives.

In 2010, Paul's eclectic and ever-evolving coaching and therapy service, QEPR (Quantum Emotional and Physical Release), was awarded the prestigious 'Holistic Treatment of the Year' by a panel of industry experts for his outstanding contribution to excellence in his field.

Over the years, he also developed his own ever-popular, stress-relieving, life enhancing light exercise class – 'Emer-gizes', which incorporates self-Shiatsu Makko Ho and Do-in exercises, Qigong, and Energy Medicine amongst others.

Paul frequently travels internationally helping thousands of clients from around the world from America to Australia with companies such as Chevron, Credit Suisse, and Turkey's Richmond (Nua). He's coached from billionaires, politicians, top CEO's and doctors to Royalty, Rock and pop Stars, even Hollywood and Bollywood actors.

He has been featured extensively on TV channels such as Fox, Sky and TNT; on the popular CH9 show *Celebrity Overhaul;* regularly on radio shows such as *Qatar Foundation Radio;* in international magazine and newspaper editions of *Vogue, Marie Claire, Harper's Bazaar, Cosmopolitan, Gala, Women's Health, Men's Health, Sydney Morning Herald, Millyet, Hurriyet,* the *Financial Times* and was featured in the bestselling book, *Ultimate Spa and Spa Treatments.*

He provides coaching or therapy either one-to-one in person, or via Skype, group workshops, QEPR Practitioner training courses, seminars and retreats.

Paul is author of the eBook and forthcoming hard copy, *Simple Stress and Anxiety Relief - Quick and Easy Steps to Stress Management with EFT.*

For more information, you can also connect with Paul at:
paul@quantumepr.com
www.quantumepr.com/blog
www.youtube.com/quantumepr
www.twitter.com/qepr
www.facebook.com/paulemerycoach

CHAPTER 42

TECHNOLOGY THAT VASTLY PRE-DATES SOCIAL MEDIA: THE CRYSTAL BALL

BY ERIC J. CHRISTESON, PhD

The crystal ball. A symbol known around the world for clairvoyance and seeing the future, might challenge your notion of items normally found in a business office. On the other hand, centuries ago no one would have grasped the concept of a tweet, a post, a blog or using social media to drive the decisions of one's company.

I am not crazy about social media, but I will accept that much about it can be leveraged with the use of just two eyeballs and a crystal ball. You can't solve every problem, or at least not every problem all at once, therefore your secret has to be how to prioritize and how to filter an easy and proper solution that works. Hence, enter the Crystal Ball: technology that vastly pre-dates social media.

Seers are said to see images of the future in the crystal, however, some seers purport not to see images, but to instead use the crystal as a means of clearing their minds so that the future can be made known to them. The latter is the approach you need when using your crystal ball in your business. All you need are your eyes, your conscious mind and an inexpensive crystal ball or some other clear object.

Additional information does not always help our decisions; in many cases, it hinders our decisions.

CRYSTAL BALLS TO QUIET THE VOICES

Social media creates too much buzz in the background; it allows us unmitigated access to too many people's opinions simultaneously. Your crystal ball, on the other hand, eliminates the background noise and gets down to the business of assessing and decision-making. What does a crystal ball really represent? Clarity. We see in it what we already know, but through a different lens. It warms to the touch, and when placed in direct sunlight, its prismatic affect can cause spontaneous combustion… setting fire to your world. Most importantly, the crystal ball takes YOU out of the equation.

Let's go a little further to examine how people talk to others about themselves. How we present ourselves to others is frequently not the same way that others would evaluate us. Would you describe yourself as a tidy person to live with? Would your spouse describe you as tidy? If you are laughing right now, we are on the right track. We know how other people see things. The people closest to us are present in our minds as unspoken advisors all day long. When we eliminate the background noise, through the all-powerful crystal ball, we are able to hear the trusted inner circle whose opinions actually do matter. We inherently know what they will tell us, even without asking.

My crystal ball sits prominently on my desk watching over me: listening to all my telephone conversations, and making sure that I keep to my diet. It has an all-knowing personality. Inside its perfectly round visage, there are a multitude of little crystal ball bubbles, each one working on a different question that I've posed. I simply speak to a different bubble to hear back the progress it has made on its assigned task.

It has more decision-making capability than Congress.

Am I being facetious? Maybe, but only a little.

What I advocate is decision-making based on the coordinates of today, not the analysis-paralysis from too much information from which so many entrepreneurs suffer. The crystal ball is the best decision-maker because in many cases choosing *something* will start the process moving forward, at the very least. Before social media clouded our judgment with the desire to have too many people's biased opinions, we sought counsel with less acquiescent things. How, then, will we use our crystal balls to keep us moving forward?

CRYSTAL BALLS TO PROBLEM-SOLVE

It was a dark and moldy moment…

Where are we now? When the calendar no longer tells you where you are and what you should do next, it's time to figure out where you and your business really are.

When you move forward, you have no choice but to move forward from your actual location, not where you ideally wanted to be. This means that when you make a mistake, admit it, change course and start over. You cannot simply pick up the plan where you left off; this is where people and businesses find themselves in dark and moldy moments. By the time that you figure out Plan A didn't work; you are already past the point where you developed plan A to begin with. Let me give you an analogy. A football coach calls a passing play when his team is at a certain position on the field; let's say they are on their own 25-yard line. The coach plans for the receiver to be open and for him to score a touchdown. That's the plan. By the time they tackle the receiver, he has made it to the opponent's 40-yard line. The coach has to call for a plan B play here, because, although his team did not score the touchdown, their position has changed. He has no choice but to assess "Where are we now?" and change plays based on the current team position.

Now, if the play he called went poorly, he has to assess how they got where they are before he makes a decision. Did the quarterback improperly execute the play? Was it the receiver's fault or the team's fault? Was the pass incomplete because of interference from the opponents? Did the opponent react differently to the play than was originally anticipated?

It is incumbent on entrepreneurs to be cognizant of the time to call a new play for the team. He or she has to interpret what has happened, good and bad in the business, predict the future on another course and create a plan. It is equally important to know where your competitors think you are.

Where would my opponent (or competitor) think we are?

As valuable as knowing your own coordinates in your business, you also need to know where your competitor sees you. Think back to your high school debate days. One of the best ways in which to clarify your own response to a situation or concern was to formulate the potential responses of your opponent. These anticipatory responses bring clarity to your argument and solutions to your problem. Deep down, you already know the answers; you just need to illuminate them.

How did we get here?

Is our current location a product of internal or external influences? My personal predicament in my business as I write this chapter is a telephone glitch induced by an office move. Despite all the best laid plans by my trusted assistant and the assured cooperation of the telephone company, our office telephones are still not operating six hours into the first day at our new location. We can use this conundrum as our case study for the moment. Did we execute the play properly? Some problems can only be resolved by a good funeral. Having ruled out the dysfunction or incompetence of my staff, I know that an external factor is to blame for the debacle. I know that my phones are not working, and I know that this is costing my business money while it inconveniences many of my staff, my customers and my shareholders. So, where do we go from here? We need to examine where we need to be—with functioning telephones so that business can transpire—and determine the logical next step.

Take responsibility now. DECIDE what happened and determine what potential actions could help pinpoint a future-saving alternative.

What are the alternatives?

While our telephones are down, business still needs to transpire. Therefore, we look for alternatives to complete as much business as possible until we meet our overall goal. We can still complete work that uses a computer or email. Therefore, we might opt to email our clients to explain the situation and transact business that way.

Another option is to ask the telephone company if they can forward any of our lines to a cellphone or two so that we will not completely miss all of our incoming calls. We can also access our company databases to obtain client telephone numbers and use those same cellphones to call our clients.

Our goal has not changed. We still desire a functional telephone system, in the same way that the football coach still wants a touchdown. Since the telephone company did not fulfill its original contract as specified, however, we are at a different position and we must change our next play. The football coach, when confronted with an exceptionally aggressive defense that keeps him from his goal, might use his crystal ball to select a running play after multiple pass interceptions. In any scenario, we choose the next best alternative.

Select the best alternative.

Once you select the best of the alternatives available to you, you have already changed position. The change in position automatically negates the original plan. Our inactive telephones today changed the position my company had planned to be in today into where we *actually* are today. I planned for one thing but another occurred. Continuing on a course that has already reached a dead end involves dreaming and wasted time. Out comes the crystal ball. What will the all-knowing crystal ball encourage me to do? The crystal ball tells me to move forward. Therefore, I call the next play.

Where do you desire to be or to go?

People will do almost anything, provided you give them a clear plan of where you want to go and what you plan to do. You are the leader, the coach; call a play. In the case of my telephone system, I know that my company cannot transact business or make money as effectively without our telephones. As the coach, I determined that my employees were not the reason for the inactive phones. This means that an outside influence determined my fate. It's time to regain control. I direct my attention to my available resources.

What are our resources?

What are my resources to remedy the problem of no working telephones?

I have logical options from which to choose:

> A) I can check with my current telephone company to see when they expect to be able to resolve the problem of my dysfunctional phone lines.

> B) I can contract with another company if one is available to complete the work and get my telephones operating in a shorter time.

> C) I can do nothing and lose money.

The crystal ball, having my best interest at heart, tells me that doing nothing equals failure. Option C, thus, is ruled out. At this point, my telephone provider reports that my telephones will be operational within 4 hours. Their competitor tells me they cannot have anyone at my office to connect new phone service until two days from now. My decision just became clear. I choose option A. In the meantime, I can focus on alternatives to use while they repair the original situation.

Let's roll.
The crystal ball is right. The next step is forward motion. Roll forward. Assess. Repeat. The crystal ball prevents you and your business from practicing the definition of insanity by repeating the same activities and hoping they net different results. The crystal ball—and the tiny bubbles within it—are a collection of filters. Use them as trusted sources in determining your next step. "Hey Ralph," I say to my crystal ball, because his name is Ralph, (I name most everything "Ralph.") "What do you think I should do about the telephone issue?" I can also ask Ralph, "How do you think Fritz (one of the more-experienced, tiny bubble filters and also a friend) would solve this problem?"

Everyone needs a crystal ball. Why? Have you ever tried reading a map without knowing where you are going? Absolutely a sure cure for insomnia. The crystal ball clarifies your end goal and enables you to predict – based on all your data points – the best method, given the road conditions that day, to get there. Personal growth equals the ability to remove yourself as an impediment to your own success.

Crystal balls offer a way to handle every problem that comes your way by removing yourself from the situation so that you are no longer an impediment to the solution. You use your subconscious mind to guide you to the answers you already possess. It really doesn't matter if you use an actual crystal ball, your favorite coffee mug or the Rolex watch you bought for yourself when you paid off your student loans. We *expect* crystal balls to predict the future. Removing notions of the past when you are looking at the crystal ball simply focuses you on predicting the future for yourself.

INCANTATIONS TO THE CRYSTAL BALL

"Oh crystal ball, seer of all and banisher of dark and moldy moments… enlighten me."

How should you talk to your crystal ball? While many a fortune-teller or magician has offered mystical words over a crystal ball in hopes of obtaining answers, I speak plain English to mine. As mentioned before, I named my crystal ball Ralph. You can name yours anything you choose.

My prediction is that the name is already waiting in the wings for your psyche to call it forth. Address your crystal ball like the old friend it is; you have known each other a long time. I promise you, as with any old friends, the awkward silences won't last long and you will be back to familiar banter with a team of trusted advisors in less time than it would take you to tweet or post a status update.

Ask your team, "How would your best friend handle this...?"

About Eric

Eric J. Christeson, CPA, MBA, PhD, DBA founded Dynamic Interface Systems Corporation (DISC) in 1982. As Chairman of the Board, Eric has spearheaded a team effort to cultivate strong sales and earnings growth while ensuring stability and long-term survival by acquiring or developing easy-to-learn, affordable, technologically-advanced products to assist the financial lending industry.

Prior to leading DISC, Eric spent twenty years in senior financial and line management positions in both small and Fortune 100 companies. During his tenure as CFO of a troubled, high-tech electronics firm, Eric restructured and refinanced the firm that then regained its NASDAQ listing and subsequent acceptance on the American Stock Exchange (AMEX). His additional experiences include controller of the $400-million division of a Fortune 100 company and several years as a contractor with the U.S. Department of Defense.

While in the U.S. Air Force, Eric obtained a Top Secret Cryptographic "codeword" Clearance. He has a B.A. degree in Russian from Syracuse University, a B.S. degree in Accounting from San Jose State University, and an M.B.A. with a concentration in Marketing also from San Jose. Dr. Christeson's Ph.D. in Economics and D.B.A. in Marketing Management both were conferred by Canterbury Christ Church University near London, England.

Despite a work ethic and schedule that would make lesser men cry "Uncle," in 2004 Eric was met at the door by his wife and his son as he arrived home from the office. He was greeted with the words, "Alex wants to join the Cub Scouts, Dear." Not one to shy away from a challenge, Eric began what he then-called his "second full-time job" as leader of a 160-youth Cub Scout pack for the Boy Scouts of America. Of his experiences in Boy Scouting, too numerous to mention, Eric says, "Scouting has changed my life forever, just as Scouting has changed the lives of boys everywhere forever."

As often happens when one excels at one's job, the Boy Scouts soon asked Eric to build a district leadership team as District Chairman—comprised of 6,000 youth and 2,500 adult leaders, for finance, training, membership, advancement, OA, camping and many more committees. He recently received the Silver Beaver Award from the Boy Scouts of America; "The Silver Beaver Award is made for service of exceptional character to boyhood by registered Scouters, Cubbers, and Explorer leaders…" Eric sums up his Boy Scouting experience by stating, "Nothing is more rewarding than watching a group of kids coming up the trail with smiling, dusty faces."

In his free time outside of work and volunteering in Boy Scouting, Eric sits on the Board of Directors for several other organizations. He and his family have been quiet, contributing members of the Unity Church of Unity Village, Missouri for the past 12 years.

CHAPTER 43

BE THE BIG FISH IN A SMALL POND

BY ROBERT KEIL

Give me a man who says, "This one thing I do."
and not, "These fifty things, I dabble in."
~ Dwight L. Moody

Imagine for a moment that you suffered from a critical sports injury. Maybe you tore your ACL. An injury of that nature requires a skilled orthopedic surgeon to perform the surgery needed to ensure a complete recovery. Obviously, the doctor's services won't be cheap and in this day and age we are all concerned about medical expenses.

So what would you do if your family doctor raises his hand and tells you he will perform the same operation for half the cost? You certainly like your doctor. That's why you have him perform your annual physical and see him when you are not feeling well, but chances are you will not have him fix your torn ACL. Why?

Because your doctor is a generalist and in order for you to have the best chance to regain full use of your knee you need a specialist that has plenty of experience with this specific injury.

The medical profession illustrates that the more specialized you are, the more you and your services will be in demand.

While this makes sense to almost everyone it seems that the vast majority of small business owners ignore this fact. As a result they never really get their business off the ground or, at the very least, struggle much more than they need to.

Just have a look at the ads you run across. Most of them are trying to get everyone to respond. And desiring to appeal to everyone, most ads just say something to the effect of, "I am the best and the cheapest." The result of this approach is that they mostly attract price shoppers who will haggle over price and are difficult to deal with. As soon as someone else offers a lower price, they will leave you for a competitor.

If you are the owner of a small business, you can likely relate and you wonder how to break this vicious cycle. In my practice as a business coach, I find that most entrepreneurs have great difficulties to define the corner of their market where they have less competition and generate larger profits.

In the remainder of this chapter, I will share with you the specific steps that have helped my clients to set themselves apart from their competition. I will sprinkle in some specific examples that illustrate how this has worked in real life.

UNDERSTAND WHAT BUSINESS YOU ARE IN

A big mistake many business owners make is that they define their business by what they do. Instead they need to define their business by the benefits they bring to their customers. Talking to your best clients will yield some interesting insights.

I recommend you talk about this with as many of your customers (that represent the top 20% of your clientele) as possible. In most businesses, these top 20% account for 80% of the company's income and therefore they are ones we need to pay attention to.

A landscaper might find out that his best customers found that they worked with him, because he was able to create the most relaxing and vacation-like setting in their backyard. Understanding this can lead the business to expand its offering. In addition to the traditional landscaping services, he could add fountains and outdoor lighting. He also found that while these clients enjoy a backyard that rivals a park or botanic garden, they often don't have the time or desire to maintain it. Chances are that a good number of them would gladly have the company that installed it all also maintain it. And, most importantly, they will make that decision without spending tons of time trying to find someone who can do it for a few dollars less.

Understanding what business you are really in will help you to determine if you are giving your most desirable clients all they want. The more products and services you add that cater to that segment of the population, the less competition you will have, because most of your competitors are only generalists.

UNDERSTAND WHO YOUR IDEAL CLIENT IS

Another key factor in creating the niche you can dominate is to understand who your ideal clients is. Again, it is a worthwhile exercise to examine the top 20% of your clients to determine what they have in common.

This exercise typically reveals a number of things our best customers have in common. Learn about them as much as possible. What is their gender, age and educational background? What sports do they like? Where do they vacation?

The more detailed you can get the better. Use your findings to create an avatar of your ideal customer and keep it in mind when you do your marketing and when you have any kind of interaction with them.

At the core of everyone's buying decision is emotion. Chances are that the more your marketing message relates to the wants and desires of your ideal target market, the better your chances are to cause in them the desire to buy from you.

As you figure out this critical detail you will notice how more and more of your customers are like the medical patient mentioned at the outset of the chapter who happily turns down the generalist who is willing to do the work for half the price.

LEARN FROM YOUR COMPETITION

Most of my clients had a major break-through when they took a closer look at their more successful competitors. Take a look at them and learn what they are doing differently. Who is their target market? What makes potential customers choose them over you?

Often this will give you some ideas that you can implement without copying exactly what they do.

One client of mine owns a photo studio and faced the same challenges that resulted in a declining business. She attracted a lot of price shoppers and over the last few years experienced more and more competition from smartphones. In the past, students needed to get their yearbook pictures taken by a professional. These days anyone with an iPhone can take yearbook pictures for free.

In looking at her competition, we found one photographer that was very successful despite this challenge. The way she did it was by creating an experience that the students would not forget anytime soon. First they would get their hair done by a professional. Then a make-up artist would prepare them for the photo shoot. In a nutshell, for a few hours these kids feel like movie stars.

This insight helped my client to create a new offering that is virtually without competition. She created a gift package for the woman that already has everything. Here is the gist of the offering. In my opinion, it is a great anniversary gift where your wife can be treated like a movie star.

In the morning a limo will pick her up and take her to a spa for a facial or a massage. Then she will be taken to a nice restaurant for lunch. After that she will get her hair and make-up done in preparation for a photo shoot. Once that is finished the limo will bring her to a restaurant where her husband meets her for dinner.

By creating this niche she eliminated almost all competition. After all, who do you compare her to? The spa, the hair salon or a photographer? You really can't compare her to any of them, because she is in a category of her own.

Learn from your competition and you will come across ideas that will transform your business.

WHAT IS YOUR UNIQUE SELLING PROPOSITION (USP)?

Having one or more clear USPs is critical to the success of your business. The USP is a clear and easy-to-understand statement that gives your prospects the reason(s) as to why they should do business with you rather than anyone else.

You may have heard the term "elevator speech." If you were to step into an elevator and someone asks you "What do you do?" you would give your elevator speech in response. Since an elevator ride doesn't take very long, you need to be able to deliver your message in 30-60 seconds.

A good elevator speech triggers the response: "How do you do that?" The answer "I am a landscaper." will not get this response, because everyone knows what a landscaper is. However, if you state, "I am helping home owners to create a vacation-like experience in their own backyard." you are more likely to solicit the "How do you do that?" response which invites further conversation.

In my experience, USPs that attract the right kind of client cover one or more of the following areas:

- The Buyer
  Again, the more specific you can be here the better your chances are to attract the customer you want to deal with. If your services are targeted towards a gender, age group, profession or genre, let your USP reflect that.

- The Product or Service
  Do you offer something that is so unique that your prospects cannot get it anywhere else? Make sure you clearly point that out.

- The Performance Guarantee
  Every consumer is afraid that they might not receive what they are paying for. Can you put their mind at ease with a specific performance guarantee? The better your product, the more powerful your guarantee can be.

- The Time Factor
  Can you deliver your service faster than your competitors? Do your products get faster results than anyone else's? Let your customer know.

- What You Are Not
  Sometimes your uniqueness in the market can be better explained by outlining what you are not. Are there no contracts or up-front fees? No late fees? No foul language is used by technicians doing the actual work? If this applies to your business emphasize how your approach is different from the competition.

Getting your USPs right will make a huge difference in how effective your marketing is.

SOME CONCLUDING THOUGHTS

Knowing and understanding your target market is absolutely essential for success in business. It has often been said (and it is so true in business) that it is better to be a big fish in a small pond than a small fish in a big pond.

This approach has given birth to some very successful companies. There is a long list of successful companies that started out that way and are now dominating their market. Take Whole Foods as an example. We already had plenty of grocery stores that were generalists. Along came Whole Foods and they started to target people that want organic and natural foods. They happily pay more for groceries that meet their specific needs. When you talk to a typical customer you find that they are raving fans and shopping there is part of their way of life.

Finding or creating your niche can have some other side benefits that will send you on the Winning Way. Catering to a specific market segment and forming an emotional bond with customers will result in more referral activity. When you deliver your product in a way that satisfied a true emotional need your customers will send more business your way, especially if you run some effective referral promotions.

Once you found and conquered your niche find another one. A financial planner could specialize in small business owners and at the same time can become an expert catering to retirees. If you have more than one niche make sure you market to each group separately.

Lastly, finding that unique target market and mastering it can lead to some additional income opportunities. Licensing or franchising your way of doing business to other players in your field can provide a meaningful passive income without creating more competition.

Now go and become a big fish in your small pond. You will find that you will attract better customers, have less competition and ultimately have much more fun with your business!

About Robert

Robert Keil has always been an entrepreneur at heart. He grew up in Germany and in his youth he played a lot of tennis. He found that many of the other club members needed to have their racquets strung. So he saved up some money and bought a tennis racket stringer. A few ads on the club's bulletin board got him his first customers and pretty quickly he added to the product offering in the form of tennis balls, shoes and clothing. His school mates always wondered how he could afford more than most of them.

When he moved to the US he returned to his entrepreneurial roots and started a commercial cleaning company. Within two years he had over 20 employees and then successfully sold the company. Thereafter he honed his business skills in Corporate America. Eventually he was responsible for $400 million in annual revenue for a business line of a top 5 bank. He managed several nationwide sales teams, marketing and for a while, the product development.

While he enjoyed his time in the corporate world and gained much valuable experience, the desire to run his own business surfaced again. He started a real estate investing business eight years ago to create a stream of passive income while working for the bank. He still owns this company.

In 2012, his paths crossed with Brian Tracy's FocalPoint organization and eventually he decided to join them. He became one their certified business coaches and sales trainers. This change has allowed him to spend more time with his family. At the same time he is able to follow his passion of helping entrepreneurs grow their business in a predictable and systematic way.

He is using a powerful program created by Brian Tracy and combines it with his own business experience. This allows him to relate to the needs of small companies just starting up as well as large companies with hundreds of millions in revenue. He can provide assistance in the fields of Marketing, Sales, Time Management, Leadership and Exit Strategies.

Robert lives with his family in the Minneapolis area. They enjoy traveling as a family and regularly spend time in Europe. Additionally, they enjoy a wide range of activities from attending sports events and concerts to visiting museums, fine dining and movies.

He would be happy to help you create a blueprint for your business that will allow you to create your niche market. You can reach out to him via his website: www.robertkeilcoaching.com or you can call him at 952-472-9804.

CHAPTER 44

"YOU MUST WANT TO WIN OR IT'S GOODBYE"

BY ROBERT PUTNAM

Winning isn't everything. Wanting to win is.
~ Catfish Hunter, Baseball Player

Wanting to win, as I see it, is a deep desire for your business to stay open. If you are not the CEO of a business, then your wanting is to keep your job. You want to keep the income coming in so you can support yourself and others.

If you have any doubts about the impact of jobs lost, then think of all the stories you've heard. Notice I said heard, first hand, and not something you read in the papers or online. Whether we realize it or not, the desire to keep your job, keep the business open, is in our bones; always in the back of our minds. Since you can't ignore it, you better figure out a way to win and make it part of your daily and long-term goals.

Threats to any business need to be analyzed and not allow your fears to get the best of you. That leaves us with threats or risks from disasters or an economic crisis. On one end of the scale, it means going out of business or the business closing. Think you can "react" to the situation as it develops? Think again.

Research shows the number of businesses that closed after the Sandy storm (October, 2012) is staggering. We all know what happened after Hurricane Katrina (August, 2005). Stories abound of the local troubles still in place in Fukushima, Japan (2011). Add in tornadoes and fire, and you quickly realize that the probability of a disaster severely affecting your business is high enough to warrant a continuity plan, a winning plan to stay open, no matter what.

Take a look at the number of economic and marketing changes we have been through recently and throughout history. The Great Recession touched everyone and "What to do?" goes back to The Great Depression. The point here is, if you are still thinking that you can react to the crisis and get through, this not right thinking. The old saying about knee-jerk reactions is true. Most immediate reactions have long term consequences that are best avoided. Put "bail out" or "government hand out" out of your mind and start thinking of a way to avoid all this.

How you plan to keep your business running will determine if you make it through the crisis. Prepare for that fight like it is a title match. Statistics show us that many businesses will close in a long disaster lasting two weeks or more. When I say business, think community, city or any group that wants to stay open, in business, through any crisis.

Developing and implementing a continuity plan is going to be the toughest thing you will do. Still want to win? Remind yourself of this every chance you get. Draw inspiration from outside the business world by looking at sports. Name one successful sports team that claimed, "We don't know how we did it." They knew, they had a plan and they executed that plan no matter what hurdles got in their way.

United wills make a fortress.
~ Author Unknown

In order to win, the business needs to be a fortress. This is not too harsh of word. Everyone, from the CEO/Owner to the essential group of employees, will need to be united on building this fortress. Let me say what this fortress is not.

It is not a "Castle." The Age of Castles died long ago, as they didn't adapt to the changing world around them. There was no benefit to the general population or merchants, despite changing to "Manor" homes.

It is not a military style fortress. Think of all the frontier forts in United States history. What good does a fort on the Kansas frontier do today? A nice tourist attraction perhaps. "Man your battle stations" is not meant to be a motivating statement nor part of the business continuity plan.

It is not a "retreat." Using the word retreat for anything never sat well with me. It is a word used when you are going in the wrong direction. Current use of the word can mean a survival retreat that doesn't amount to more than a fortified bunker. This is another bad idea. No business or family group can win or survive in what most retreat or bunker scenarios have planned.

What you need is a fortress for the twenty-first century. I call it the "Fortress21" concept. A Fortress21 plan creates a holistic environment that includes the basic needs of the worker and the business so they can stay open through, and survive, the crisis. Survival means keeping the business open in a way that works for the company, the employees and the customers that depend on that business. Not an easy mission as you will see below.

The business continuity plan should include fortress features. It has to include a place for everyone to live and work. Housing can include condominiums and apartments on site. It should include a suite hotel or extended living facility. All of the people have to eat so restaurants, fast food, and a farmer's market are needed. Plan for a courtyard in the center of the site for eating out and/or exercising. Office and convention space is needed so that the business is conducted on site or within short walking distance. During a crisis, everyone needs some level of medical attention. The site doesn't need to have a full-blown hospital but it can have an urgent care facility or clinic of some kind. Branching off on a tangent here, but we tend to put elder care facilities "out of sight." Why not plan for that to be part of this complex. I think you see where I am going with this.

A Fortress21 in a Garden City is a win for the local community and the businesses in that city. If this fortress becomes too much of a stand-alone facility, then it loses the benefits originally planned. A way to improve this and tie together many fortresses would be to create or adapt a current city or town into a Garden City. Sir Ebenezer Howard used this term in his book, "Garden Cities of To-morrow" (1902). It starts us down the path of looking at urban planning in a whole new light. When we talk about uniting the wills into a fortress business, the same can be said for uniting a city into a Garden City.

Urban planning for a Garden City (fortress business) still considers the basics: Land use, open spaces, natural resources, housing, transportation, recreation, infrastructure and public services. It plans for all this from a different viewpoint. The chances of a "cookie-cutter" concept or plan that can be duplicated in other locations is remote and not worth attempting. What environment is your city and business located in and what makes it unique? Figure out how to take advantage of your environment in an intelligent manner. Several cities in the United Kingdom, Canada and the United States of America are on the right track. The same is true for businesses looking to go "Green" and what to do with their large cash balance.

Go to: www.3cfortress.com and look at the picture of Windsor Castle in Great Britain. I ask you to play a small trick on your brain, as you look it over. Think about how this can be a business fortress, with all that I mentioned before, located in a Garden City with people able to walk to work, home, and play.

What a picture. Left tower equals the office spaces. Right tower is the suite hotel. Condominiums and apartments located on the facing second level and beyond. Retail shops and entertainment located on the ground level. Parking can be underground along with a secure storage facility. Imagine what the courtyard in the center looks like. The footpaths, places to stop and eat, with all the fresh air you can take in. Overall health improves, as you want to go for a walk through this site. Your parents and the kids grandparents could live somewhere in this complex. A working farm that supports the food supply can be just beyond the trees. Urban planning is transformed into a more holistic approach. **Walk, walk, walk** to business, home and entertainment. Every time I look at this picture I think of all the places that this concept could be adapted to and make life just a little better for all of us.

We don't rise to the level of our expectations,
we fall to the level of our training.
~Archilochus

Training is key to making any plan work. It has to be done incrementally or you end up with confusion, possibly failure. Train everyone on your communication plan and test it before you have a full-blown exercise. Have a "picnic" day at work (on site) to test your food and water plans. Have a "Family Get-Away Weekend" at the local hotel to test out the housing piece of your plan. Over that weekend, have training be fun events that involves the whole family.

AdIOS – *Adapt Improvise Overcome Survive*
~ Modified quote by Robert Putnam

This acronym, which means 'goodbye' in Spanish, is my way of planning to win. We started off stressing that a plan is needed and as you write your plan, take these four points into consideration. If you don't, then it will be **goodbye** to your business.

Ad – Adapt is to adjust oneself to different conditions, environments. With the current conditions in business, finance, and social networking changing so fast, it comes down to adapting to stay ahead of these changes. Adapting in the face of stress or adversity is resilience. Not only can this be considered step one, adapting is needed in just about any other step towards winning.

I – Improvise is to invent, compose, or perform with little or no preparation. Another way to put it is making do with whatever materials are at hand. One could argue that improvise is what happens when you fail to plan. I disagree, as the point here is that many plans can fall apart when it comes time to execute them. Improvise doesn't have to mean "knee-jerk reaction." Improvise is having the courage to perform under stress, leading up to the next point. What you learn needs to go back into the plan, the training, so that you learn from it and can apply it the next time.

O – Overcome means to gain victory; win; conquer; by any means possible. Think back to the beginning of this chapter and think about your chances of overcoming without a desire to win or without a plan. Doesn't sound good! Create a plan to win with a Standing Operating Procedure (SOP) or playbook that takes a cold hard look at what needs to be done so that your chances of success are greatly improved.

S – Survive means just that. Win, endure or live through an affliction, adversity, crisis or disaster. This is the bottom-line or the objective or your plan. Another "S" word can be Sustain or Sustainability. All of this must to be done in a way that promotes long-term balance.

Adapting a current plan or editing it is a start in the right direction to win. Improvising is continually assessing the situation and making the adjustments while executing the plan. Overcome means you see the end-state that you have been working so hard to reach. Survive/Sustain means you win and accomplished your mission. Beyond any personal pride in all this, think of the benefits to the associates at your business, their families, and the customers this helped get through the crisis.

Stating that your business or family needs to have a "fortified" plan in order to win, stay open and survive a disaster or crisis and get moving in the right direction. Plans shouldn't sit on the shelf. Once everyone commits to the plan, you practice and rehearse it so it is relevant and everyone knows what to do. This is my manifesto to the world and I hope to be part of this change.

About Robert

Robert Putnam leads teams to achieve that next level of excellence. After graduating college he was commissioned a Marine Corps Infantry Officer. He led infantry, reconnaissance, and Special Operations units. After getting a second bachelor's degree in Computer Science, Robert was the Project Manager for a wireless telecom. These projects were for Call Center and Retail Store applications. Robert took time to work as a Private Security Contractor in Iraq leading a multi-national guard force at the U.S. Embassy. Robert is currently working for FEMA in Disaster Recovery middle manager role.

Robert's current work with FEMA enables him to hone business continuity, crisis planning, and disaster recovery skills. In the military it was called support operations and contingency planning. At a Forward Operating Base in Iraq, staying in business presented several logistical and security challenges. Add it all up and Robert understands how to stay in business despite a changing market place or when a crisis presents itself.

Robert is a graduate of Missouri University (in Columbia) and Missouri State (in Springfield) majoring in Computer Science and Political Science respectively. Robert authored a memoir book about his father, *The Life and Times of R.L. Putnam, Jr.* All of his thirty years of experience goes into how to make tomorrow better than today. Yet with all this experience, Robert is committed to a lifetime of learning. In this Just-in-Time world, it is never too late to learn a new way of getting things done.

After starting an online blog and business, Robert is passing on his expert skills at his website: www.Fortress21.com and www.3CFortress.com. Connect with him at the web site or email: rwputnam@consultant.com.

CHAPTER 45

THE END OF THE PILL ERA: HOW CHIROPRACTORS ARE BRINGING BACK NATURE'S WINNING WAY.

BY SOREN MAJGAARD

Inadvertently, I read that the fascinating mayor of New York, Michael Rubens Bloomberg, told the British Prime Minister David Cameron that, "the worst combination of things is, not to do the right thing and to lose. Then you have nothing to hold your hat on."

 He was right. because I realized, that even if I had just written a book to commemorate D. D. Palmer, the founder of chiropractic 100 years after his death, I hadn't finished. There was more to do.

The writing of the book, '**D.D. Palmer's Testament**', had given me an opportunity to explain D.D. Palmer's 'winning way,' the biomechanical mechanisms as well as the fundamental chiropractic principle: _Function over Structure_, so that people suffering from pain could understand why chiropractic was not just a treatment of symptoms, but a treatment of the very cause in most neuromuscular skeletal cases. Chiropractic is part and parcel of Nature's Winning Way and that is the reason why chiropractic is so effective.

I had explained why the stability of the vertebral column is based on a natural _suction/vacuum principle_ as well as a _tripod principle._

The meniscus in joints functions like a piston in a syringe. If the piston/meniscus doesn't function, the vacuum doesn't form and the ligament and muscle tendon attachments to the bone-tissue become inflamed and painful. Muscle acidity may give pain too, but not discs, nerve-roots and joint cartilage, so don't operate and don't kill the nerve roots with phenols, etc.

I'll say it this way: It's an unneccessary expense for the taxpayers.

We in chiropractic acknowledge and strengthen those principles nature uses, and stability will be in danger, when the disc is operated on, and it isn't a good idea to operate if not absolutely neccessary, because pain doesn't come from the discs, nor the nerve roots. A hernia operation would eventually improve a nerve's impulses to the muscles, but lead to complications in 50% of all the disc operations (Johns Hopkins, April 20, 2012). Therefore, a disc operation should be looked upon as a failed procedure that is not only dangerous, but also costly, and even more so if the costs of the complications are calculated into the equation. Traction under anesthesia is also a failed procedure. Chiropractic decompression is the only safe way.

Dr. Reckeweg's Disease Evolution Table, which you can see on Google's www.heelusa.com/Practitioners/docs/DET_Chart_en1108.pdf reveals that the medical profession understands the academic principles of the disease evolution.

We chiropractors apply these principles in a very practical biomechanical way, combining our treatment with sound dietary advice and special excercises – Nature's way. The chiropractic treatment gives the body a better chance to fight inflammation and heal disturbed organ functions by itself. We do our utmost to help the patient fight and win, so that the condition doesn't turn into disease. We realize that only the body can heal. We trust Nature has an inborn genetic ability to fight disease when we have helped to remove the blocks —just as a car runs better when the handbrake is released. We never ignore to help the body follow it's own 'winning way' when it asks for help and says so with a symptom. The symptom is very often pain, and in 80% of all sorts of pain, the condition is referred pain from neuromuscular skeletal conditions.

I also realized that 'The Winning Way' was a philosophical gem, because everybody by upbringing, education or religion, think that they have the right 'Winning Way' without having taken a moment to ponder if 'their way' is ethically or morally acceptable and in harmony with nature. We know that for some, 'The Winning Way' is a Stash o' Cash and they are absolutely fine with that.

It suddenly made sense why - when we are on our 'winning way' and we're opposed - we press harder to be heard and also why we must try to find consensus, because we can only get that consensus when what we say and do makes sense to the listener or the spectator. So it's no wonder why we all too often can't get to terms with each other when trying to make the blind see and the deaf hear.

That is a serious problem. Because in philosophical terms, we can't say that we're winning if we can't explain it simply and clearly enough to get consensus. Can we?

Chiropractic has been practiced for over one hundred years. Actually, since D.D. Palmer gave a patient a treatment that not even D.D. Palmer knew should be the first chiropractic treatment ever – because the name 'chiropractic' had not been coined yet. Not even D.D. Palmer knew what it was. He was only gradually turning a discovery that he had stumbled over into a new professional method, principle and philosophy, building the foundation of chiropractic up on his clinical observations and experiments. And he paid for it by two jail sentences in 1903 and 1906.

You may say that clinical observations are regarded as less important than large–scale controlled trials. That is highly debatable, because an astute observer can have developed a laser-sharp and useful understanding of a patient's therapeutic needs, like D.D. Palmer did, and therefore give you better care, than can be obtained by giving a treatment, where there is statistical evidence saying that it works.

Significance or positive evidence can be very small indeed. Controlled research in spite of what you may be told, is not necessarily leading to better care, because it has become the gold standard and now must fit all. We are not test tubes. We are living beings, not cadavers. We don't react the same way to the same treatment. We're reacting in a myriad of different ways, depending on different genetics and psyche, diets, age, living style and environment, culture, body dynamics and sleep as well as stress. So can you be sure that the research covers all variables, and fits your needs before you have tried it?

You can't.

Much of the medical research is being given a value it doesn't merit, in spite of all precautions. If the research builds on a principle and <u>a biomechanical mechanism Nature uses</u>, the positive evidence could be high. If it's built on a biochemical synthesis that only can be patented because it works differently from Nature's own way, it's outcome and effectiveness is much more dubious. Because then you want to force a biochemical process to work in reverse, Because that's what is is, when the patented product or medicine turns spectrophotometric light left, while it must turn it right to work in your living biochemical body. But then you can't patent it.

That's why it is unsettling that the medico-pharmaceutical industry is subsidizing 'organisations against quackery' to attack the chiropractic profession working diligently with Nature's principles, and calls cooperation with Nature dangerous, when in fact, they break all the rules of the laws Nature has been using for millions of years, just to have their own products patented.

It's therefore food for thought that a Science-Ethical Committee for Copenhagen and Frederiksberg Municipalities in Denmark has found that 75% of all published medical-scientific material was no more than promotional material and rated fraudulent. Some companies promoted synthetic hormone preparations, which were contra-indicated.

In another promotion, the principal scientific author of the scientific material hadn't even read what he had 'written,' but he had been paid.

Clinical Evidence Publication from a British Medical journal, showed positive and proven effect rating was a mere 3%. But how can it be otherwise, when scientists work squarely against Nature and fill the scientific magazines with scientific material, written by communication bureaus on material coming from pharmacists in such companies.

A vice president from one of the largest phamaceutical companies in the world admitted that 90% of their products didn't work. Another big company admitted that they couldn't prove or substantiate what they claimed: That their products worked against diseases such as cancer, heart diseases or female hormone diseases, when in fact they didn't. Money is king – one winning way. Or, is there a better winning way?

I think we chiropractors have a better winning way. We observe Nature closely. We help Nature to do it's own unparalleled healing. We can't heal. We can only adjust, so nature can repair, when given the right conditions to accomplish what is genetically built into your body. Of course, I can't rewrite a 535 page book in 2000 words, but I can bring you the essence of the principles. Otherwise blame me, that I don't understand it:

24 vertebrae are stacked on top of each other. With the exception of the upper one, each vertebra forms a tripod and the front leg of the tripod rests on a very strong pillow, the so-called disc. The disc may look bad if herniated, but should be left alone instead of being operated on, because an operation weakens the structure . The tripod-vertebra is the engineering marvel. It produces stability in spite of a torn disk, whereas four legs would fail. The disk is placed and anchored to the vertebra below and above, beginning at the sacrum, which is a bone made of five fused vertebrae.The sacrum is stabilized at it's right and it's left margin by a long and strong ligament, we treat to keep the sacrum movable without compromising the stability of the pelvic ring. The two other legs of the tripod form the hind-legs of the tripod and they are covered with strong cartilage. They form the joints with the two posterior tripod legs sticking up from below. There are no pain receptors in the disk, the nerve root, or the joint cartilage. So the pain doesn't come from there. The pain comes from somewhere else.

The covering of the bone is very sensitive. Therefore the ligaments, which are anchored in this covering, called the periosteum, will give off pain, when the ligament- and muscle-attachments are overstretched, or in part, or totally ripped off.

A weakened ligament is by reflex helped by neighboring muscles, so they function as active stabilizers, but they have a 'trick up their sleeve,' because they send distress signals to the brain and these are amplified in the brain's cortex and signals are sent back to the cells in the pertinent areas of the spinal cord. Nerve circuits of impulses go from the spinal cord to the muscles. But instead of stimulating the nerve impulses of these circuits, the impulses are suppressed, so that less impulses reach the muscles. When the healing has taken place, we can often restore normal nerve emission from the spinal cord.

Obviously the muscles are being protected this way from use. Because the lowered impulse emission from the spinal cord acts as protection from further damage. It even spreads to neighboring muscles, thereby adding to the protection. But to make sure that you don't move, one more trick is coming out of the sleeve: Pain. To assure, that muscles function, they must be supple, so that they can contract and move fresh blood coming from the lungs into the muscles. The chemical that does just that, is ATP produced in the energy factories of the muscle. But the factory can't produce without energy, like when an electric grid is 'down.' That energy has been blocked by the brain impulse mechanisms, and we now have muscle stiffness, because the muscle can't get fresh alkaline blood in and lactic acid out, so acidic metabolites accumulate. When the acidity reaches the pH of 5, you always have pain. We call it referred pain. You need to rest to recover, so use a cold compress and stay put. If you don't want to respect Mother Nature, you can take a pill and play macho. Some sports people have done that, and quite a few have paid the highest price: With their life.

Where does the chiropractor come in?

He looks for the cause of your misery. The meniscus in the periphery of the joints is the mechanism allowing movement and at the same time assures a degree of stability, by creating a vacuum, when the joint movement sucks it in! A good normal vacuum in a healthy joint is up to 2,5 atmospheres, and is created during the joint movement. It is a masterpiece of creation. But alas, it is not infallible. With age or following an accident, you may have lost the vacuum and now the joint is less stable, inflamed or even full of liquid. The joint movements will hurt and damage the anchorage of the ligament into the periosteum, making things worse. And the muscles may give in as well, at their insertions or at their triggerpoints. So you see how re-establishing a good vacuum is very essential. Naturally, we can also improve the ligament attachments and also help the muscles. That's actually what we do every day. By listening to and understanding what Nature wants, we have helped millions of patients for more than one hundred years, and because we aim never to violate Nature's intentions, our safety record is the highest in the 'Health Industry'..

About Soren

SOREN MAJGAARD, DC, MSc

You may not believe this, but my Mother pushed me! She wanted a doctor she could trust. So luck more than my own desire sent me to the USA to study chiropractic.

I had no idea what it was, but actually chiropractic would propel me into a hobby more than a job.

I have come to love this work so much that I'm still working at an advanced age of 77, but that's not uncommon for chiropractors. They are a group of devoted – should I say fanatics – so they stay on the job until they die.

In 1970 or so, I helped assist the Anglo-European Chiropractic College in its start up and I enjoyed teaching Chiropractic and Special Pathology.

In 1985, I jumped ship to work in France after I had written a book in Denmark about chiropractic and had worked with the CEO Bent Brylle of a mattress company, who accepted my wish to cooperate with me and make a mattress to be called 'Marie Tudor', which meant in French, 'You sleep, Marie.' In other words, a wonderful mattress to help an ailing back. It was patented in Europe and the CEO Lars Larsen of Jysk, bought half of the company and initiated a five million kroner campaign – a good sum at that time – to promote chiropractic, because I became the galleon figure although I was now in France. This attempt to promote chiropractic was immediatly rewarded with a 5000 kr fine from my professional association. I declined to pay and quit the organization, but having understood that my sole purpose was to promote chiropractors, in the same way that dentists are promoted by fluoride toothpaste, I was forgiven. My mattress was certainly healthier than the fluoride toothpaste.

You can read about this and my study for a Master's Degree at Life University in Georgia over the period 1997 – 1999, in my thanks to D.D. Palmer. My book is written 100 years after his death (Oct. 20 1913). The book, I called *D.D. Palmer's Testament,* and I owe the book to this awesome man, not only because of my career, but especially because it has saved millions of patients from pain and misery.

I returned to Denmark in 2001, and then I went to France again in 2008 only to settle down in Coevorden in 2011. The work included working with young Soccer players in the 100 year old soccer club, Germanicus. I did enjoy it, but it also made me realize that the sport is more challenging, than I had hoped. The players continued to play on pain relief like Diclophenac, even when I wanted them to stop until they recovered. I remember my last game, where a wonderful and talented player was run down and paid for his bravery 15 minutes before 'game over' and he had to have his knee operated on.

That's why I stick with what I know I can handle.

www.screening.eu. com

CHAPTER 46

FIVE POINTS THAT FARMING TAUGHT ME

BY STEPHEN A. STACK

How does a farm boy get into sales, especially in the financial planning industry? This question has always made me think of the journey and be thankful for the very same. You see I was a farmer's son, and have memories back to age three when my father was a farm manager. He had returned to farming after a short time working for Dunlop Tire and Rubber in western New York.

My father only had an eighth grade education but a great work ethic. He was the middle of three boys while my grandfather was the oldest of eight who immigrated to the USA in 1916 and chose farming. Well, farming was all they really knew as they came from the Czech Republic as we know it. They were crop farmers and dairy farmers. This all came about as my grandfather tried to get work on the docks in Pittsburgh, but our then name was of the Slovak decent and did not afford him the opportunity as they favored Irish and English workers. The name was changed to allow my grandfather and his brothers jobs on the docks, but farming was the ultimate love. My father purchased a farm from my grandfather and moved our family – my Mom, brother, Dad and myself – to this new location and this is where my development began.

As a five year old, I was given chores in the barn. I was to carry the milk the length of the barn and place into cans. We later went to using a large bulk tank to store and cool the milk. We were the first in the county to obtain such a device. We made hay bales and stored them, cut wood to warm the home, cleaned the barn by hand and even put up the winter supply to feed the animals by hand. Automation was on the horizon.

Tractors got more powerful to handle the need for equipment; larger equipment was being produced to aid the timely and quick methods needed to increase production for the increased need of our products.

Things were starting to move at a faster pace and change was coming. The lifestyle was fantastic for a young man to start his development as a person of values. We enjoyed the years, didn't complain, and waited patiently for things to come full circle. We usually had most of our hay up before the fourth of July, and would get rewarded by going to the lake for a weekend. We drove back and forth after the milking. The animals don't care if you are not there. They start to drop their milk. We conditioned the animals to be milked at the same time to make it easier for the process. It was a great life we had. We knew what we had to do, when we needed to be there and looked forward to the reward after we finished, only to repeat it daily and yearly. The work ethic was being put into place.

In November of 1958, a serious accident happened to my father that would make or break the family unit. My Dad lost his left hand in a farming accident. I remember my feet hitting the road while getting off the school bus and the sensation that something serious was wrong. The silence in the air, the lack of farm activity that should be present and NO family member there to greet two elementary school boys at the drive way.

We had a system though. If no parent was home, we were to go up the road to the neighbors and stay with them until Mom and Dad got home and we did just that. Being curious about this unusual event, I started to ask questions as to what may have taken place. This is the time in my life when I understood the art of sensing things. I could tell on the face of the neighbor lady and the tone in her voice that something serious had happened. I later was told of the accident my father had had, he lost his hand in a field chopper and had walked a quarter mile to get help. He did not panic as it would have cost him dearly and finally got another farmer to take him to the hospital.

We tried to continue farming for a while. The neighbors would take turns milking, families made meals, others watched my brother and I while all the work still needed to be completed. I became my father's strength at age seven. I could handle a hundred-pound bag of feed and hold the hitch while Dad backed up the tractor. I was now the main strength my father had lost.

This lasted about a year and Dad lost interest and we sold the farm. We lived on a rented place until Dad decided what he wanted to do. I watched him closely as he was my leader. There were times I thought he would quit all together. All he needed was some time to clear his mind and refocus and he did.

My family bought another farm. Dad was the "Outstanding Young Farmer" for the county, Mom had got her passion back to sing and play music at the church. She was doing opera locally and auditioned for the "Met" and she decided to stay home as a family; all of us were making a comeback. My brother and I were now older and enjoying the fruits of sports and the lessons they had to offer.

Sports seemed to be my outlet for my emotions and hurt from my Father's loss. I took his accident very hard and it was difficult at times. Mom and Dad decided to help my brother and me by switching to a farming practice that would allow for us to play more sports. At the time, we had sixty cows and five hundred chickens and sold the extra eggs. They decided to sell the cows and get more chickens. Who would have thought we would end up with one hundred thousand laying hens and produce over one thousand dozen eggs per day? We became one of the largest eggs farmers around. Again the farming industry had given us our lives back. My brother and I were able to excel in sports up through and beyond graduation. Athletics allowed me to transfer my farming work ethics to all aspects of my life.

I went to college right after graduation, and a year later the poultry business ceased as there was no one to run it – as both my brother and myself had gone off to get an education. Well, this only lasted for about three years and we both came back to the farming industry with Dad. He started a machinery business in 1973. This was a bit harder to get going, but we did it. I left Dad for a year and a half. He called me up on a Sunday morning and wanted to talk. I agreed and he offered me a chance to own the business and said if I could make it go, he would give me part ownership, a dream come true for me.

I started to put my stamp on the business. I took over selling, ordering, collection, demonstration of equipment and ordering of parts – all aspects of this business were under my direction. The business had done an admirable $600 thousand before my efforts. In four years, we were doing $1.2 million in receipts and I went to Dad and asked for my interest in the business. This was my first lesson in business as he said thank you but I don't owe you anything. WOW!!!

Normally, this would have devastated me, but his training and my work ethic provided me an opportunity to start a new business. Dad showed me earlier that life sometimes is not what we think is fair. While I was running the family business, I discovered the love of machine operating, especially the combine. This is a machine that harvests the grain we eat and the grain for animals feed. You may have seen them in Farm Aid events.

I bought my first machine by borrowing the money from my own life insurance policy and repaying it after one season. I had no customers. I did however have those valuable life lessons from farming and from my Father. While looking for farmers that would hire me, I offered them two things they could count on. I would get all of their grain possible, and it would be the cleanest you had seen. This promise never wavered and the grain elevators could tell when grain from my machines came in. It meant a premium to the farmers for their product. This part of my life took another unexpected turn. I was offered a consultant's position with a major farm machinery line in 1978 to follow the wheat caravan from Texas to Saskatchewan, Canada. I declined the offer as I had an infant, my first child, and it would have been difficult to carry them along in a trailer.

Things kept going well for all. Dad's business was going well, mine was increasing and I added a new dimension to my business of growing and marketing corn. I was up to about three thousand acres of growing and harvesting going into the tumultuous decade of the 80's. Interest was at an all-time high. It was costing me 22 percent to borrow money to grow my crops, fuel was going up and we had a political event looming over us. Russia had invaded Afghanistan and President Carter was not going to have that. He put an embargo on Russia and the USA did not fulfill the contract of 220 million metric tons of corn to Russia. There was a huge backlash and the price dropped 50%. The loss of money and a wet harvest bankrupted me. I lost $250,000 in less than six months, just another setback for me.

I took a year to decide what I wanted to do with my life. An ad appeared in the classifieds and I answered it. It was for Life Insurance sales. I thought about it for a couple of months and went ahead and said yes to the training. They had to let me finish the harvest from the previous fall and they had me.

I never thought for a moment that this would be my life's other passion. I had the passion for farming and how would I transfer the lesson from farming to Insurance and Financial planning? After I made the commitment, I knew that farming and animals are a totally demanding fulltime pledge of your time, I took educational courses. I knew I did not know this field and I was determined to be the best I could be. That is a tenet I carry from the farming industry. I started getting courses from the American College and passing taxation, economics, social security, the planning process, whatever it took to get the designation saying I was proficient in this new craft I was entering. I tried my hardest to get the best possible grade. This was my only way of measuring my progress. I did whatever was asked of me and totally placed myself in a position to learn all I could absorb.

I have obtained many designations for my education and knowledge, and have applied many aspects of the learning process to everyday life situations. I came from a very simplistic way of life on the farm and I am committed to transferring it to clients. The 'no quit' attitude my Father had when he lost his hand was pervasive in my style as well. He never took NO for an answer and I carry that same tenet in my life.

Education became more of a tool to allow me to transfer knowledge to others than a measure of achievement. Maintaining your credibility is maintained by taking ongoing classes. I would take other courses to broaden my view and increase my knowledge base.

I dropped out of college to go back to the farm to work. I have since gone back to obtain both a Bachelors and a Masters for my sake as well as for those I work with.

So, the five points farming taught me have allowed me to achieve many fun things. I got to play semi-pro sports, become a state champion, and hold scoring records and the like. These are all part of a great journey, and farming taught the lessons that allowed me to achieve.

1. Farming taught me to not give up on my vision. It showed me how to persevere when things didn't look very good. There were many times family and friends thought I should get a normal job. My pledge helped me stay the course. I told them that "JOB" was not a real word. It's like "GOLF" – in that golf stands for Gentlemen Only Ladies Forbidden. That's where that word came from and JOB stands for Just Over Broke. I can't honestly say it never crossed my mind, but it's not an option.

2. It taught me to respect my craft and to know it well. If you don't know it well, get plenty of education. There are two kinds of knowledge. That from books and classrooms and the other is from the school-of-hard-knocks. Farming gave me the school-of-hard–knocks knowledge; formal education gave me a wider horizon.

3. Love what you do so you look forward every day to go do it. I love going out to see my clients. Each day presents another challenge and I like to walk down the path with each and every person I work with.

4. Patience is a virtue alright. Farming taught me patience. Put your money into the ground in the spring and hope you get a crop in the fall to pay it off. That's what farming was like for me. Not only was there patience, but I also had the opportunity to experience faith. I had faith in farming and patience to see it through. Today, when I work with a larger client, I display the patience for them to make the right decision, and they have faith in what I do. I have had the pleasure to work with some very important individuals who have done things in this world that made huge differences – from men who help fix little children's faces to financiers who averted major airline strikes. It has been an honor to be a part of their lives and see it through to the next generation.

5. The largest point of all is gratitude. I am so grateful for this opportunity to have a chance to do this with a life that had no path when I look back. I started out as a dirt farmer, took all the lessons farming had to offer. I then added some foundational knowledge and have a life that I love to live and get up every day and pinch myself. That's gratitude and an awesome opportunity.

About Stephen

Stephen A. Stack is a Best-Selling Author and founder of Homeland Estate and Financial Services. His experience and qualifications have established him as one of America's leading financial professionals.

Stephen is licensed to practice financial services in North Carolina and other states. He is a Chartered Life Underwriter, a Chartered Financial Consultant, a Certified Senior Advisor™, a Charitable Advisor, a Registered Financial Consultant™, a Certified Estate Planner™ and a Master Certified Estate Planner™. He now focuses on and is devoted to Estate Planning, Retirement Planning and the preservation of wealth.

He works with his clients to obtain the maximum income with the minimal taxes that afford his clients a desired life style. He has worked in this arena for over 32 years. He has taught many classes and has spoken in seminars on Estate Planning, Retirement Planning, Annuities, Revocable Living Trusts, Long Term Care and Wealth Accumulation.

Growing up on a farm taught Stephen the dedication, hard work, and attention to detail one needs to have success in life. He applied those same skills as he transitioned from farming to finance after finding his passion for helping others reach their financial goals. Stephen graduated from American College with a CLU and ChFC designation, and from Strayer University with a Bachelors in Business Administration. He has also garnered the designation of CEP™ and MCEP™ from the National Institute of Certified Estate Planners, and has his Masters of Science in Financial Services, MSFS, from The Institute of Business and Finance.

CHAPTER 47

TWELVE COMMITMENTS TO GIVE YOUR LIFE GREATER SIGNIFICANCE

BY TAMARA WORD-MAGALOTTI

Last night at my son's basketball game, I ran into someone who had been a big part of my life for a very long time. As I sat in the bleachers cheering my son on, this person walked right by me, looked me straight in the eye and kept on going without saying a word. Although I no longer had any romantic feelings for him, it was still sad to see how low this relationship had gone. My best friend leaned over and whispered in my ear, "The best revenge is to live a very successful and authentic life."

I don't know about getting revenge, because that is just not my nature, however, living an authentic and successful life sounds like the right prescription for me. After some thought and quiet contemplation, I decided to commit to a truly successful and authentic life that will change how I feel about myself, past relationships and my future.

That journal entry marked the turning point in my world and the development of a success strategy anyone can follow. I decided that night not to allow that silent exchange to make me feel insignificant. The silent exchanges, whether within ourselves or with someone else, often are responsible for eroding our faith in ourselves, and our abilities. Each of us should live the life we crave, a life with purpose and significance. The only thing stopping most of us from achieving those goals is a plan.

As a business banker who secures loans and lines of credit for businesses and commercial loans for commercial properties, I meet people daily who have big dreams and no plan. Most of the time they have fantastic business ideas and big dreams powered by years of imagining, but they lack direction. For myself and for those clients of mine who refuse to let the world make them feel insignificant, I developed twelve commitments. These twelve commitments can be introduced over a year's time, but the commitment to live them will last a lifetime.

COMMITMENTS TOWARD AUTHENTICITY

1. Commit to Health and Wellness

You may be rich as King Midas, but your health can make you poor as a church mouse. Stress-related diseases steal quietly into people's lives, creating a stronghold when no one is minding the castle walls. Stress can trigger or exacerbate heart disease, headaches, diabetes, depression and gastrointestinal problems. Maintaining optimal health by eating well and exercising and reducing stress can ward off disease that might otherwise derail your life or career.

2. Commit to Helping Others

Helping others and showing patience, kindness and compassion enriches our lives. Let something bigger than you guide you. Sometimes we become so engulfed in our own problems that we do not realize how insignificant some of them really are.

Helping others changes your perspective. When you volunteer at a food pantry, your inability to upgrade your computer this year becomes less important. Looking beyond yourself to the world around you provides freedom from your own head and grants space for new ideas to take hold.

3. Commit to Creating your Own, Unique Spiritual Path

Spiritual life is a well of strength from which to draw. It enriches our lives by providing us a focus outside ourselves, thus keeping us from becoming too egocentric. I have always known that I can go to God when I have a problem, just as if I were talking to a friend. No matter what you call the higher power in your life, the belief in something more powerful than you will keep you grounded. The structure of spiritual beliefs and dogma to follow encourages integrity. Integrity provides stable footing in our lives and businesses.

4. Commit to Career Success

Each person defines career success differently. Strive for integrity in your career. Define your career goals and establish how you choose to build your business. The difference between you and everyone else is how you conduct yourself. Zig Ziglar said, "Honesty and integrity are absolutely essential for success in life - all areas of life. The really good news is that anyone can develop both honesty and integrity."

Define your career goals. If you do not know what your next step or goal should be, consider finding a mentor or hiring a career coach. Talk to people whom you respect and whose job you would enjoy having to find out how they got where they are. What would you do if you thought you could not fail?

5. Commit to Living without Fear

How do we let go of fear? One way to give up fear is to give up the trappings that cause our fears to begin with. Many times, we fear losing a job or a relationship, not because we love it and cannot imagine life without it, but because we fear losing the goodies that go along with it. Living without fear also means giving up what is unimportant. Ask yourself, what do I have to accomplish today? I once heard that when presented with a difficult decision or situation, the best course of action is to do that which is directly in front of you. Ultimately, living without fear means living in truth and living for yourself and for your needs.

6. Commit to Education

If an undergraduate or graduate degree from a university is within your budget, pursue one. Keep in mind, school is not the only way to attain an education. The purpose of education is to expand your thinking, thereby expanding the possibilities you see in the world around you. Pick up the classics and read them—not because a high school English teacher ordered you to—to learn what Dickens and Hemingway might teach you about yourself. Teach yourself new techniques in your field. If you are a salesperson, study different closes so when the next big deal comes to the table, you have a larger repertoire of hooks to catch the big fish.

7. Commit to Looking your Best

It is important in both business and your personal life to look your best. Can you picture the woman or man who walks past you and their look just screams…Power!? They are so put together that you cannot help but look at yourself and use them as the barometer by which to measure your own attire. We all want to know their secret. Their secret is authenticity. How can you look your best on the outside if you are not living authentically? The inner discord caused by continually burying who you really are is exhausting and aging.

People who are living the dream tend to look younger and take better care of their looks. Why? They have the emotional energy to invest. Conversely, people who are not true to themselves and their needs often do not have the energy to care for their looks as they once did. Some even eat to resolve inner, negative feelings. In addition to my friends and clients who gained substantial amounts of weight at jobs they disliked or in relationships that were unhealthy, I have personally fought the weight battle due to discontent. Whom would you rather see in the mirror, the person who looks vibrant and successful? …or the person who looks a frumpy, unkempt mess?

People who dislike their jobs are not the only ones that might benefit from taking the time to look their best. Busy professionals are notorious for not making time to manage their appearance. If you are feeling trepidation each time you pass a mirror, take action. Make the time in your planner to head to the hairstylist or barbershop. Visit an aesthetician for a facial or take a refresher course on applying business-appropriate makeup.

8. Commit to Creating a Financial Plan

After years in the financial business, I am still surprised at how many potential customers come into my office with a wonderful business idea and zero financial plan to accomplish their goal. People spend more time planning their vacations than they do their financial future. They ask for loans, yet have no idea how much money they currently make. They have no idea where they want to be in five years because they can barely tell where they are today.

The Internet is a wonderful place to begin designing a personal or a business financial plan. There are many resources online to set you on the correct path. Create a budget if you do not have one. Find the areas in your budget where overspending occurs. Create a plan to deposit the value of one latte per week into your personal savings account instead and watch your savings grow while your waist whittles. Chart a course for not only where you want to be but also how to get there.

9. Commit to Mentoring Someone

Commit to mentor someone else to help them better themselves. This might mean helping someone to change careers or to grow in their current position. Everyone has something to give. Even stay-at-home parents or retirees can mentor someone else. Taking a younger co-worker or college student under your wing to offer guidance or to relate to their struggles can help them immensely. At one time, you were the novice. Gather your list of things you would have done differently, "if you knew then what you know now." Share those insights with someone, especially if sharing will benefit them. You will be very surprised how mentoring someone else will benefit you.

10. Commit to Becoming Better Everyday

Seek to do one thing better everyday. If you are constantly late to meetings, work or your children's events, practice leaving ten minutes earlier, even if you have to set your clock ahead to manage it. If you tend to let laundry pile up, create a schedule and stick to it. Do you need better organization of your work files? Purchase a set of file folders that will entice you to create a new level of organization.

Keep a list of the things you want to improve in your life. Practice those things that you wish to improve for at least 21 days before giving up. You may not succeed, but you become better every time you *try* to be better. You may want a separate list for career improvements and one for personal improvements. If you are feeling overwhelmed by all the changes, try alternating the items you are working to improve.

11. Commit to Learning a New Skill

New skills change the person you are today into the person you will be tomorrow. Everyone can learn a new skill. Surely, each of us has a new skill we have always dreamed of mastering. Think back to your childhood. Did you want to learn to play tennis or to ski? No matter how old you are, you can still learn. You can do this even if you were not the athletic kid in school, in fact, especially if you were not the athletic kid in school. Learning to play a sport now gives you the opportunity to prove that elementary P.E. teacher, and yourself, wrong. Do not give in to the self-talk that says you cannot do something.

If you never learned to cook, have friends show you how to make their favorite recipes or take a cooking class at the local community center. Ask your great-Aunt Betty to teach you to knit. Every new skill you acquire brings you a step closer to reaching your full potential and to being the person you desire to be.

12. Commit to Relaxation and Renewal

Renew yourself mentally and physically. Vacation to you might mean trekking through the Himalayas or across the Sahara. It could mean lying in a hammock tied between two palm trees in a tropical paradise and sipping Mojitos. We sometimes view vacations as a reward for working hard. Vacations restore our vibrance and reset our bodies. They are the prescribed antidote to the ills of long workdays at the office, at home with the kids or in front of client after client. If you never recharge the batteries, eventually you run out of juice. Vacation also brings you full-circle to your #1 commitment to health and wellness. Health deteriorates rapidly when a person burns the candle at both ends.

I have a favorite quote that is the reason I ask you to *commit*:

There's a difference between interest and commitment.
When you're interested in doing something, you do it only
when circumstances permit. When you're committed to something,
you accept no excuses, only results.

Commit to giving your life purpose and significance by taking control and adopting a plan that helps you grow everyday. Your journey through these twelve commitments will help you to discover who you are, what motivates you, what you value, and where you are going, so you can live your best possible life: authentically, vibrantly and powerfully.

About Tamara

As a business banker, the philosophy that Tamara Word-Magalotti always maintains is to continuously treat your clients like precious golden nuggets, and you will reap the rewards one thousand fold. Growing up with a family of missionaries presented Tamara with the unique opportunity to find her niche in the business world. Deeply influenced by her family's faith, Tamara wanted to find a position that would truly help others in a profound way. As Tamara always says, "Business Banking gives others the unparalleled opportunity to reach their financial potential in a very positive way."

Tamara is the Founder and Owner of Tamara Magalotti & Associates, LLC., a consulting firm that helps businesses and individuals reach all of their financial possibilities through their unique product offerings, as well as their specialized attention to each and every client. Tamara is also CEO of TriCity Business Management, LLC., a firm specializing in telecommunications, energy, and essential services for both residential and business clients. Her goal is to help small businesses provide customers with a professional touch. TriCity Business Management, LLC., meets the ever-changing needs of small businesses by offering a complete line of essential services, including phone service, natural gas and electricity, and simple and affordable credit card processing. Services are tailored for a company's individual needs and are designed to grow right along with the business.

Tamara attended San Francisco State University until she found her passion in the Fashion Industry working and traveling worldwide with such giants as Chanel, Dior, Versace, Calvin Klein, Donna Karan and many others. She was also selected as one of America's PremierExperts®.

Tamara is also very passionate about giving back to the community as well, with 5% of all company profits going to St. Jude Children's Research Hospital.

You can connect with Tamara at:
Tamara.Magalotti@gmail.com
www.facebook.com/TamaraWMagalotti

CHAPTER 48

REAL ESTATE IS THE WINNING WAY

BY TONY HORNER

When I graduated high school at 17, I went into the military – the United States Air Force. I stayed four years in the Air Force, got out and got a great paying job at the railroad. People with more years experience were fighting to get in at the railroad because of the high paying wages. I was fortunate because of my prior military training enable me to get hired. Once I got there, I found out why the pay was high. Working at the railroad was no cakewalk. I worked the third shift 11 pm to 7 am with Tuesdays and Wednesdays off – we worked outdoors in the hot sun or the cold weather – if it was 95° or it was 10° outside. You know, I just could not see myself working until I was 65 with Tuesdays and Wednesdays off in the hot sun or the cold winter weather with no real chance for promotion. It seemed like a dead end job to me.

So I began to explore ways out, because I could not simply quit my job. I had a house and a car. I had bills like everybody else. I might be young, but still had responsibilities. I came to believe that real estate was my way out, so I started reading books – anything I could get my hands on the subject. I studied for 1½ - 2yrs but I didn't take any action. Finally, fed up with the railroad, one day I decided to take action. I made a goal and took some action, I made some offers. Six months after I made that decision, I bought a duplex, a triplex and a single-family house. My second year in the business, I bought 28 houses, and over the next four years I averaged about 36 houses per year. To this date I have bought over 400 houses. I know that seems like a lot of houses, but using my system really allows you to do a lot of volume in a short period of time. It is a great wealth creation formula.

Why the real estate business? What are benefits?

The Real Estate business has created more millionaires than any other business. Benefits of real estate are Income, Tax Benefits, Appreciation and Depreciation.

1. **Passive income** is income that you make when you're not working. Tenants paying Rent to you is a form of passive income. You don't have to do anything to be owed that money. It is owed to you regardless if you do something or not.

2. **Tax write-offs** – many institutional investors buy real estate for the tax write offs. They use the tax benefits of real estate to write off their high incomes – resulting in paying less taxes. Please consult your tax attorney for your specific situation.

3. **Appreciation** – Historically, real estate goes up in value and this is a solid strategy for creating wealth using appreciation. Typically in real estate, single family houses will go up 3-10% per year in good neighborhoods, this equates to thousands of dollars in your homes increased value. This appreciation of 3-10% happens without you doing anything. It really is making money while you sleep. Yep, that is a unique benefit of real estate. When someone mentions appreciation in Real Estate, I talk about how it changed my bloodline and it could change yours also. I'll give you an example. If you just bought ten houses over five years and the ten houses appreciated 7% per year for five years. Each house value is currently $170,000.

$170,000 value at 7% appreciation after one year = $11,900 in increased value per house or $11,900 increased value the first year. Multiply this 7% increase per year for five years and the value increased through appreciation is $59,500.

$170,000, the original house value, plus $59,500 equity buildup = $229,500 is the house value after five years. Multiply this scenario times 10 for each house you own. That equals $595,000 of Appreciation or equity build up. $595,000 is not a bad income after five years for something you didn't have to do – it just happened through appreciation.

Now what happens if you get serious and buy 20 to 30 houses. Yep, you can do the math. You can create generational wealth that you can pass on to your children's children, and if you do the numbers, you can see why this one benefit of real estate can change your bloodline – from being average middle class American to wealthy upper class American.

YOU'VE GOT TO LOVE THE BUSINESS.

Cash flow is the reason most people get involved in real estate. Cash flow is defined as the difference between the debt or mortgage that you pay out to the bank and the income collected on your rent – that is what we call cash flow. This cash flow attracts many people into the real estate business. Investors will need to exercise disciple to keep more of what you earn. Discipline to keep more of the cash flow that you earned should come first. Set up a plan to get out of debt with the cash flow you earned, paying your house and your cars off, and have a mandatory savings plan. This is referred to as: better to live within your means than above your means. This is a basic principle of creating wealth and becoming a millionaire. Well you got me excited now! So tell me, how do we get started exercising these principles? To get into action what must I do? I can give you some simple steps to follow.

First you must decide if you are going to flip or hold. Of course, the long-term benefits of holding real estate far outweigh flipping for cash today. On the other hand, flipping pays today's bills. When I first got started I did both, I would flip three out of four houses I bought, keeping one for long-term and wealth creation. As I progressed to longer in the business, I would keep two and flip two, and so on and so forth. Your cash flow, needs and personal situation can determine how you use the formula. So now that you've decided strategy to use – Fix and Flip or Buy and Hold – now we need to get you deals to come to your door. You will learn to deal with motivated sellers.

YOUR POSTURE IN REAL ESTATE

Are you chasing deals or are deals chasing you? There is a *Big* difference in this distinction. I'll will say it again, are you chasing deals or are deals chasing you? I don't have to tell you that if the deals are chasing you, you will have a higher success rate for 'bought' and 'closed' houses. The old or traditional real estate investor will go out and knock on doors, cold call people in foreclosure, look in newspapers for people that are behind on payments and in foreclosure. Many of these people do not want to be contacted, so the success ratio of getting a deal done using this method is typically not as high as getting them to come to you. However, I have developed strategies where you can attract the seller to you, using specific techniques.

We call the people we attract *motivated sellers*. A *motivated seller* wants to sell their house. You don't have to say anything slick or tricky to get them to sell – no long sales presentations and usually they don't want top dollar. They are very open to the investors 'no money down' strategy that you give to them. *Motivated sellers* are the people you want to deal with, and dealing with them makes for a long, successful real estate career.

Motivated sellers can be people that fell behind on their payments; their houses were in need of repair and they don't have the money to fix it up; people that may be getting a divorce and need to dispose of their home quickly; people that have lost a job or have a job transfer and need to sell quickly; people that are over-leveraged in their homes and need to do a short sale. Many situations like this and more are the fuel to make that person motivated to sell the property. This is an opportunity for an educated investor to come in and help the sellers solve their situation and get their house sold – while the investor can make a profit at the same time. This is what we call a win-win transaction. The seller gets what he wants (a sold property) and the investor gets what he wants (a profit).

FUNDING YOUR DEALS

Great! So where do I get the money to do deals, you are asking? This is where creative financing comes in to play. Most of financing strategies have been used for decades, so they may not be new, but they are very effective for getting you in the door for very little or no money and getting the seller out of their difficult situation. Again, we call that a win-win transaction.

<u>Home Equity Credit Line</u> – Before I bought my first investment property, I bought my first house to live in. Before you know it, equity was building up in this house that I lived in for only three short years. Remember, I talked about the Appreciation Strategy earlier; that is what happened to me on my first property. Three years later I received a letter in the mail offering me a Home Equity Line of Credit and all I had to do was to come in and talk to a representative at the bank. They did an appraisal on the house and found out it went up $21,000 over the past three years. They also went on to say that I would be able to get an equity line of credit at a low interest rate and a $21,000 second mortgage Home Equity Line of Credit on my property. I could use this $21,000 for whatever purpose I needed. I could use it for down payment money to buy new property, repair money if something went wrong on it, investment property, or if a tenant didn't pay one month, I had a cushion to pay the mortgage payment. This was the start of building my confidence to go out and make that first deal and have a little cushion if I did make a mistake, I would be okay. And that's what I did to get started.

VA Vendee Loans – the VA vendee loan is a mortgage loan guaranteed by the US Department of Veterans Affairs. The VA loan allows veterans 100% finance without private mortgage insurance or a 20% down payment although you do have to qualify for this loan and you can always check with your local VA office for the qualifications and regulations that apply in your area of the country. I was able to use this loan to buy VA properties in my local area with no money down. The VA in my case was actually doing financing at a very low interest rate with no down payment – no outside banks and qualifications were needed. Pretty great program.

Hard money loans – these are short-term loans, the funding criteria is based on the value of the real estate used for the collateral on the loan. A low loan-to-value is what most hard moneylenders look at. Most don't even pull your credit. Hard moneylenders typically have much higher interest rates than banks but they offer more flexibility in terms of financing than conventional lenders. Hard moneylenders are a great source of money; they have deep pockets and can fund many of your deals. However, this source of financing is very expensive and it is very common for the hard moneylenders to charge points and very high interest rates to do business with you, so you must use them sparingly. You can find them by attending your local investment club meetings or try googling them (hard money lender), in your local area. I have used hard moneylenders several times. I found the best use of these hard moneylenders was when I was flipping houses. They would provide the short-term financing usually 4 to 12 months. This would give me enough time to buy, fix up the property, market the property, find a buyer and close for a profit.

Partners – Partnering up is a great way to fund the deal also. When I started, I didn't have any money so I was looking for partners. When I would say to the potential partner if I found a great deal would you put up the money and partner up with me then we could split the profit. You be surprised how many partners I got to say yes on that. There are a lot of people that have money that don't look like they have money. A lot of people overlook family friends and acquaintances. Again, once you start to look, you'll be surprised at how many people have the ability to partner up with you if you're willing to share in the profits.

Buying houses 'subject to' the existing loan. This is my favorite way to buy property for little or no money because there is no credit check, no loan committee to approve you, no underwriting requirements and no appraisal. You simply take over the payments on the existing sellers debt. These are a lot of the benefits of buying houses 'subject to'. The seller wants debt relief and is willing to let an investor take over the payments that they are no longer able to make – even though the loan will remain in the seller's name. I have bought at least 200 houses using this method alone. This strategy allowed me to buy the properties for very little money. Here is an example: seller's monthly payments are $750. They fell behind two payments. I was able to make up those two payments or pay $1500. The seller would sign over the deed to me, I give the $1500 to the bank and bring sellers payments current. Once the seller deeded their house over, they have transferred ownership over to me So I was able to capitalize on buying a house from a motivated seller for $1500 in back payments. Now, of course, I had to keep the payments current from that point on since it was my house now. My exit strategy: I rented that house out for $925 per month – keeping the spread between what I paid out, $750, and what I collected, $925, making $175 per month on the spread.

Like I said, you gotta love this business ☺

www.TonyHorner.net

About Tony

Tony Horner has been a full time real estate investor since 1998 – actively investing in 30-45 properties a year. He is the past Vice President of Tidewater Real Estate Investment Group, and has been featured in the National magazine *Black Enterprise* for his investment strategies. He is a sought after national speaker and teaches seminars on his "no money down" purchasing techniques. He has been a landlord since 1998 of single-family homes, commercial properties and owner of large apartment complexes. He won the outstanding investor award in 2003.

When Tony is not fulfilling his time with the Real Estate Investing, Tony spends his time with his wife and two daughters. He also occasionally works on improving his golf handicap, working out and catching a movie.

CHAPTER 49

OUR LIVES NEED A NIP AND TUCK: CONFESSIONS OF A PLASTIC SURGEON

BY DR. MICHAEL W. PAYNE

It is well reported that when you experience more happiness, more success, more spiritual peace, more energy and more physical health – you feel better. I am always wondering why some people live a fulfilling life and why sometimes, although the same factors are present for myself, they do not match my own expectations for my life. I think that every day we are searching for these elements to achieve more in life.

Working in the world of plastic surgery for years, I never clearly understood why some patients are over the moon with their results, and others, although given a major improvement, are unhappy.

I am always searching to find the right answer for potential patients - should they have surgery or should they not? Is a nip here and a tuck there really the answer to their problems? Or is it really a minor change of their lifestyle that they need to lift their spirits and provide them with the happiness they seek? (I ask myself these same questions and in some ways am trying to practice what I preach to allow myself to live a richer and fuller life.)

I then looked at my own life and asked myself the questions about what makes me happy and what is fulfilling me, and none of the so-called things one can buy with money have these credentials, it is only when I am serving people when I am giving back, that I realize this makes me happy for a longer time, if not a lifelong time, and nourishes my soul.

So I started to give back abroad in underdeveloped countries, performing plastic surgery for free to patients who had no one to help them. But I soon realized there are so many possibilities of helping in our own communities and close surroundings and this is so fulfilling. This is how I grow happiness by giving when I have a personal choice.

The most interesting, fascinating and fulfilling thing about being a plastic surgeon for me is the variety of my work. This includes – starting from head to toe – from reconstructive to cosmetic surgery, from operating on children with birth deformities to adults with wound-healing problems, and gaining insights from the world of celebrity cosmetic procedures to traumatic burns.

The same is true for the vast array of characters and personalities you get to meet and the stories of unbelievable value and interest – be it in the rich metropolitan world or in poor underdeveloped countries. This, combined with the ability to help in a surgical way to either create confidence or reconstruct functional bodies, to help find inner beauty and change lives, is a great honor, but also a gift you have to deliver and serve in the right human way.

So instead of only treating patients as individuals considering surgery, I try to go the extra mile by looking deeper into their issues, building their confidence and opening up their minds to the possibilities of making small changes in their life.

I have found that besides plastic surgery for their outside bodies, they need the removal of emotional scars and an injection of positive beliefs, removal of unhealthy nutrition and an injection of organic-tolerated nutrition, a removal of physical trash and an implementation of routine exercise regimes, a removal of sleep deprivation and a fueling of energizing sleep. This is what I call my *plastic surgery detox* with cosmetic surgery to the five key areas of life – (1). Confidence, (2). Nutrition, (3). Exercise, (4). Sleep and (5). Mindset.

The most important challenge on which we have to perform cosmetic surgery is our own system of beliefs and unbeliefs. We have to work on our self-acceptance and become more at peace with ourselves. Every time change comes into our life, we tend to first look at the negatives instead of seeing the positives in it. If we accept ourselves and are at peace in our minds, we can show our vulnerability and learn and accept the change from deep within.

We all want to be happy but we have to work for happiness, it can't just be found. You can't remove unhappiness with a scalpel. Happiness needs to be created consciously on a daily basis. Living our fast-paced life in this Internet-driven techno-crazy world, we forget to stop and be present in the moment.

As soon as we become present in the moment, we feel more alive and can go deeper into relationships with friends and family. The people we are surrounded by deserve our full attention. We all want to be loved, but to be loved by somebody else means that we have to give love to others too, so the circle can close.

Another major factor is to be grateful for what we have, who we are and our general life. We forget all the best moments by not recognizing the things we should be grateful for. We also need to be optimistic about the future. Any circumstance we find ourselves in, we sometimes have to accept that it was our choices that got us there, and that we alone can change any direction we want to go in at any time. We are a rare breed of species in that we can choose the direction of our life in the next moment. Our mind has more power than our physical body, and we can escape any situation and change course.

The key aims of my *plastic surgery detox* are to improve all areas of your life from the inside out. The core of the system is to get you thinking about how you can make small changes in your day which will then in turn have a big impact on your life. It's also about helping you to look at yourself differently, become more confident and follow your dreams.

The core areas it covers are:

1. Confidence
   Nobody is born with confidence. We learn it first when we grow up, then through our education system, through our family and friends, in

our workplace and finally in the relationships we build. The hope is that this will lead to a confident person. But this does not mean that a confident person in one area will be confident in all areas. Confidence can be achieved by working on your competence in these specific areas.

2. Nutrition

We are constantly being bombarded by the creation of different diets, and like everything else in life, it will suit some people to eat one way and not suit others. There is some agreement on what is healthy, but also there is much opposition amongst various food sectors about what we should or shouldn't be eating. In general it is a very individual choice and everyone has to look at what works for them and what they like to eat, what energizes them after eating, what drains their energy and what will help them to improve their lifestyle. I am a big believer of adding good nutrition to the meal plan, and to prepare what to eat for the week or the day so that you avoid sugar cravings.

3. Exercise

Recent research demonstrates that to live longer and to live healthier our body and our brain need signals of us moving around and not retiring from life – to help rebuild our cells and keep our body young. Studies have shown that it helps to reverse the ageing process by taking regular exercise. Again there is a lot of conflicting information about how long and how often you have to train and how to achieve the balance between cardio exercises and muscle-building exercises. Only with hard work will we improve our body shape with the hope that this will give us the confidence to be more radiant on the inside and outside.

4. Sleep

In general most people do not sleep enough, or they think they do not require more sleep and a vast majority feel tired during the day. Sleep is the time when our body cells are recharged and regenerated, and if we do not pay attention to this then we accept a different level of presence during the day. Yes, you can function under these conditions, but to be vibrant and alert is a different feeling.

5. Mindset

I think we are conditioned to listen more to bad news than good news. Media that only tells us good news are deemed as not financially viable, and many news channels sell because of negative or catastrophic and sensational news. This affects how we feed our brain with information and how we look at different and new situations. I wish I could remove the limiting beliefs in my patients' lives, as I can see the potential they have, but they cannot mirror it themselves.

These five core elements need applying and for this we need three principal steps: Action, accountability and consistency. First to take action, second to act consistently and third to act consistently with accountability.

Take action: No action is worse than imperfect action. If you do nothing, there is no chance for change whereas if you act on something, the worst-case scenario is that you make a mistake, you learn from it and you continue on. This is what we were taught when we learnt to walk, learnt how to play an instrument or play a game.

Accountability: This is the major key for gaining success in any area. If you shout your goals out to the universe or your accountability partner, you are more likely to fulfill them. That's why deadlines work so well, because you know you only have a certain amount of time to complete the task.

Act consistently: We learnt about consistency while growing up. If we consistently do our homework we finish school well. If we consistently do anything in life and work hard we get better at it and the compound effect comes into place.

To improve all five areas of your life, you need to be consistent with them and choose positive messages. If you think of the five areas for your life and give them a place in your weekly schedule and plan it monthly, your year will be more successful and your life lived to the fullest.

About Dr. Michael

Dr. Michael W. Payne is a highly educated and experienced specialist plastic surgeon with a proven track record within the plastic and aesthetic surgery industry across the UK and Germany.

Born in Seesen, Lower Saxony in Germany, Michael was initially educated at the University of Cologne, before going on to study Human Medicine at the University of Berlin in 1987. With a keen interest in sports – especially handball, athletics, high jump and javelin – Michael ventured off to run a windsurfing school in Sardinia, Italy for a period of time. Following that, he secured work at Disney World in Florida where he spent a year meeting new people and building relationships. Becoming a fully qualified Doctor in 1996 and enjoying training at the University of Pittsburgh, Lancaster Hospital in California and the Mayo Clinic in Rochester, Michael followed his passion by exploring his growing interest in plastic surgery.

Holding these positions allows him to deliver his specialty to hundreds of individuals across the UK and Germany, including a growing list of celebrity clients. Michael's passion does not detract from his moral compass of ensuring that prospective clients are advised and guided correctly regarding specialist procedures, ensuring that he remains ethical and authentic to his craft and purpose.

Being a focused and driven individual with a flair for cosmetic surgery, Michael has mastered his skill over a decade of practising in this industry having studied in Berlin, Frankfurt, Hagen and Vogtareuth before moving to the UK in 2004. As a specialist surgeon with The Hospital Group, Michael performs hundreds of surgeries annually, carrying out a range of procedures from breast augmentation to plastic and hand surgery. Such is his reputation within the sector; he was headhunted by BHZ Vogtareuth in Germany who offered him the position of Head of Department of Plastic Surgery, Breast Surgery and Hand Surgery which he fulfilled from 2008 up to March 2010 before returning to the UK.

A true believer in giving something back, Michael undertakes regular charity work with Multiple Interplast Plastic Surgery Aid Camps in India, Tanzania and Paraguay.

As a way of relaxation, Michael enjoys travelling, sport and literature.